D0891868

RISE UP, WOMEN!

RISE UP, WOMEN!

The Militant Campaign of the
Women's Social and Political Union
1903–1914

Andrew Rosen

Department of History
California State University, Long Beach

Routledge & Kegan Paul
London and Boston

66943

First published in 1974
by Routledge & Kegan Paul Ltd
Broadway House, 68–74 Carter Lane,
London EC4V 5EL and
9 Park Street, Boston, Mass. 02108, USA
Set in Monotype Walbaum
and printed in Great Britain by
Unwin Brothers Limited
The Gresham Press, Old Woking, Surrey
A member of the Staples Printing Group
Copyright Andrew Rosen 1974
No part of this book may be reproduced in
any form without permission from the
publisher, except for the quotation of brief
passages in criticism

ISBN 0 7100 7934 6

Library of Congress Catalog Card No. 74–81317

To My Parents

Contents

Plates

A*

Acknowledgments

I would like to thank the following individuals and institutions for permission to quote from copyright material: the Earl of Balfour for the Balfour Papers; the First Beaverbrook Foundation for the Lloyd George Papers; Miss Fiona Billington-Greig for the papers of Teresa Billington-Greig; Mr Mark Bonham Carter for the Asquith Papers; Mrs H. N. Brailsford for the correspondence of H. N. Brailsford; Mr B. I. R. Davidson, Mr D. R. Davidson, Miss N. M. Davidson, and Mrs R. D. Jeanes for letters written by Emmeline Pankhurst to Dame Ethel Smyth; Sir William Gladstone for the Viscount Gladstone Papers; Mrs Emily Maud Harben for a letter written by H. D. Harben; Viscount Harcourt for a letter written by the 1st Viscount Harcourt; Miss Esther Knowles for correspondence of Lord and Lady Pethick-Lawrence; Viscount Long for a letter written by the 1st Viscount Long; Mr Geoffrey Mitchell for the typescript autobiography of Hannah Mitchell; the National Library of Scotland for the Haldane Papers; Dr R. K. P. Pankhurst for the papers of E. Sylvia Pankhurst; Miss Grace Roe for letters written by Emmeline Pankhurst and Dame Christabel Pankhurst; Viscount Samuel for a letter written by the 1st Viscount Samuel, and Shepheards and Bingley (solicitors) for the journals of H. W. Nevinson.

I would also like to thank the following institutions for permission to quote from collections owned by them: the Beaverbrook Library; the Bodleian Library, Oxford; the British Library of Political and Economic Science, the London School of Economics and Political Science; the British Museum; the Fawcett Library; the Internationaal Instituut voor Sociale Geschiedenis, Amsterdam; the London Museum; the Manchester Public Library; and the National Library of Scotland. Quotations of Crown-copyright records in the Public Record Office appear by permission of the Controller of Her Majesty's Stationery Office.

I would also like to thank the following publishers for permission to quote from books published by them: George Allen & Unwin for *Age of Equipoise* by W. L. Burn and *The Anti-Corn Law League* by N. McCord; Edward Arnold for *Memories of a Militant* by A. Kenney; Ernest Benn for *What I Remember* by M. G. Fawcett; William Collins & Sons for *The Political Diaries of C. P. Scott* (T. Wilson, ed.); Victor Gollancz for *My Part in a Changing World* by E. Pethick-Lawrence and *I Have Been Young* by H. M. Swanwick; Hutchinson Publishing Group for *Unshackled* by Dame C. Pankhurst; William Heinemann and C. & T. Publications for *Winston S. Churchill*, vol. 2 and *Winston S. Churchill*, vol. 2, Companion, Part 3, 1911–1914, by R. S. Churchill; Heinemann Educational Books for *Divorce in England* by O. R. McGregor; Longman Group for *The Suffragette Movement* by E. S. Pankhurst; MacGibbon & Kee for *The Strange Death of Liberal England* by G. Dangerfield; Manchester University Press for *Primitive Rebels* by E. J. Hobsbawm; Marshall, Morgan & Scott for *The Lord Cometh!* and *Pressing Problems of the Closing Age* by C. Pankhurst; Nisbet & Co. for *More Changes, More Chances* by H. W. Nevinson; Routledge & Kegan Paul and Humanities Press for *Prosperity and Parenthood* by J. A. Banks; and George Weidenfeld & Nicolson for *Mid-Victorian Britain, 1851–1875* by G. Best.

I would also like to thank The Trustees of the London Museum and The Mansell Collection for permission to reproduce the illustrations.

I would also like to thank the many persons who aided me in the research and writing of this book: Miss Jessie Kenney, Miss Grace Roe, Miss Kathleen Pepper (formerly private secretary to Dame Christabel Pankhurst) and the late Miss Stella Newsome all gave generously of their time and knowledge. Mrs Mary Beatrice Blackman, of Chettle, Dorset, arranged a visit to Chettle so that I could examine the papers of Mrs Teresa Billington-Greig in her possession.

I am also particularly indebted to Mrs Alice Prochaska and Miss Susan Davis, both former Keepers of the Women's Suffrage Collection at the London Museum, Mrs Sally Kington, Public Relations Officer of the London Museum, and Miss Jean Ayton, Archivist of the Manchester Public Library, for their very substantial assistance, and to Mrs Pamela Rearden, who helped tabulate the marital status of WSPU subscribers, Miss Lee Goldberg, Miss Susan Levitt, and Mrs Penelope Davies, whose copy-editing saved me from numerous infelicities of style, and Mr David Bennett, who typed the manuscript with consummate care.

   Finally, I would like to thank Dr L. Perry Curtis, Jr, of Brown University, Providence, for detailed and helpful criticism and suggestions throughout the writing of this book, Dr Sheldon Rothblatt, Dr Ulrich Knoepflmacher, and Dr Alex Zwerdling of the University of California, Berkeley, for their extensive comments and advice, and my friend Susan Minter for many suggestions. Finally, I am deeply indebted to my wife, Adrienne, for bringing her own skills to bear on the final stages of the writing of this book.

Andrew Rosen

Introduction

In British history there are relatively few topics of broad interest which have not, at some time, been written upon. The militant campaign of the Women's Social and Political Union is certainly no exception; women's fight for the vote has been described in numerous autobiographies, in secondary accounts of a popular nature, and in general works on the history of the women's suffrage movement as a whole. The most important of the autobiographies written by those who were active in the WSPU have been Annie Kenney's *Memories of a Militant* (1924), E. Sylvia Pankhurst's *The Suffragette Movement* (1931), Emmeline Pethick-Lawrence's *My Part in a Changing World* (1938), Frederick William Pethick-Lawrence's *Fate Has Been Kind* (1943), and Dame Christabel Pankhurst's *Unshackled* (1959).* Without doubt, the most widely-read secondary account of the suffragettes has been that contained in George Dangerfield's *The Strange Death of Liberal England* (1936).† A more recent but less penetrating account is Antonia Raeburn's *The Militant Suffragettes* (1973).‡ Finally, the standard works on the women's suffrage movement as a whole – that is, general works describing the movement from its inception in 1867 to either 1914 or to the winning of the vote in 1918 – have been Ray Strachey's *The Cause* (1926), Roger Fulford's *Votes for Women* (1957), and, more recently, Dr Constance Rover's *Women's Suffrage and Party Politics in Britain, 1866–1914* (1967).§

* For comments on *The Suffragette Movement*, see fn. *, pp. 15–16.
† For comments on *The Strange Death of Liberal England*, see p. 213 and fn. *, p. 237.
‡ Largely an anecdotal account of the personal experiences of individual suffragettes. The author does not attempt to capture the complexity of the WSPU, her approach to which is both simplistic and uncritical.
§ *The Cause* and *Votes for Women* are both surveys primarily based on secondary sources. The brief biographies contained in the appendix of *Votes for Women* are, however, invaluable. *Women's Suffrage and*

Curiously enough, despite the number of books devoted
entirely or in part to the history of the fight for women's enfranchisement, no full length scholarly monograph based on extensive research into archival source material has yet been devoted
to the Women's Social and Political Union. The explanation for
this somewhat curious lack is not hard to come by; as recently as
1966, when I first became seriously interested in the WSPU,
militant feminism was still regarded by most professional
historians as something of an historical curiosity – interesting
enough in its own right, but certainly a most minor tributary to
the main streams of social history, if, indeed, a tributary at all.
As a result of this attitude, professional historians had paid no
more than passing attention to women's suffrage movements,
with the consequence that, as none of the existing works touching on the suffragettes had been grounded in extensive archival
research, many of the most important sources for the history of
the WSPU had never been used. To give but a few examples,
neither the journals of H. W. Nevinson, nor the secret correspondence between Christabel Pankhurst and A. J. Balfour, nor
the Arncliffe-Sennett Collection, nor the papers of Teresa Billington-Greig, nor the reports of the Metropolitan Police, nor the
Sylvia Pankhurst Papers deposited at the Internationaal Instituut
voor Sociale Geschiedenis, Amsterdam, had been made use of by
anyone writing on the WSPU. Moreover, a number of published
but obscure sources, such as Emily Wilding Davison's essay,
'The Price of Liberty' (see p. 199), were completely unknown,
the annual reports of the WSPU had not been mined, and the
myriad ephemeral articles, speeches, and statements to the
press which had emanated from the leaders of the WSPU
remained buried in a host of forgotten newspaper columns.
Finally, the papers of those politicians most affected by the
militant campaign – Asquith, Lloyd George, Herbert Gladstone,
and their colleagues – had not been consulted with regard to the

---

Party Politics in Britain, 1866–1914, is the most recent and the most
scholarly general treatment of the various women's suffrage organizations and the vexed political situation they encountered. Dr Rover is
insufficiently empathetic with the Liberals' very real political dilemmas,
but hers is the only published work to date which has attempted to
dissect political parties' attitudes towards the women's suffrage question. For additional comment, see fn. *, p. 9.

light they might shed on the Liberal Government's reaction to
the suffragettes.

In making use of these and other sources, I have been particularly interested in the origins and underlying patterns of
militancy, the political efficacy (or inefficacy) of the WSPU's
tactics, and the effect of those tactics on the ideology and organizational structure of the WSPU. I have also been concerned with
the Union's almost intimate relationship with those politicians
who, by blocking the passage of women's suffrage legislation for
so many years, were directly responsible for bringing about the
exasperation of the suffragettes at the apparently complete
inefficacy of conventional methods of agitation. Finally, I have
attempted to assess the character of the final and most extreme
phase of militancy – the arson campaign of 1913–14 – and I have
been struck by the extent to which the WSPU in its two final
years came to resemble, in certain respects, millenarian movements of other eras.

In writing this history I have striven to construct an account
which is faithful not only to the facts as I found them, but
faithful in affect as well – I have tried to write history which is
evocative as well as accurate. In connection with this effort, a
few questions of usage arose in which decisions that were to
some extent arbitrary seemed called for.

With regard to the use and non-use of the prefixes Miss and
Mrs, I decided to follow the usages generally prevalent within
the WSPU: for example, Mrs Emmeline Pankhurst and Mrs
Emmeline Pethick-Lawrence were known to all but a few
intimate friends as Mrs Pankhurst and Mrs Pethick-Lawrence,
and they have been referred to thus in these pages, whereas
Christabel Pankhurst and Sylvia Pankhurst were usually
referred to as Christabel and Sylvia – there were, after all,
three Misses Pankhurst in the WSPU – and I have frequently
referred to them by their first names. Neither disrespect nor
undue familiarity will, it is hoped, be construed from this
practice. To have referred consistently to Christabel Pankhurst
by her full name would, I think, have established a degree of
formality not present in the WSPU, and would have failed to
convey a sense of that intimacy through which, as Christabel,
she became idolized by her followers.

A question of usage also arose with regard to direct quotations from newspaper accounts of speeches: Edwardian and Georgian newspapers, in reporting speeches and interviews, frequently changed first person pronouns to third person pronouns – 'I' and 'we' became 'she', 'he', and 'they', and corresponding changes in syntax were made. For example, on 4 July 1896 the *Manchester Guardian* quoted Mrs Pankhurst as saying, 'she was aware when she spoke that very likely proceedings would be instituted against her.' Despite the lack of complete fidelity to all the original words, such newspaper reports often constitute the most accurate available accounts of important statements, and I have on occasion quoted such reports rather than resorting to para-phrase. I have, on the other hand, completely avoided the use of any of the highly suspect dialogue introduced into so many personal memoirs by WSPU members – such memoirs were usually written twenty to forty years after the words quoted were allegedly spoken, and I have found that over such lengthy periods the unaided human memory is an unreliable recorder of events, let alone of what people actually said.

Matters of usage aside, some definition of topic may be help-ful: my subtitle – 'The Militant Campaign of the Women's Social and Political Union, 1903–1914' – is intended to describe accurately the subject of this book. I have not attempted to chronicle the doings of the non-militant National Union of Women's Suffrage Societies, nor have I attempted to analyse with any completeness the history of women's suffrage legisla-tion, though I have discussed in some detail the necessarily close relationship between political leaders, parliamentary affairs, and the tactics of the WSPU, and I have also analysed in detail the factors which led to the passage of women's suffrage legislation in 1916–18.

In conclusion, I would add that in my subtitle and elsewhere I have used the word 'militant' as it was used by the women of the WSPU: by militant I do not necessarily mean illegal or violent – though most of the activities called militant were illegal, and many were violent – rather, I refer to a wide spectrum of tactics chosen by the WSPU precisely because its leaders knew that conventional society would regard those tactics as acts of social and political bellicosity when employed by women. Broadly defined, militant tactics were those tactics sufficiently combative as to be widely regarded as shocking, and therefore worthy of comment – comment being exactly what the WSPU sought; the militant campaign was based on the perception that the use of 'shocking' tactics, by evoking discussion, would create substantial public interest in a cause which had previously seemed virtually moribund.

1 Antecedents

In mid-Victorian Britain, a woman of the middle or upper class was not expected to earn her own living; she was supposed to remain forever dependent upon a man – first as a daughter and then as a wife. After she married, her economic dependency was enforced by law, for prior to the Married Women's Property Acts of 1870, 1874 and 1882, a married woman was not permitted to own property in her own right – her estate passed to her husband on marriage.* Victorian women could not easily change the property laws, or any other laws affecting their lives, since they could not vote in parliamentary elections, and thus were governed by laws made by men alone.

During married life, the middle-class wife was expected to provide her husband with a domestic sanctuary, a peaceful haven to which he could repair from the world in which he earned his family's living. She was expected to be what Coventry Patmore called 'the Angel in the House', a creature unsullied by intimate involvement in the competitive arena in which money was made and affairs of state decided upon.[1] She was not expected to perform even the work of her own household, for during the 1850s and 1860s maintenance of middle-class status increasingly came to require the keeping of several domestic servants,[2] with the result that the household duties of the middle-class wife

* The harshness of the common law was mitigated, however, for the daughters of the rich. W. L. Burn has written, 'Among the upper classes it was customary for an elaborate settlement to be executed in anticipation of marriage. Such a settlement was likely to give the wife a right to a specified amount of pin-money and, broadly speaking, to separate her property in law from her husband's. . . . The fact that, as Dicey put it, "the daughters of the rich enjoyed, for the most part, the considerate protection of equity" while "the daughters of the poor suffered under the severity and injustice of the common law" may well have delayed legislative intervention' (W. L. Burn, *The Age of Equipoise*, p. 252).

became limited to what O. R. McGregor has referred to as 'supervising, and complaining about, her servants'.[3] The *Saturday Review* of 15 February 1868 claimed that:[4]

> the usual method of London housekeeping, even in the second ranks of the middle-classes, is for the mistress to give her orders in the kitchen in the morning, leaving the cook to pass them on to the tradespeople when they call. If she is not very insolent, [sic] and if she has a due regard for neatness and cleanliness, she may supplement her kitchen commands by going up stairs through some of the bedrooms; but after a kind word of advice to the housemaid if she is sweet-tempered, or a harsh word of censure if she is of the cross-grained type, her work in that department will be done, and her duties for the day are at end. . . . Many women boast that their housekeeping takes them perhaps an hour, perhaps half an hour, in the morning, and no more.

Some part of the rest of the day might be devoted to music, reading, or to varieties of sewing which Geoffrey Best has aptly described as 'ornamental, strictly *useless* needle-work for the most part; the *useful* stuff, the men's shirts and women's dresses and underwear, was done by working women.'[5] The number of hours devoted to sewing was no doubt increased by the frequency with which pregnancy and, thus, confinement occurred: whereas the average number of live births to women who married in Great Britain between 1925 and 1929 was 2·19, the average number of live births in England and Wales to women who had been born between 1841 and 1845 was 5·71.[6] Eight or more children were born to fully 33 per cent of marriages taking place 'about 1860'.[7] We will never know the inner feelings of more than a comparative handful of Victorian women regarding the frequent child-bearing so many of them went through. In 1841, one perhaps not completely atypical Victorian woman – the Queen – wrote to the King of the Belgians:[8]

> I think, dearest Uncle, you cannot *really* wish me to be the 'maman d'une nombreuse famille', for I think you will see with me the great inconvenience a *large* family would be to us all, and particularly to myself; men never think, at least seldom think, what a hard task it is for us women to go through this *very often*.

Outside her home, and beyond the concentric circles of family life, the scope of a middle-class married woman's activities was severely limited. She might venture abroad to pay morning calls, play whist, perform works of charity, and attend tea-parties, yet whatever the scope of such activities, she rarely worked for remuneration, because almost no suitable careers were open to women whose social class precluded factory work or domestic service. A middle-class woman could not enter medicine, engineering, the clergy or the army, her chances of becoming an architect or accountant were negligible, and the worlds of finance and big business were equally impenetrable. The bars that prevented her entering either the professions or business, on any scale larger than shopkeeping, were kept securely bolted by the widely accepted belief that women were by nature unfitted for most serious occupations, being innately inclined to be unworldly, impractical, and, unlike men, led by their emotions rather than by reason. Effectively prevented by both lack of education and lack of opportunity from acquiring competency in worldly pursuits, many Victorian middle-class women were indeed as helpless as Respectable Opinion expected them to be.

Though mid-Victorian laws and practices affecting middle-class women appeared at the time to be fairly stable, those laws and practices were based on the fallacious assumption that virtually all women had husbands. In fact, a large number of Victorian women did not have husbands. Of the 10,380,258 women of all ages resident in England and Wales in 1861, there were 1,537,314 unmarried women aged 20 and over and 756,438 widows aged 20 and over.* The source of financial support of the 2,293,752

---

* *Census of England and Wales for the Year 1861*, vol. 1, p. 5; and vol. 2, p. xx. That a society which exalted marriage as a social norm included a singularly large body of unmarried women seems to have been the result of at least two basic factors: first, whereas there were 10,380,258 women resident in England and Wales in 1861, there were only 9,825,246 men, a discrepancy that resulted from the higher mortality rate of men (and of male children in particular), from preponderantly male emigration overseas, and from males' serving abroad in the armed forces. Second, as J. A. Banks has pointed out, in mid-Victorian England maintenance of genteel status required a newly married couple to

adult women without husbands varied considerably, since among these women were employed working-class women, girls in their early twenties living at home, and elderly women living on funds bequeathed by deceased husbands. Nevertheless, among the over two million adult women without husbands were a great many women whose economic and psychological needs were simply not catered to by the pitifully few varieties of gainful employment open to them – the few careers that were open to the unmarried middle-class woman carried extremely limited potential either for monetary gain or for intellectual development, and entailed a social status that was uncertain at best.* For example, according to the 1861 census,

---

achieve a standard of living considered appropriate to their social station. Hence, many young gentlemen of limited means postponed marrying until their finances permitted beginning married life with the approved standard of living. The consequence was that 'the average age of those clergymen, doctors, lawyers, members of the aristocracy, merchants, bankers, manufacturers, and "gentlemen" generally, who married between 1840 and 1870 was 29·93 years' (J. A. Banks, *Prosperity and Parenthood*, p. 48). See also pp. 30 and 45. Banks cites C. Ansell, Jr, *On the Rate of Mortality at Early Periods of Life, the Age at Marriage . . . and Other Statistics of Families in the Upper and Professional Classes*, 1874, p. 45.

* The problem of 'surplus' or 'redundant' middle-class women was treated by a number of mid-Victorian commentators: W. R. Greg wrote that there was a 'disproportionate and quite abnormal' number of single women in the nation, and that these 'redundant' women were 'chiefly to be found in the upper and educated sections of society' (W. R. Greg, 'Why are women redundant?' *National Review*, April 1862, as reprinted in *Literary and Social Judgments*, pp. 276 and 288). Greg portrayed unmarried middle-class women without satisfactory employment as 'beautiful lay nuns, involuntary takers of the veil, who pine for work, who beg for occupation, who pant for interest in life' (*ibid.*, p. 277). Far from advocating wider employment opportunities for such women, however, Greg wrote (*ibid.*, p. 302):

those wild schemers – principally to be found on the other side of the Atlantic, where a young community revels in every species of extravagant fantasies – who would throw open the professions to women, and teach them to become lawyers and physicians and professors, know little of life, and less of physiology. . . . The cerebral organization of the female is far more delicate than that of man; the continuity and severity of application needed to acquire real *mastery* in any profession, or over any science, are denied to women, and can never with impunity be attempted by them;

72.5 per cent of teachers were women – but teaching was ill-paid, low in social status, and offered no chance of advancement.[9] A spinster could also become a governess, but being a governess was fraught with all the disadvantages of teaching, and had other marked disadvantages of its own.[10] If, as one contemporary commentator wrote, women were driven to become governesses 'by great pecuniary necessity',[11] it was because the handful of other careers open to the unmarried middle-class woman – writer, artist, and actress – required special abilities possessed by few women. In the 1850s and 1860s, there was simply no career offering any degree of intellectual scope, pecuniary reward, and social respectability open to an unmarried middle-class woman, unless she happened to have special artistic talent. It was primarily as a reaction against the manifest lack of opportunities for unmarried middle-class women that organized feminism began in Britain.

In 1865, a small group of London women with a common interest in higher education began to meet regularly in a discussion group called the Kensington Society. Most of its members were young, intelligent, middle-class and unmarried. Of the eleven members of the society named in H. Blackburn's *Record of Women's Suffrage*, nine were unmarried.[12] That the society consisted of a specially gifted group of women is attested by the achievements of many of its members: Mrs Barbara Bodichon (who was already well-known as the editor of the *Englishwomen's Review*) and Miss Emily Davies went on to found Girton College. Miss Frances Mary Buss founded the North London Collegiate School, and Miss Dorothea Beale founded the Cheltenham Ladies' College. Miss Jessie Boucherett led the Society for Promoting the Employment of Women. Miss Elizabeth Garrett (later Dr [Mrs] Garrett Anderson) became famed as one of the first recognized woman doctors in England. And the outspoken stepdaughter of John Stuart Mill, Miss Helen Taylor, also belonged to the Kensington Society.

---

mind and health would almost invariably break down under the task.

The chief solution for female 'redundancy' was, Greg proposed, female emigration overseas to the colonies, where an adequate supply of potential husbands was, he believed, to be found.

Mill was elected MP for Westminster in 1865, the same year that the Kensington Society was founded. He mentioned women's enfranchisement in his election address, and on 28 April 1866 three members of the Kensington Society, Mrs Bodichon, Emily Davies, and Jessie Boucherett, drafted a petition – the first of its kind – asking for the enfranchisement of 'all householders, without distinction of sex, who possess such property or rental qualification as your Honourable House may determine.'[13] The petition implicitly excluded married women, for married women could not be householders, since all property rights belonged to their husbands. The petition was signed by 1,499 women, including Harriet Martineau and Mrs Josephine Butler, and was taken to Mill at Westminster. On receiving the petition, Mill exclaimed, 'Ah, this I can brandish with effect', and he and Henry Fawcett presented the roll to the Commons on 7 June 1866.[14]

The small group of women who circulated the first enfranchisement petition for signatures was succeeded by a provisional committee which, in November 1866, issued a petition asking for the vote on the existing rental and property qualification. The committee tried to persuade women householders to sign the petition. On 3 January 1867, Emily Davies wrote to Lydia Becker of Manchester, a forty-year-old spinster who was president of the tiny Manchester Ladies' Literary Society, and had written a paper in favour of women's suffrage,*

We have received the signed Petitions & I send you by this post some more copies . . . a Committee is in process of formation at Manchester & as soon as they get into work it will probably be most effective to work with them. They intend, I understand, to canvass all the female householders in Manchester, so you will be sure to hear of them. I suppose they will also announce themselves in some way in the newspapers.

* Archives, Manchester Public Library, box M/50, E. Davies to L. Becker, London, 3 January 1867. I have found no evidence to support the claim of Sylvia Pankhurst (in *The Suffragette Movement*, p. 30) that a women's suffrage society was formed in Manchester in 1865 or 1866. Were such a society already in existence, Emily Davies surely would have mentioned the fact in her correspondence with Lydia Becker.

The committee referred to by Emily Davies was formed at a small meeting at the Manchester home of Dr Louis Borchardt, on 11 January 1867, with Jacob Bright, the brother of John Bright, in the chair. The committee met again on 13 February, and appointed Lydia Becker as Secretary.

On 5 July 1867, the provisional London committee became the London National Society for Women's Suffrage, and, in August, the Manchester committee became the Manchester National Society for Women's Suffrage. At a special meeting held on 6 November 1867, the two groups, together with a newly-formed Edinburgh society, formed a loose federation called the National Society for Women's Suffrage. The executives, constitutions, and funds of the constituent societies remained separate.[15]

On 14 April 1868, the Manchester National Society for Women's Suffrage sponsored the first public meeting on women's suffrage ever held in Britain, in the Assembly Room of the Free Trade Hall in Manchester. At the meeting, a resolution was passed which asked for the vote 'on the same terms as it is or may be granted to men.'[16] In a second resolution, the society pledged itself to support the NSWS by 'all practical and constitutional methods'.[17] Extension of the franchise on the same terms on which it was then held by men would have given the vote to no married women and to relatively few lower-class women, for most such women (i.e. most women) lacked the requisite property qualification.* The leaders of the NSWS were, however, primarily concerned with middle-class women, and with middle-class widows and spinsters in particular. Indeed, printed on the stationery used by members of the provisional London committee in April 1867 was the remarkable letter-head:[18]

Enfranchisement of Unmarried Women & Widows.
Possessing the Due Property Qualification.

---

* Speaking in the Commons on 12 June 1884, in support of a women's suffrage amendment to the Representation of the People Bill, Sir Stafford Northcote said, 'We believe there will be 400,000 or 500,000 women who will be so admitted [to the franchise] . . . 400,000 or 500,000 women who are at the heads of households and are managers of property' (*H.C. Deb.* 3s. vol. 289, 12 June 1884, c. 193).

Barbara Bodichon had said, in October 1866:[19]

> Let each member of the House of Commons consider . . .
> all the properly qualified women of his acquaintance, and
> he will see no reason why the single ladies and widows
> among his own friends should not form as sensible opinions
> on the merits of candidates as the voters who returned him
> to Parliament.

Lydia Becker, too, was an apologist for the widows' and
spinsters' franchise. Moreover, in a letter for which, unfortunately, no date has survived, she wrote: *

> What I most desire is to see men and women of the *middle
> classes* stand on the same terms of equality as prevail in the
> working classes – and the highest aristocracy. A *great lady*
> or a *factory woman* are independent persons – personages –
> the women of the middle classes, are *nobodies*, and if they
> act for themselves they lose caste!

The middle-class character of the NSWS was not just a matter
of the severely restricted franchise it sought, for its political
tactics were based on the tactics of the Anti-Corn Law League.
Some of the most important leaders of the NSWS had been
influenced by the League: Lydia Becker had grown up in
Lancashire, and her sister later wrote that 'the stormy discussions connected with the Anti-Corn Law League were reproduced
in miniature in our juvenile circle!'[20] Barbara Bodichon had
also been influenced by the League – one of her co-workers
later wrote of her that 'the first public movement with which,
when almost a child, she was actively associated, was the great
Anti-Corn League [sic] struggle of Cobden and Bright.'[21]
Richard Cobden himself believed in female suffrage, and his
daughters Annie and Jane became active feminists. John Bright

---

* H. Blackburn, *Record*, p. 42. The recipient of Lydia Becker's letter is
not given. That Lydia Becker could so baldly describe factory women as
'independent persons' would seem to corroborate O. R. McGregor's
observation that 'the conditions under which working women lived and
laboured were beyond the knowledge and sympathies of most mid-
Victorian advocates of women's rights' (O. R. McGregor, *Divorce in
England*, p. 87).

was not a convinced suffragist, but his brother, Jacob, who had taken the chair at the first meeting of the Manchester committee, subsequently became a member of the executive committee of the Manchester National Society for Women's Suffrage, and after Mill lost his seat in 1868, Jacob Bright became the leader of the suffragists in the Commons. *

The tactics of the Anti-Corn Law League had included the retaining of itinerant lecturers, the holding of indoor public meetings, and, after 1839, the production of a 'steady stream of tracts, handbills and propaganda devices of all kinds which was to grow in later years to a torrent.'[22] The League sought to influence candidates in parliamentary elections, and encouraged a flow of petitions to both Houses of Parliament, the League's Manchester Association being ready to supply printed petitions to any free-trader who wished to make use of them.[23]

In turn, the Manchester National Society for Women's Suffrage utilized many of the same tactics: it too made use of lecturers, indoor public meetings, handbills, and tracts, its members were asked to bring the women's cause 'under the notice of Members of Parliament, whenever they appear before their constituents', and, again like the League, it sponsored a flow of petitions to Parliament.[24] In January 1869, Lydia Becker published a leaflet entitled *Directions for Preparing a Petition to the House of Commons*, in which she gave detailed instructions for the composition and handling of a petition and added, 'Let women all over the country promote petitions for the suffrage, and diligently ply Parliament with them throughout the Session.'[25] In 1869, a total of 255 petitions for women's suffrage, with 61,475 signatures, were presented to the House of Commons. Eighty-seven of these petitions, signed by 21,132 people, were sent by members and friends of the MNSWS.[26] The vogue for petitions continued through the 1870s; in 1874, a total of 1,273 petitions was presented in favour of a private member's Bill.[27]

In their continued attempts to persuade the Commons, the societies of the NSWS supported both private members' Bills

---

* See C. Rover, *Women's Suffrage*, pp. 61–2. To my knowledge, Dr Rover was the first historian to point out how extensive were the connections between the first generation of suffragists and the Anti-Corn Law League.

and the amending of electoral reform Bills. During the 1870s, private members' Bills were introduced in every year except 1875, but these Bills made little headway. Jacob Bright's Bill of 1870 passed a Second Reading by thirty-three votes, but was subsequently rejected in Committee after Gladstone opposed it; almost all of the other Bills were easily defeated on Second Reading.

Certainly the 1870s were not without strain for the NSWS. In 1874, the organization became severely divided over the proposed addition to that year's Bill of a clause that *expressly* excluded married women from the franchise. Lydia Becker and some of the London members successfully fought for inclusion of this clause, with the result that some of the original supporters of the MNSWS, including Jacob Bright, became estranged from Lydia Becker. In 1877, when Bright again became the sponsor of the suffrage Bill, the clause was dropped, but Lydia Becker and her closest associates remained proponents of the widows' and spinsters' franchise.

The climax of NSWS efforts at persuading Parliament through private members' Bills and amendments to (male) franchise Bills was reached in 1884, when on 10 June, William Woodall, a Liberal, introduced a women's suffrage amendment to the Representation of the People Bill. Both Gladstone and Northcote, the Conservative leader in the Commons, stressed the non-party character of Woodall's amendment. Gladstone described women's suffrage as [28]

> One of those questions which it would be intolerable to mix up with purely political and Party debates. If there be a subject in the whole compass of human life and experience that is sacred, beyond all other subjects, it is the character and position of women.

In the face of general agreement that women's suffrage ought not to be made a party issue, the voting on Woodall's amendment was not along strict party lines. The amendment was defeated by 136 votes, after Gladstone opposed it on the grounds that the proposed extension of the male franchise already involved 'as much as . . . it can safely carry. The introduction of what it cannot safely carry endangers a measure which the heart and mind of the country alike desire and assent to.'* The amendment's defeat made the ineffectuality of the NSWS policy of attempting to influence backbenchers without converting the Cabinet cruelly apparent, for of the 271 MPs, mostly Liberals, who had voted with the Government against the amendment, 104 were what the NSWS called 'known friends' – men who had previously said that in principle they were in favour of women's suffrage, but who had voted against Woodall's amendment in order to avoid displeasing Gladstone.

The occasion was by no means unique. Between 1884 and 1914, a large number of the Liberal backbenchers who were at least nominal supporters of women's suffrage quite frequently allowed their tepid enthusiasm for the women's cause to be overborne by a variety of political considerations, one of the most important of which was that Gladstone and Asquith were both steadfast opponents of women's enfranchisement. Both Prime Ministers repeatedly helped to block the progress of women's suffrage measures through the various stages of parliamentary approval. (In 1870, for example, Gladstone had prevented the further progress of a Bill which had passed its Second Reading.) In contrast, Disraeli, Northcote, and Balfour all voted in favour of limited measures of women's suffrage, but were unwilling to seek their party's support for the Bills because they knew that a majority of Conservative MPs were against enfranchising women. Mrs Fawcett later rather piquantly

---

* W. E. Gladstone to W. Woodall MP, 10 Downing St, 10 June 1884, as quoted in H. Blackburn, *Record*, p. 163. While Gladstone pleaded expediency in opposing the women's suffrage amendment of 1884, he was not more sympathetic to similar legislation on other occasions. His opposition seems to have stemmed primarily from his desire to preserve the existing character and social role of women. On 11 April 1892, in a letter to Samuel Smith, MP, he gave as his reasons for opposing that year's Bill not only that the Bill excluded married women, and that women were 'generally indifferent' to their own enfranchisement, but that the Bill would effect 'a fundamental change in the whole social function of women'. Domestic life might be modified injuriously, and women's nature might be sullied – 'The fear I have is, lest we should invite her unwittingly to trespass upon the delicacy, the purity, the refinement, the elevation of her own nature, which are the present sources of its power' (W. E. Gladstone, *Female Suffrage. A Letter from the Right Hon W. E. Gladstone, MP to Samuel Smith, MP*, [pamphlet] London, 1892, pp. 1–7).

said of the Liberal and the Conservative parties that 'from the suffrage point of view the first was an army without generals, and the second was generals without an army.'*

After the major defeat of 12 June 1884, the societies of the NSWS entered a period of discouragement and decline, during which the women's suffrage movement was increasingly afflicted by internal divisions and political impotence. Also, in the wake of the Corrupt Practices Act of 1883, canvassing and other election work ceased to be salaried, and women became welcome as unpaid workers for the major political parties. The founding of the women's auxiliaries of those parties – the Women's Council of the Primrose League in 1885, the Women's Liberal Association in 1886, and the Women's Liberal Unionist Association in 1888 – diverted the energies of many feminists, who, given opportunities to play even supporting roles in party politics, seized those opportunities. Between 1886 and 1892 the Commons did not even debate women's suffrage. Lydia Becker died in 1890, and no leader of similar capacity and stature emerged in the years immediately after her death. On the whole, the period from 1884 to 1897 marked the nadir of the women's suffrage movement in Britain.

It would be easy to fail to appreciate the independence of mind of the first generation of British feminists. Considering the extremely straitened role of mid-Victorian women, the actions of the early feminists in forming organizations, giving speeches, circulating petitions, and so on, involved far more originality and courage than may now be readily apparent. The overriding fact remains, however, that the genteel tactics of the NSWS were not particularly effective. Organized feminism declined after 1884 because the NSWS had neither aroused public opinion nor induced more than a handful of MPs to take women's

* M. G. Fawcett, *The Women's Victory – and After: Personal Reminiscences, 1911–18*, p. 125. (Regarding Mrs Fawcett, see p. 25.) In the division of 12 June 1884, ninety-eight Conservatives supported Woodall's amendment, and only twenty-seven opposed it, but the vote was atypical; the Conservatives' motive for voting on this occasion in favour of an amendment which they knew had no chance of passage had more to do with a desire to 'dish' Gladstone than with any concern for women's suffrage.

suffrage seriously. The failure to arouse Parliament was due in part to the narrowness of the franchise sought; widows and spinsters were a relatively easily dismissed segment of the population, of questionable electoral potential. Many Liberals feared, and not without reason, that the relatively small group of propertied women who would actually be enfranchised by extension of the existing qualification would, on balance, vote Tory.

The overriding handicap, however, was that the NSWS employed means of publicity that were simply too conventional to stir prolonged and heated public debate. As long as public opinion was not greatly stirred, Parliament was not really interested in women's suffrage on any franchise. As the vote of 1884 had so clearly demonstrated, most of the so-called 'known friends' of women's suffrage in the Commons were men who had no intention of doing more than state principles. During the 1890s, only a handful of MPs gave any indication of taking the issue seriously.

B

2 Enter the Pankhursts

One of the most fervent male supporters of the MNSWS during its first years was the Manchester barrister Richard Marsden Pankhurst. The son of a Baptist Dissenter, and himself a teacher in Baptist Sunday schools during his youth, Pankhurst had gone on to study at Owens College, Manchester, and had received from the University of London the (external) degrees BA in 1858, LLB in 1859, and LLD in 1863. Known thereafter as Dr Pankhurst, or 'the Doctor', he had already become well known in Manchester as a supporter of educational and social reform when, soon after being admitted to the bar at Lincoln's Inn in 1867, he became a member of the executive committee of the MNSWS.[1]

In April 1868, Dr Pankhurst was one of the speakers at the first public meeting in favour of women's suffrage. In 1869, he acted as counsel in Chorlton v. Lings, a suit in which women's enfranchisement was sought on the basis of ancient statutes. The Court of Common Pleas ruled that the uninterrupted usage of centuries had greater weight than the statutes cited. In December 1869, at the second Annual Meeting of the MNSWS, Dr Pankhurst moved that Jacob Bright and Charles Dilke be asked to introduce a women's suffrage Bill during the next session of Parliament. Dr Pankhurst subsequently drafted the Women's Disabilities Removal Bill that was introduced by Bright in 1870:[2]

> That in all Acts relating to the qualification and registration of voters or persons entitled or claiming to be registered and to vote in the election of Members of Parliament, wherever words occur which import the masculine gender, the same shall be held to include females for all purposes connected with and having reference to the right to be registered as voters, and to vote in such elections, any law or usage to the contrary notwithstanding.

For the next four years, Dr Pankhurst continued to take an active role in the MNSWS, serving on the executive, speaking at meetings, and corresponding with Lydia Becker with regard to the legal aspects of women's suffrage. In 1874, he was one of the members of the executive who opposed Lydia Becker's support for amending the private member's women's enfranchisement Bill of that year to exclude married women expressly. The quarrel was so heated that after 1875 Dr Pankhurst ceased to take part in the activities of the MNSWS.

Dr Pankhurst had resolved to remain unmarried so that he could devote himself completely to work for the public good.[3] He lived with his parents until 1879, when, at the age of forty-four, he married Emmeline Goulden, the twenty-year-old daughter of a Manchester manufacturer who was also an amateur actor and (for a time) the owner of the Prince of Wales Theatre in Salford. Emmeline Goulden's grandmother, Mary Goulden, had been a member of the Anti-Corn Law League, but Emmeline herself had been educated in France, and had no experience of politics. * The Pankhursts' first daughter, Christabel

* See E. S. Pankhurst, *The Suffragette Movement*, pp. 53–7. The first 164 pages of Sylvia Pankhurst's mistitled autobiography were devoted to a detailed account of the Pankhurst family during the late nineteenth century. Virtually no Pankhurst family papers survive from the years 1867–1903, so it is highly unlikely that the work of any professional historian will ever take the place of Sylvia's extensive autobiographical memoirs of this period. Only those details relevant to the birth of militant feminism will be dealt with here, and the reader interested in an extended account of the domestic life of the Pankhursts, and the numerous causes espoused by Dr Pankhurst, would do well to read pertinent chapters of *The Suffragette Movement*. The work is reasonably accurate in so far as those subjects that are a matter of public or documentary record are concerned. Regarding all family matters, however, Sylvia's strong biases must be taken into account, in particular her idealization of her father. She saw him as a selfless and saintly doer of good for his fellow men: 'Our father, vilified and boycotted, yet beloved by a multitude of people in many walks of life, was a standard-bearer of every forlorn hope, every unpopular yet worthy cause then conceived for the uplifting of oppressed and suffering humanity' (*The Suffragette Movement*, p. 3). She also exaggerated his importance: 'Thus brilliantly equipped with academic distinction, he was to become, for forty years, the most outstanding public personality in his native city. His abilities

Harriette, was born in September 1880. Whereas Mrs Pankhurst's subsequent offspring were handed over to a nurse, Christabel remained her mother's charge. Christabel was followed by Estelle Sylvia in May 1882, Henry Francis Robert in February 1884 (he died at the age of four, of diphtheria), Adela Constantia Mary in June 1885, and Henry Francis in July 1889.

In 1885, the Pankhursts moved to London. Later that year, Dr Pankhurst stood for Parliament, under the sponsorship of the Rotherhithe Liberal and Radical Association. He was defeated. During the next few years, Dr and Mrs Pankhurst became increasingly involved with the then fermenting world of London radicalism that included William Morris, Tom Mann, and Annie Besant, all of whom attended quasi-political gatherings at the Pankhursts' home in Russell Square. Grant Allan, William Lloyd Garrison, and Louise Michel, the 'petroleuse' of the Paris Commune, also visited the Pankhursts, and as early as 1886 Dr Pankhurst's radical republicanism began to give way to newer and more fashionable doctrines – he began to advocate the nationalization of land, and he also began to speak

---

never passed unperceived. Office was always refused him; honour never' (*ibid.*, p. 6).

It was, of course, possible to view Dr Pankhurst in rather a different light. Some years after his death, an anonymous contributor to the *Manchester City News* (12 April 1913) wrote, in a somewhat patronizing memoir:

> There were two characteristics of Dr. Pankhurst which beyond all others stick in the memories of those who knew him, his smile and his voice. . . . The smile was not the smile of gaiety, nor of amusement. It was not the twinkle of the humorist. It was a smile of universal kindliness and goodwill – such a smile as the visage of St. Francis may have worn. The voice was a natural alto, a thin piping treble, heaven knows how many octaves above the normal pitch.
>
> It used to be amusing, in a way, to hear the Doctor, with that smile and in that voice, propounding the most blood curdling theories of government, and denouncing wrath to come on Kings, and Priests, and Aristocrats. You knew that he would not hurt a fly, much less a fellow creature. . . .

A certain streak of noble ineffectuality seems to have characterized Dr Pankhurst; even his adoring daughter Sylvia later wrote that he was 'inapt for any sort of manual effort. "I am a helpless creature!" he often said, handing over even the carving of the joint to his energetic spouse' (E. S. Pankhurst, *The Suffragette Movement*, p. 90).

in favour of independent labour representation in the manner of
the Irish Nationalists, whom he much admired. Dr Pankhurst said
to a conference sponsored by the Fabian Society in June 1886:[4]

> Let Mr Morris . . . train up among his socialistic young
> fellows a handful of men to go to parliament in that spirit
> [the spirit of the Irish Nationalists] & they would do noble
> work.

Between 1885 and 1893, Mrs Pankhurst acted as hostess for
any number of quasi-political gatherings in her home, and she
gradually acquired more and more political knowledge of her
own. Soon after her marriage, she had been made a member of
the Married Women's Property Committee, but she had not
been an active member of that committee – she did not become
seriously involved in work for women's rights until after the
last of her five children was born. In 1889, after the birth of
Henry Francis – who was turned over to a nurse – she and her
husband helped to form the Women's Franchise League, the
council of which included Jacob Bright, Jane Cobden, Josephine
Butler, and Elizabeth Cady Stanton. The League originated as a
reaction against the established suffrage societies' preoccupation
with the enfranchisement of widows and spinsters, and it
placed primary emphasis on equal voting rights for married
women and equal divorce and inheritance rights. To the
Women's Disabilities Removal Bill originally drafted by
Dr Pankhurst, the League proposed a clause to the effect that no
woman – married or unmarried – should be disqualified for
election or appointment to any office. The League also espoused
one of Dr Pankhurst's pet schemes, the abolition of the House of
Lords, going so far as to publish a pamphlet which he had
written, *The House of Lords and the Constitution*, that had no
immediate bearing on the women's suffrage question.[5] The
League was regarded as a radical and impractical organization
by less adventurous suffrage societies, which raised the cry 'Half
a loaf is better than no bread!' against the League's proposals.[6] In
turn, the League rather unkindly referred to its rivals as 'the
Spinster Suffrage party' and accused them of pursuing a
'cowardly policy'.[7]

The Women's Franchise League disbanded in the early 1890s
because of a lack of funds and the ill-health of several of its

leading members, including Dr Pankhurst, who had begun to
suffer from gastric ulcers, which necessitated periods of rest and
recuperation. He was now also affected by financial difficulties,
which stemmed in part from his illness and in part from
Mrs Pankhurst's financially unsuccessful attempt to manage a
fancy goods shop – called Emerson's – on aesthetic rather than
commercial considerations. The family suffered an additional
reverse when the lease on its Russell Square residence ran out.
Much of Dr Pankhurst's legal work had continued to be on the
northern circuit, and in 1893, the Pankhursts returned to
Lancashire.[8]

During the London years, the political views of Dr and
Mrs Pankhurst had become increasingly radical. After returning
to Lancashire, Mrs Pankhurst became a member of the executive
of the Lancashire and Cheshire Union of Women's Liberal
Associations, but both she and her husband were drawn towards
the recently formed Independent Labour Party. A particularly
attractive facet of the ILP, from the Pankhursts' point of view,
was that women played a central role in its affairs. The Conservatives had formed the Primrose League and the Liberals had
formed the Women's Liberal Association, but in neither party
did women play major roles in formulating party policy or as
party spokesmen. In contrast, the ILP did not form a separate
women's auxiliary, and women played important roles both
as itinerant lecturers at the ILP branches' innumerable outdoor meetings, and as members of its National Administrative
Council. The most important of the ILP's women lecturers
were Katherine St John Conway (who became Mrs Bruce
Glasier and was responsible for bringing her husband into the
ILP), Caroline Martyn, and Enid Stacy. These three young
women were well known to the working-class audiences that
gathered on Sundays in the public parks of Lancashire and
Yorkshire textile towns. They also played important roles in
administering ILP affairs – Enid Stacy and Caroline Martyn
were both members of the National Administrative Council, and
Katherine Conway was for a time the editor of the ILP's weekly,
the *Labour Leader*.* In view of the fact that the rank and file

---

* *Independent Labour Party, Directory and Branch Returns*, Glasgow,
1896. Caroline Martyn died on 23 July 1896 at the age of twenty-nine.

of the ILP was largely composed of working men, and the majority of its parliamentary candidacies were undertaken by men of limited formal education, it is particularly interesting to note that two of the three women lecturers were highly educated – Katherine Conway had been a student at Newnham College and had passed the examination for a Cambridge BA, and Enid Stacy had received a BA from the University of London. That the ILP did not restrict the activities of its women members was one of the decisive factors that led the Pankhursts to join the party in September 1894.*

Three months later, Mrs Pankhurst was elected as ILP candidate to the Chorlton Board of Poor Law Guardians. Subsequently, in May 1895, Dr Pankhurst was adopted as ILP candidate for Gorton, an industrial suburb of Manchester. The Liberals put up no candidate, but Dr Pankhurst lost the by-election to a Conservative, 5,865 votes to 4,261. In view of the fledgling political status of the ILP, the candidacy had been fairly successful, and later in 1895 Dr Pankhurst was elected to the party's National Administrative Council. Subsequently, in the spring of 1896, he and his wife became deeply involved in an acrimonious political dispute which proved to be of signal importance in the political development of Mrs Pankhurst and her daughters.

The park called Boggart Hole Clough lies about three miles north of central Manchester. In 1896, the Clough, as it was commonly called, comprised sixty-three acres. The Manchester City Council had acquired the land for public use, and had placed it under the jurisdiction of the city's Parks Committee. From 1892 until May 1896 the Manchester ILP had held meetings in the Clough every Sunday during the summer months. These meetings normally took place in a cleft between two hills, a natural amphitheatre where audiences sat on hillside ridges which rose in tiers on either side.

In May 1896, the Parks Committee decided to put an end to ILP meetings in the Clough. The decision was probably based on political considerations, for in a recent election the chairman of the committee had been opposed by an ILP candidate, John

* Regarding the Pankhursts' decision to join the ILP, see E. S. Pankhurst, *The Suffragette*, p. 5.

Harker, but the justification given for banning the meetings was that they detracted from the serenity of the Clough. On Sunday 10 May 1896, ILP speakers were told by the police that if the meeting was not stopped, they would be booked. The meeting continued, and the names of the speakers were taken by the police, but formal charges were not preferred.

News of the incident spread rapidly, and on the following Sunday about 1,200 persons came to the Clough. This time, John Harker was given a summons for holding the meeting, it being alleged that he was guilty of 'occasioning an annoyance'.[9] Defended in court by Dr Pankhurst, Harker was found guilty and fined ten shillings. Dr Pankhurst appealed against the verdict.

On 24 May, seven persons were given summonses at the Clough, again for 'occasioning an annoyance'.[10] They too were defended by Dr Pankhurst, who stated that the ILP had held meetings in the Clough for four years without any previous attempt to 'put them down', and that 'the holding of a meeting was a lawful act, and a lawful act could not be an annoyance.'[11] Again, the defendants were found guilty. Harker was fined £5 and costs, and the other defendants were fined 40s.

On 7 June, nine people, including Harker and Mrs Pankhurst, were given summonses for 'occasioning an annoyance' in the Clough. At their trial, a constable testified that 4,000 people had come to the park, that the grass had been badly damaged, and that after the meeting the main avenue had been completely blocked. The case against Mrs Pankhurst was dismissed, but two of the defendants who refused to pay fines, Harker and Leonard Hall, received prison sentences of one month. Not long afterwards, Fred Brocklehurst, the president of the Manchester ILP, was convicted of a similar offence, refused to pay a fine, and was also sent to prison for a month.

On 21 June, Mrs Pankhurst spoke at the Clough to a crowd of 12,000 on 'The Life of William Cobbett', a topic selected because Cobbett, who had himself addressed great outdoor meetings, was the grandfather of the Manchester Corporation's prosecuting lawyer. Mrs Pankhurst again was given a summons for 'occasioning an annoyance'.[12] At a subsequent meeting of protest, Dr Pankhurst said that his wife 'would accompany, no doubt, their excellent comrades Hall and Brocklehurst to prison, for nothing that could be undergone to maintain the sacred right of free speech was too great. He, very probably, would be one of the next to follow.'[13]

Mrs Pankhurst was tried on 3 July. In her defence, she said that she was[14]

> fully prepared to take the consequences of her act in speaking at the meeting, and she was aware when she spoke that very likely proceedings would be instituted against her. If the magistrates decided – illegally as she thought – to convict, she would not pay the fine, and she would be very indignant if anyone paid it on her behalf. She would not be bound over to keep the peace, which she had not broken. She put upon the bench the full responsibility of committing her to prison, and she was determined to repeat her conduct upon the first possible occasion.

The magistrate adjourned the summons for a week, saying that the course he would pursue depended upon what happened the following Sunday.

On the evening of 3 July, a crowd of 10,000 gathered to protest at the prosecutions. Keir Hardie, Tom Mann, and Mrs Pankhurst all spoke. Mrs Pankhurst said she had gone to court 'prepared to pass the night in Strangeways Gaol, and it was no fault of hers that she was not there.' Keir Hardie said that the only reason Mrs Pankhurst had not been imprisoned was that she was a 'woman of the middle class', and the magistrate feared the public indignation which would result if he sentenced such a woman to prison.[15]

On Sunday, 5 July, Dr and Mrs Pankhurst, their daughters Christabel and Sylvia, and Keir Hardie, who wore his tweed cap, drove to the Clough in an open barouche. Between 25,000 and 40,000 people awaited their arrival, and those who sat on the highest ridges could neither hear the speakers nor see them clearly. During the meeting, Christabel (aged fifteen) and Sylvia (aged fourteen) collected money, as they had done on previous Sundays. On 11 July 1896, the *Labour Leader*, the ILP weekly which Hardie edited, published sketched portraits of Christabel, Sylvia, and Mrs Pankhurst.

When Leonard Hall was released from Strangeways on the morning of 11 July, a crowd of 300 greeted him at the prison gates. Most ILP supporters had to work during the day, so that

B*

evening a second gathering was held near the prison, and 10,000 people assembled there. A little girl gave flowers to Hall, who made a short speech. Then Hall was seated next to Mrs Pankhurst in a wagonette, a procession was formed behind a brass band, and all moved off to a meeting of welcome held in Stevenson Square.

Fred Brocklehurst was released from Strangeways on the morning of 18 July. He was immediately escorted to a ceremonial breakfast, the guests at which included the Pankhurst family. The other events which honoured him on the day of his release were essentially the same as those which had honoured Leonard Hall.

With all the ILP leaders free, the controversy over the use of the Clough began to abate. On 5 August, the Manchester City Council passed a new by-law which prohibited public meetings in Manchester parks without express permission of the Parks Committee. In view of the character of the new ordinance, all previous summonses for 'occasioning an annoyance' were withdrawn. The Parks Committee had no intention of giving the ILP permission to hold meetings in the Clough, but the Home Secretary subsequently refused to sanction the new by-law, and the City Council was forced to permit the holding of public meetings in Manchester parks.

As far as the history of the ILP is concerned, the dispute over the use of Boggart Hole Clough did not prove to be of signal importance. In the wake of the victory over the Parks Committee, two members of the Manchester ILP were elected to the City Council, but after the controversy died down attendance at ILP meetings in Manchester dwindled rapidly. The dispute over use of the Clough was, however, pivotal to the political apprenticeship of Mrs Pankhurst and her daughter Christabel. The controversy had exposed them to the use of political tactics markedly unlike those used by the women's suffrage societies then in existence. Whereas the NSWS utilized conventional methods, the leaders of the Manchester ILP had refused to submit to legal rulings that they thought unjust, and on being convicted had refused to pay fines, choosing to go to prison instead. By arranging protest demonstrations during imprisonments, and by conducting tributes and parades when its leaders were released, the ILP had gained substantial publicity. Through such means, a party so poor that its members chalked notices of meetings on pavements in order to avoid unnecessary printing expenses had received column after column of extended coverage in Manchester dailies. The ways in which the ILP had dramatized the sense of martyrdom evoked by imprisonments incurred for the sake of a just cause, and the extent to which that dramatization had brought the ILP support, had not been lost on Christabel and her mother, and nine years later Christabel was to decide that deliberately sought-after imprisonment (provided the deliberation were not revealed) would reap substantial publicity for women's enfranchisement, a cause that had failed to receive extensive or clamorous public support through conventional methods of agitation.

3 The Founding of the WSPU

For the Pankhursts, the five years after the fight for the use of Boggart Hole Clough were not years of extensive political activity. In 1897, Dr Pankhurst's stomach ulcers grew more severe, and he died on 5 July 1898 at the age of sixty-three. His death was a traumatic experience for his wife and daughters, and Mrs Pankhurst subsequently withdrew from virtually all political activities.[1] She retired from the Chorlton Board of Poor Law Guardians, to which she had belonged since 1894, and took on the nonpolitical post of Registrar of Births and Deaths. For a time, she also ran a fancy goods shop – again called Emerson's and again a commercial failure. Between 1898 and 1901, Mrs Pankhurst was not active in any feminist organization; her only political work was as a member of the Manchester School Board, to which she was elected in 1900. The revival of the Pankhursts' involvement with organized feminism was initiated not by Mrs Pankhurst but by Christabel, who in 1901 met Eva Gore-Booth and Esther Roper, the guiding spirits of the North of England Society for Women's Suffrage.

To W. B. Yeats in 1894, the Gore-Booths of Lissadell, County Sligo, had seemed 'a very pleasant, kindly, inflammable family', who were 'ever ready to take up new ideas and new things'.[2] By 1896, the aristocratic, adventuresome, and somewhat erratic Gore-Booth daughters had 'taken up' women's suffrage, holding in that year meetings in Ballinfull schoolhouse and at Drumcliffe.[3] Earlier in 1896, Eva Gore-Booth had travelled on holiday to Italy, where she met Esther Roper, who was involved with women's suffrage work in Lancashire. In 1897, Eva joined Esther Roper in Manchester, a city that had long been the commercial centre for a conglomeration of textile towns and villages in which the majority of cotton operatives and the majority of cotton trade unionists were women. In 1902, Lancashire and Cheshire textile factories employed 289,000 women and

181,000 men. 206,000 of the women and 134,000 of the men were over the age of eighteen.[4] As Eva Gore-Booth later wrote, the region was the natural home of a women's movement.[5]

By 1900, Eva Gore-Booth, who was then thirty, had become co-secretary of the Manchester and Salford Trade Union Council, an organization which sought to foster women's trade unions, and Esther Roper had become the secretary of the North of England Society for Women's Suffrage. The NESWS was one of the sixteen autonomous societies affiliated with the National Union of Women's Suffrage Societies, the organization that had been founded in 1897 to succeed the NSWS, which had split in two in 1888. The NUWSS was led by Mrs Millicent Fawcett, who became, in effect, Lydia Becker's successor.

In 1901 the North of England Society for Women's Suffrage received £745 from approximately 350 subscribers. The stated object of the NESWS was 'to obtain for Women the Parliamentary Franchise on the same conditions as it is; or may be, granted to men.'[6] This goal would seem to have been identical to that of the old NSWS, but the import of the demand had become substantially broader following the Franchise Act of 1884 and the Local Government Act of 1894. Qualified (rate-paying) spinsters had been permitted to vote in borough elections in 1869, and for town councils in 1882, and in 1888 their enfranchisement had been extended to county councils. The Local Government Act of 1894 had opened the existing local franchises to married women, and also stated that women who were qualified to vote were also qualified to be elected to town and county councils.[7] (The scope of the Act was restricted, however, by the fact that wives were not allowed to derive occupation from their husbands, i.e. husband and wife could not qualify with respect to the same property.) As a precedent, the Act had put an end to any lingering hopes for the parliamentary enfranchisement of unmarried women and spinsters alone.

The North of England Society for Women's Suffrage differed fundamentally from the defunct MNSWS in that it sought to gain the support of working-class women. In 1900 and 1901, the principal work of the NESWS consisted of collecting signatures of working-class women for petitions to Parliament asking for women's suffrage. Eva Gore-Booth, Esther Roper, and their co-workers held open-air meetings in factory districts, spoke to women at mill gates, and canvassed from house to house, distributing about 30,000 leaflets each year. In 1900, they obtained from women cotton operatives 29,359 signatures to a petition that was duly presented to Lancashire MPs at the House of Commons.[8]

After 1901, the newly-founded Labour Representation Committee's practice of arranging for its constituent organizations to finance parliamentary candidacies independently furnished the NESWS with its most oft-repeated argument. The LRC was not adverse to making use of the donations of women trade unionists to elect and maintain MPs. In 1900, there had been 96,820 women and only 69,699 men in textile trade unions in England.[9] The textile trade unions became affiliated with the LRC in 1902, and agreed to an affiliation fee of 10s. per thousand members. In addition, 4d. was to be levied each year on each member, women included, for Labour representation. Of the 4d., 1d. per member was to go to the fund for maintenance of Labour MPs.[10] Thus, women trade unionists helped pay the election expenses and salaries of MPs for whom they could not vote. In one case, women trade unionists even paid more than half of a Labour MP's salary: after David Shackleton was elected to Parliament in the Clitheroe division in 1902, 18,000 Clitheroe unionists, more than half of whom were women, paid sixpence per member into a special fund for his salary.[11] The anomalies involved in collecting assessments for parliamentary representation from those unable to vote in parliamentary elections were not confined to women's helping pay the election expenses and subsequent maintenance of Labour MPs: in 1902, the Card and Blowing Room Operatives, numbering 20,000 women and 5,000 men, gave £27 to the Parliamentary Committee of the TUC, and, in 1903, the weavers' unions, with 75,000 women and 33,000 men, gave £123 to the same committee.[12] Such anomalies were eagerly publicized by the NESWS. In 'The Cotton Trade Unions and the Enfranchisement of Women', Esther Roper wrote:[13]

The Trade Unions have, in one form or another, adopted the principle of the Direct Representation of Labour. They have agreed that Labour Members of Parliament should be paid directly by the Unions to uphold their interests in the

House of Commons. . . . The women pay, why should their
interests not be attended to?

If it is as necessary, as the men say it is, for men to be
directly represented in Parliament, how much more
necessary must it be to women, the only entirely
unrepresented workers, to have the protection and power
of a vote?

The women's best chance of winning their own enfranchisement is through the Cotton Trade Unions of the North.

From 1901 to 1904, Christabel Pankhurst served her political
apprenticeship in the NESWS, under Esther Roper and Eva
Gore-Booth. During those years, a close friendship developed
between Christabel and Eva Gore-Booth, of whom Sylvia
Pankhurst later wrote:[14]

Tall and excessively slender, intensely short-sighted, with a
mass of golden hair, worn like a great ball at the nape of
her long neck, bespectacled, bending forward, short of
breath with high-pitched voice and gasping speech, she was
nevertheless a personality of great charm. Christabel adored
her, and when Eva suffered from neuralgia, as often
happened, she would sit with her for hours, massaging her
head.

As the political protégé of Eva Gore-Booth, Christabel became
both a member of the executive of the NESWS and a member of
the Manchester and Salford Trade Union Council. By the summer of 1902, at the age of twenty-one, she was speaking in
public under the auspices of the NESWS. In July 1902, she
spoke in Lancashire towns on at least four occasions, and in
November she addressed the Glasgow ILP and the Sheffield
ILP.[15]

Mrs Pankhurst had revived her ties with the ILP the previous
spring; in June 1902, she had become a member of the newly-
formed central committee of the Manchester ILP. Christabel was
also a member of the ILP, but her political outlook had been
strongly influenced by Eva Gore-Booth's and Esther Roper's
stress on the anomalies of Labour representation, and her first
speeches and writings were tinged by more than a touch of
scepticism with regard to the prospects of somehow gaining votes

for women through the LRC. In March 1903, Christabel wrote
to the editor of the *Labour Leader:*[16]

> what is the Labour representation movement going to do
> for that large section of the working-class which, by
> reason of its lack of political power, is unable to secure
> direct representation?. . . . thousands of workers are
> disenfranchised merely because they happen to be women.
> . . . It will be said, perhaps, that the interests of women
> will be safe in the hands of the men's Labour Party.
> Never in the history of the world have the interests of
> those without power to defend themselves been properly
> served by others. . . . I hope the women of England will
> not have to say that neither Liberal, Conservative nor
> Labour parties are their friends.

In May 1903, Christabel rebuked an ILP candidate for Preston
for failing to include women's suffrage in his election address,
and added, 'It is not enough to have supporters who are merely
"in favour". A majority of the House of Commons is "in favour"
now of giving political rights to women, but with no result. We
want friends who will do something practical.'[17]

Christabel's acerbity was not limited to the public arena.
After Isabella Ford, one of the nine members of the ILP executive, told the Pankhursts that the executive was not more than
lukewarm with regard to women's suffrage, Christabel took to
questioning sharply ILP leaders who visited the Pankhursts'
home, with regard to their views on women's suffrage. Bruce
Glasier, then chairman of the ILP, who argued that it was not
important for women to have the vote as the interests of working
women would be defended by Labour MPs, was received with
'bitter resentment'.[18] Christabel soon gave further vent to her
irritation in the leading article of the August 1903 issue of the
ILP News:[19]

> As a rule, Socialists are silent on the position of women. If
> not actually antagonistic to the movement for women's
> rights, they hold aloof from it. One gathers that some day,
> when the Socialists are in power, and have nothing better
> to do, they will give women votes as a finishing touch to

their arrangements, but for the present they profess no interest in the subject. . . . Why are women expected to have such confidence in the men of the Labour Party? Working-men are as unjust to women as are those of other classes.

During August 1903, there was mounting unemployment of women workers in Lancashire cotton mills. Women cotton operatives were among the best paid women workers – their salaries were almost forty per cent higher than the average salary of all women workers – but the cotton industry was subject to marked cyclical changes.[20] In the late summer of 1903, unemployment was caused in part by a shortage of raw cotton that stemmed from a cornering of the cotton market by American financiers. Some mills went on short time and others closed completely. By September, at least 4,000 operatives in the Oldham district alone were receiving relief from the Cotton Operative Spinners' Association, and the Burnley Weavers' Association voted £5,500 to its members. At the beginning of October, the trade correspondent of the Board of Trade estimated that in the cotton industry of England and Wales, 450,000 operatives out of a total of 580,000 were on short time.[21]

Mrs Pankhurst had looked on Christabel's work in the NESWS with considerable interest, and had herself spoken on behalf of the NESWS on two occasions, but she had not become more than marginally involved in its activities. During the summer and early autumn of 1903, however, as the unemployment and short-time employment of women cotton operatives mounted, Mrs Pankhurst began to talk of the need for a new organization which would fight for the interests of working-class women. In North Salford, the ILP had been building a hall that was to be named after R. M. Pankhurst. Sylvia Pankhurst helped decorate the hall, and while working there found that a branch of the ILP that was already using a finished part of the building did not accept women as members, ostensibly because the branch was affiliated with a social club that did not admit women. Pankhurst Hall was formally opened on 3 October, when Philip Snowden and Bruce Glasier addressed a crowded evening meeting. Snowden was hostile to women's suffrage, and, at the meeting, Christabel refused to speak to him. But she was engrossed with the NESWS, and, in addition, had just embarked on a course of legal studies at Owens College of the Victoria University, Manchester, and it was Mrs Pankhurst, who, aware of the distress of women cotton operatives, and exasperated by the refusal to admit women as members to an ILP branch that was using a hall named in honour of her late husband, decided to form a new organization which would carry on political and social work on behalf of working-class women. Mrs Pankhurst wanted to call the proposed organization the Women's Labour Representation Committee, but Christabel said that Eva Gore-Booth and Esther Roper were taking the title for an organization they were forming (it came into existence that autumn as the Lancashire and Cheshire Women Textile and other Workers' Representation Committee). So Mrs Pankhurst selected instead 'The Women's Social and Political Union'.*

On 10 October 1903, Mrs Pankhurst asked a small group of women, most of whom were working-class supporters of the ILP, to her home at 62 Nelson Street, and the Women's Social and Political Union was formed. No reliable evidence survives of what was decided at the first meeting. The most informative surviving account of the internal affairs of the WSPU in its earliest days is contained in the unpublished recollections of Teresa Billington (later Mrs Teresa Billington-Greig),† who wrote that 'at a very early meeting I was asked to draw up a

---

* E. S. Pankhurst, *The Suffragette Movement*, p. 168. In December 1903, the newly-formed Lancashire and Cheshire Women Textile and other Workers' Representation Committee announced that it would put up a candidate, Mr Hubert Sweeney, for the constituency of Wigan at the next election (*Women's Suffrage Record*, December 1903, p. 1).

† Teresa Billington, then an elementary school teacher in Manchester, came to know Mrs Pankhurst in 1903 at meetings of the Manchester branch of the ILP. She joined the WSPU shortly after its founding, and was one of its leading members until 1907. A brief biography of Teresa Billington appears on pp. 43–5.
    The Billington-Greig Papers, in the Fawcett Library, include many pages of recollections that Mrs Billington-Greig apparently wrote as notes for a projected autobiography. Her memoirs contain information on the early WSPU not available elsewhere, but they were written many years after her bitter break with the Pankhursts in 1907, and are hardly unimpeachable sources. Unfortunately, it is not possible to write of the internal affairs of the WSPU in its first months in the light of original documents alone, since few survive.

Draft Constitution to serve as the basis on which at some later
day a Conference of members would shape the rules and regulations which the movement desired'.[22] She described the draft as a
democratic constitution, with voting members, elected officers,
and an annual conference. But there was, it seems, no great
desire that a constitution be adopted: 'From time to time the
formal shaping and passing of the Constitution came up in
discussion but it was always willingly postponed. So far as I know
there was never any distress on this account'.[23]

In addition to lack of a constitution, there seems to have been
little by way of formal procedure in the naming of officers, the
holding of meetings, or the arranging of finance. At first, neither
Mrs Pankhurst nor Christabel held any office, as neither wished
the WSPU to be discounted as 'just Mrs Pankhurst and Christabel' or known as 'a family party'.[24] The WSPU did appoint a
secretary, Mrs Rachell Scott, but the job was largely clerical. A
Mrs Harker (probably John Harker's wife) was treasurer for a
time, but no record of her work survives.

Meetings of the newly-formed WSPU were held weekly,
often at 62 Nelson Street, but sometimes in a small room located
above a warehouse in Portland Street.[25] The meetings were
attended by those women who wished to come; there was no
formal membership list. WSPU finance too was conducted
informally – at meetings, members put shillings and loose change
into a collection bag. Mrs Pankhurst supplied additional funds
from her own money and from donations by sympathizers. From
time to time, Mrs Pankhurst announced that she had received a
donation from a friend, but the Union's members were usually
told neither the source nor the sum of such donations, and there
is no extant evidence that any accounting of WSPU finances was
made to members at early meetings.[26] The normal business of
the weekly gatherings was to choose speakers to address ILP
meetings as well as trade unions, trades councils, Labour Churches,
and Clarion Clubs. During the week, letters were written from
Nelson Street asking for speaking engagements, and then at
WSPU meetings Mrs Pankhurst or Adela would arrive bearing
replies and invitations to speak, and speakers would be chosen.
At first, there were only five speakers – Mrs Pankhurst, her
three daughters, and Teresa Billington. The five women were all
members of the ILP, and though the WSPU was not officially

affiliated with the ILP, in practice it was dependent upon the ILP for publicity, lecture platforms, and audiences.

During the first months of its existence, the WSPU received little attention. Although Keir Hardie had known Mrs Pankhurst for many years, the founding of the WSPU had not been mentioned in the *Labour Leader*, which Hardie edited. The WSPU's first tentative political efforts also passed virtually unnoticed. One of the Union's first political undertakings was to ask candidates for the Manchester City Council to support a resolution that the council petition Parliament to make women eligible for election as councillors; the Union received several favourable answers, but no concrete results.[27]

In December 1903, the WSPU published, in a bright yellow pamphlet, the suffrage resolution it espoused: 'That for all purposes connected with, and having reference to, the right to vote at Parliamentary elections, words in the Representation of the People Act importing the masculine gender shall include women.'[28] The terms of enfranchisement were essentially those that Dr Pankhurst had advocated in 1869. Mrs Pankhurst persuaded the Manchester ILP to pass the suffrage resolution, and the WSPU also asked the National Administrative Council of the ILP to adopt the resolution. In addition, the WSPU sent a deputation to John Hodge, who was the chairman of the LRC and a Labour candidate for Gorton, asking him, if elected, to introduce a Bill extending the existing franchise to women. Hodge replied that he was pledged to give first place in his programme to the extension of the check-weighmen's clause to the Steelsmelters', Mill, and Tinplate Workers' Association, but that he would 'do all in his power to secure that one of the measures to be promoted in the House of Commons by the Parliamentary Labour Group shall be the above Bill.'[29] A Councillor Parker of Halifax was also approached, and informed the WSPU that if he was elected to Parliament he would put the vote for women 'first on his programme.' Neither Hodge nor Parker won a seat in Parliament at this time.

Vague pledges from candidates of a fledgling Labour coalition with only three seats in Parliament gave scant satisfaction to Christabel, who was well aware that the three Labour MPs could not possibly alter the fate of women's enfranchisement

Bills. Christabel resented more influential politicians' lack of interest in the issue, and she decided to press her case at a major meeting of the Free Trade League, to be held in the Free Trade Hall on the evening of 19 February 1904. Winston Churchill, who had spoken for an hour and a half, had just proposed that the meeting reaffirm its 'unshaken belief in the principles of Free Trade adopted more than fifty years ago', when Christabel, who had managed to obtain a seat on the platform, stepped forward and sought to propose an amendment to Churchill's resolution.[30] She asked that the Representation of the People Acts be amended so that words expressed in the masculine gender would be construed to include women. The chairman refused to allow consideration of the amendment in connection with a free trade resolution which, he said, should be received with unanimity. For several minutes, he explained his refusal to an adamant Christabel, who for a time refused to give way, but finally withdrew amidst loud cries of 'Chair'.[31] Christabel later remembered the episode as[32]

> the first militant step – the hardest to me, because it *was* the first. To move from my place on the platform to the speaker's table in the teeth of the astonishment and opposition of will of that immense throng, those civic and county leaders and those Members of Parliament, was the most difficult thing I have ever done.

Christabel's abortive attempt in the Free Trade Hall had been undertaken at her own initiative, and was not connected with existing strategies of either the WSPU or the NESWS. The WSPU was at this time almost exclusively concerned with trying to instil enthusiasm for women's suffrage in Labour organizations, and the effort of persuading such organizations was conducted by orthodox means. The WSPU's most extensive proselytizing was directed at the ILP, which was divided over the wisdom of working for extension of the existing franchise to women, as opposed to eventually including women in an omnibus measure which would enfranchise all adults. The WSPU argued for extension of the existing franchise on the grounds that an omnibus measure was desirable in principle but unobtainable in practice, there being insufficient support in either major party for a complete revision of the franchise. In contrast, Philip Snowden and other supporters of adult suffrage argued that extending the existing franchise to women would not serve the interests of the working class, as a disproportionate number of the women enfranchised would be women of property and means, who would not support Labour candidates.[33] Christabel replied to Snowden that while extending the existing franchise would indeed leave many women without votes, it was a necessary first step to complete equality.[34] Christabel disliked Snowden, and she wrote with some bitterness that he 'ought to be a woman for a while. As Miss Snowden he would never have been either a councillor or a Parliamentary Candidate.'[35]

Mrs Pankhurst had been elected to the ILP's National Administrative Council in April 1904. She subsequently used her position to secure the passage of a resolution instructing the NAC to arrange for the introduction of a limited women's suffrage measure in Parliament. Her victory had only been obtained over the stiff opposition of the adult suffragists on the NAC, and Keir Hardie, realizing that the dispute was by no means settled, sought clarification of the basic issue by instructing the NAC to send all ILP branches a questionnaire in which he sought to ascertain the social class of women already on municipal registers, on the grounds that all such women would be immediately placed on the parliamentary register if the existing parliamentary franchise was extended to women. Each ILP branch was asked to ascertain the 'number of women voters of the working class' and the 'number of women voters not of the working class' on the local municipal register. 'Working-class women' were defined as 'those who work for wages, who are domestically employed, or who are supported by the earnings of wage-earning children.' 'Wages' were not defined.[36]

Only 50 of the approximately 300 existing ILP branches replied to the questionnaire. The 50 branches reported a total of 59,920 women voters on municipal registers, of which 49,410 were 'working women voters' 10,510 'non-working women voters'.[37] Hardie asserted that the result showed that 82 per cent of the women who would be immediately enfranchised by extending the existing franchise to women would be 'working women'.[38] The statistic was worthless, for several reasons. First, the characteristics of electoral districts with ILP branches were not necessarily the same as the characteristics of the aggregate of British electoral districts, ILP branches having been established in areas favourable to the ILP. Second, though only 50 out of about 300 branches had answered the questionnaire, no inquiry had been made into the characteristics peculiar to those branches that had chosen to reply; the possibility that a disproportionate number of responding branches were in areas with a high proportion of relatively well-paid working-class women – textile manufacturing districts, for example – had not been investigated. Third, as 'wages' had not been defined, branches were free to include women employed in occupations such as school teaching as 'working women' who worked for 'wages', even though most such women were not ordinary working-class women in terms of education or social standing. Finally, no systematic inquiry had been made into the other categories of woman voter – lodgers and property owners – who would have been enfranchised by extension of the existing qualifications. * Nevertheless, the WSPU eagerly and uncritically seized upon the statistics yielded by the ILP poll, and from 1904 on, WSPU writers and speakers freely claimed, citing the poll, that extending the existing franchise would result in over 80 per cent of those enfranchised being 'working women' or 'working-class women' – both phrases were used on various occasions.† The WSPU never undertook research of its own regarding the electoral consequences of the measure of enfranchisement it consistently advocated.

On 25 and 26 November 1904, the National Union of Women's Suffrage Societies held its national convention in London. The North of England Society for Women's Suffrage was one of the constituent bodies of the NUWSS, so Christabel was *ipso facto* a member of the latter organization. At the convention, Christabel made a speech in which she pleaded for 'the franchise for women' on the ground that enfranchisement would benefit 'working women', whose[39]

---

* The two major categories not covered by the ILP poll were lodgers occupying apartments of £10 annual value (unfurnished) and owners, in county constituencies, of freehold estates or long-term leaseholds of not less than £5 annual value (see C. Rover, *Women's Suffrage*, pp. 25–7).
† See Mrs Pankhurst's speech, p. 36. See also F. W. Pethick-Lawrence, 'Women's fight for the vote', in *Votes for Women*, 25 March 1910.

position has rather gone down than up in the last generations. You find the women of Cradley Heath working at
chair-making for 2s. 6d., 4s., and 5s., a week; if you go to
the shirt makers you will hear that their conditions are
worse than when Thomas Hood wrote his famous 'Song of
the Shirt' . . . in their industrial position women have
rather gone back than forward. . . . This is my claim to the
franchise – that it will advance the industrial condition of
women.

Christabel urged[40]

that party women . . . be a thorn in the side of their
respective parties, and urge the members of their party to
make this question of the enfranchisement of women part of
the programme of their party.

Two months later, at the Labour Representation Committee's
conference in Liverpool, Mrs Pankhurst tried to persuade the LRC
to adopt a measure extending the existing franchise to women. She
went so far as to claim that under such a measure '90 per cent. of
the women enfranchised would be working women, and by working women she meant every woman who earned her living.'[41]
Mrs Pankhurst's statistics did not persuade the LRC, which
proceeded to espouse adult suffrage, 483,000 votes to 270,000.[42]
The LRC's vote notwithstanding, Keir Hardie told Mrs
Pankhurst that he would introduce a private member's Bill
extending the existing franchise to women. However, in the
private members' ballot on 21 February 1905, Hardie was not
able to obtain a place for the Bill. Subsequently, after much
chasing of MPs, Hardie and Mrs Pankhurst were able to persuade
Bamford Slack, a Liberal MP who held fourteenth place in the
private members' ballot and whose wife was a member of the
executive committee of the NUWSS, to introduce the Bill. On
19 February, Mrs Pankhurst wrote to Mrs Dora Montefiore,
complaining that the traditional suffragists had not worked to
obtain a favourable place for the Women's Enfranchisement Bill
in the private members' ballot:[43]

If women had worked in the House as the trade unionists do
we should have had Members battling for us session after
session. This time we owe it all to Keir Hardie, but we have

no right to expect M.P.'s to do more for us than they do for others. The people who secured good places for their measures have done so because they have lobbied incessantly for years. Of course, it is horrid work, but it has to be done, if we are to succeed. Mr. Hardie told Miss Pallisser that more energy was needed.

Now we must get to work to get pressure brought to bear on Members by petitions, deputations, lobbying, etc., in support of the Bill. Is it possible to form a Women's Parliamentary Committee in London to do this lobbying work? The old-fashioned and official gang will never do it. I have no confidence in them.

In March, that old-fashioned and official gang, the National Union of Women's Suffrage Societies, held a meeting in Queen's Hall in support of the Women's Enfranchisement Bill. Sylvia Pankhurst, who attended the meeting, later remembered Members of Parliament in evening dress, and ladies who spoke in nervous high-pitched voices – 'It was all very polite and very tame; different indeed from the rousing Socialist meetings of the North, to which I was accustomed.'[44] In the north, the WSPU carried on its own campaign for the Bill; Mrs Pankhurst, Christabel, and Teresa Billington spoke again and again in Lancashire and Yorkshire towns, and in April the WSPU persuaded the ILP's annual conference to carry a resolution supporting the Bill.

Slack's measure was the first women's enfranchisement Bill to be presented to the House of Commons in eight years. On 12 May 1905, the day of the Bill's Second Reading, about 300 women, two-thirds of whom had come from co-operative guilds in the London area, went to the House of Commons to await the results. From noon until 4 p.m., a measure that sought to make mandatory the fitting of lamps at the rear of carts was debated at length, and with much jocularity, by anti-suffragist MPs, who effectively whittled away the time available for debate on the women's Bill. When the Bill finally reached the floor, the aged Henry Labouchere, long a foe of women's suffrage, rose to make a lengthy anti-suffrage speech in order to use up the remaining time and make a division impossible. Labouchere's arguments were those that had been advanced again and again by anti-

suffragist politicians for the past forty years: 'In consideration of
the great problems which came before the Imperial Parliament
they [women] were certainly inferior intellectually to men. . . .
Women were nervous, emotional, and had very little sense of
proportion.' The 'vast majority' of women did not want the vote;
only women with 'masculine minds' were interested in politics.[45]
And so on. Anti-suffrage MPs greeted the familiar propositions
with laughter and cheers. Labouchere held the floor until
5.30 p.m., when debate was adjourned, with the Bill talked
out.

As Labouchere had talked away the meagre time allotted for the
Bill, the waiting women had grown dismayed and then angry.
With debate concluded, the police moved the women away from
the Strangers' Entrance. The women sought to hold a meeting
next to the statue of Richard Coeur de Lion, outside the House of
Lords, but the police again moved them on. Only on Keir Hardie's
intervention were the police persuaded to allow the women to
hold a meeting, in the safely distant precincts of Westminster
Abbey. The Pankhursts' old friend, Isabella Ford, wrote of the
occasion:[46]

> when the news came that the House had risen, and all was
> over, our Bill talked out, our indignation was stronger and
> more burning than I for one have ever seen it before. . . .
> The police finally escorted us past Westminster Abbey to
> a corner of Broad Sanctuary, and there, where in long past
> ages persons in terror of their lives could take refuge from
> their pursuers, we all stood, political outcasts, as were
> those old fugitives, while Mrs. Martel read aloud a petition
> of protest to the House, to be presented this week. It was
> carried with acclamation. We groaned for Labouchere,
> cheered Mr. Hardie, and dispersed. The police stood by us all
> the time, for our meeting was only allowed by courtesy,
> and they seemed much relieved that we went away so
> peacefully and quietly.
> In the heart of each woman there the seed of discontent
> and revolution is now too deeply implanted for us to fear
> for the future. The future is ours. Many of the Members
> laughed when they saw us in the Lobby, even as they often
> laughed before when time after time the voteless workers

and their friends passed, defeated and angry, out of the doors of Parliament.

The defeat of the Women's Enfranchisement Bill coincided with the start of the season during which ILP branches held open-air meetings throughout the north. On 7 May 1905, the Manchester branch of the ILP and the WSPU together inaugurated weekly Sunday evening meetings at Tib Street, in Manchester. In addition, on almost every Sunday for the next four months, the WSPU dispatched four or five speakers to meetings in Lancashire and Yorkshire towns. The ranks of the regular WSPU speakers had heretofore been composed solely of the four Pankhursts and Teresa Billington. These five speakers were now joined by Mrs Hannah Webster Mitchell and Miss Annie Kenney. Whereas nothing is known of the twenty-odd working-class women who came to WSPU meetings in 1903 and 1904, both Hannah Mitchell and Annie Kenney wrote autobiographies, and, as has been mentioned, Teresa Billington left extensive unpublished autobiographical fragments. The three women had much in common, and rather similar factors seem to have led them to join the WSPU.

Hannah Maria Webster had been born in an isolated farmhouse on the moorlands of the Peak District of Derbyshire on 11 February 1872. * She was the fourth child born to a poor family, and she later wrote that her mother 'bitterly resented my coming into the world'.[47] Mrs Webster was a deeply embittered woman, who hated farm life and drove the seven members of her family (two more children had followed Hannah) with an iron temper. She was periodically subject to manic fits of anger, during which the entire family fled her wrath:[48]

* At her death in 1956, Mrs Hannah Mitchell left several typescript copies of an unpublished autobiography. The autobiography was subsequently edited by her grandson, Mr Geoffrey Mitchell, and published as *The Hard Way Up*. In an introduction, Mr Mitchell stated that the text had been 'arranged in parts', but that substantial alterations had not been made (*ibid.*, p. 33). In comparing one of the original typescript copies with the published version, I have found a considerable number of changes in diction. All quotations in these pages are from the typescript copy of the autobiography of Hannah Mitchell deposited in the London Museum.

She would throw herself into violent passions and drive us
all out of the house. Sometimes we would have to spend the
night in the barn sleeping on the hay. My father seemed
totally unable to combat these storms or even to protect us.
He was always the first to leave the house when they broke,
and the last to return.
   . . . he could not shield us from my mother's virago like
[sic] temper.

Cleanliness was Mrs Webster's household deity. Farm life was
naturally dirty, but she liked neither dirt nor animals, and 'used
her leftover soap suds on washing days to scrub and wash the
pigs.'[49] She looked upon house-cleaning and cooking as a woman's
natural tasks, to be suffered through but never escaped from, and
with scoldings and beatings she drove Hannah to perform a
seemingly endless series of chores. Mrs Webster mocked her
daughter's desire for education, and Hannah Webster received
only a few months of formal schooling; her education was limited
to the simple ability to read and write that she acquired from her
father, a gentle, kindly, rather unassertive man, whose wife
'quite definitely "ruled the roost" in our house'.[50]
In 1884, when Hannah Webster was thirteen, her family's
financial straits forced her into apprenticeship as a dressmaker.
The following year, she left home for good. After leaving home,
she worked first as a maid and then as a seamstress, an occupation
which entailed long hours and meagre wages. Subsequently, in
1895, she married Gibbon Mitchell, a fellow lodger who was
employed as a shop manager. Of the origins of her marriage she
later wrote:[51]

We were both tired of living in other people's houses, and
felt that our own hearth even if humble, would be more
comfortable. . . . Married life as lived by my brothers,
sisters, and friends held no particular attraction for me
either, but I wanted a home of my own. Perhaps if I had
really understood myself, as I did later, I should not have
married. I soon realised that married life, as men understand it, calls for a degree of self abnegation on the part of
women which was impossible for me, I needed solitude,
time for study, and the opportunity for a wider life.

Gibbon Mitchell's wages were low, so Hannah Mitchell
continued to work as a seamstress. She now found that since
household work took up her leisure hours, no time was left for
the education she still desired. Her husband was a Socialist, and
brought her into contact with the nascent Socialism of the 1890s,
but, like Christabel Pankhurst, Hannah Mitchell came to look
askance at what she saw as the unthinking lip-service paid by
Socialists to women's equality:[52]

> Even my Sunday leisure was gone, for I soon found that a
> good deal of the Socialist talk about freedom, was 'Well'
> just *talk* and these Socialist young men expected Sunday
> dinners and huge teas with home made cakes, potted meats
> and pies, exactly like their reactionary fellows. . . .
>   I think I resented the Sunday work most of all, but as I
> was busy with dressmaking during the week I had to do all
> my cooking and baking on Sunday. Not being one of those
> happily constituted souls who enjoy cooking I found no
> pleasure in it.

To make matters worse, her domestic efforts were, she felt,
unappreciated: 'There being not much rich feeding to be got out
of a pound a week, neither my husband nor his family thought
much of my efforts on the kitchen front . . . he never really
valued my contribution to the housekeeping.'[53]
   Maternity only brought additional unhappiness. Hannah
Mitchell found labour extremely painful – she delivered without
an anaesthetic – and she later wrote:[54]

> Only one thing emerges clearly from much bitter thinking
> at that time, the fixed resolve to bring no more babies into
> the world. I felt that I could not face again either the
> personal suffering or the responsibilities of bringing children
> up in poverty. Fortunately my husband had the courage of
> his Socialist convictions on this point, and was no more
> anxious than myself to repeat the experience. I could not
> feed my baby and was unable to find a food to suit him. He
> was cross and miserable, so was I. So also was his father.

She had no more children.
   Hannah Mitchell joined the ILP in the later 1890s. Like Mrs

Pankhurst, she had been attracted by the ILP's women lecturers, and from Katherine St John Conway she had received 'the
beginnings of a faith which later sent me out to the street corner
with the same message'.[55] In about 1902, Hannah Mitchell
became Lecture Secretary of the Labour Church at Ashton-under-
Lyne. This post brought her into frequent contact with itinerant
ILP lecturers, who often stayed overnight with the Mitchells,
and she thus met Hardie, MacDonald, and Snowden, among
others. One Sunday, she spoke in the Labour Church on 'The
Woman's Cause', and she thereafter began to lecture regularly
from ILP platforms. In May 1904, Hannah Mitchell became a
candidate for the Ashton Board of Poor Law Guardians. Mrs
Pankhurst came to aid in the election campaign, acquaintance
followed, and Hannah Mitchell was speaking under the auspices
of the WSPU at least as early as 7 May 1905.[56]

Annie Kenney had been born on 13 September 1879, in a
Pennine village called Springhead. Almost two months prema-
ture, she was as a baby regarded as a 'weakling'.[57] Like Hannah
Webster, she grew up in a large and financially hard-pressed
family – she was the fifth of eleven children, and her father's
wages at an Oldham cotton factory were limited. Annie Kenney's
girlhood was by no means as grim as that of Hannah Webster,
but the Kenneys resembled the Websters in at least some respects.
Mrs Kenney, 'loving and affectionate, but a firm believer in
discipline', was clearly the head of the Kenney household.[58] Mr
Kenney was a kindly man who was dominated by his wife. Annie
Kenney later wrote of him,[59]

> Father never seemed to have any confidence in his children,
> and he had very little in himself. Had he possessed this
> essential quality, perhaps the whole course of our lives
> would have been changed. My mother always said she
> ought to have been the man and Father the woman.

Mr Kenney was a 'born nurse', and a proficient cook, but he
could hardly be the sole support of so large a brood, and in 1889,
at the age of ten, Annie was told by her mother that she was to
begin half-time work in a cotton factory. At thirteen, Annie
Kenney had to leave school entirely to become a full-time cotton

operative, rising at 5 a.m. to reach the factory before 6 a.m. to begin an eleven-and-a-half-hour day. During the course of her career as a 'big tenter', in charge of a pair of frames, one of her fingers was torn off by a whirling bobbin.[60]

During her adolescent years, Annie Kenney remained a rather child-like person. She still played with dolls at the age of fourteen, and, later, as a young woman, apparently lacked interest in young men her own age, preferring to live in day-dreams of friendship with God, kings, and potentates – older men of power and munificence, who regarded her in a fatherly or uncle-like fashion. (She later wrote: 'All through my life, the day's work over, I have lived in dreams.' When she was little, God, who looked like Tolstoy, 'sat for years, in the same cloudy arm-chair, waiting for me.'[61] Later, 'King Edward and I were good friends, in fact he was more like an uncle to me in my day-dreams.')[62]

By the time she was twenty, Annie Kenney had become interested in the Labour movement. She began to read the *Clarion* regularly, and discovered Ruskin, Carpenter, and William Morris. She also joined the choir of the Oldham ILP, and through that membership met Christabel Pankhurst, who came to address the Oldham ILP in the spring of 1905. Annie Kenney was then twenty-six, unmarried, living at home, and still girlish rather than womanly in character. A significant change in her life had recently occurred, however – her mother had died in early January, and 'the cement of love that kept the home life together [had] disappeared.'[63] Soon after meeting Christabel, Annie Kenney became a frequent visitor at the Pankhursts' home in Nelson Street. She quickly came to place complete faith in the political judgment of Christabel, who had almost finished her legal studies at Owens College of Victoria University, and was by now a seasoned and knowledgable political speaker. In turn, Christabel valued Annie's devotion, and appreciated the element of social balance she brought to WSPU lecture platforms – from the start, Annie Kenney was instructed always to intro-duce herself to the WSPU's working-class audiences as 'a factory-girl and Trade Unionist'.[64]

Teresa Billington had been born in Blackburn in 1877. Her father too was a genial but ineffectual man. William Billington was a shipping clerk in a Lancashire iron foundry. In his daughter's eyes, he was a*

> popular fellow outside his home, [but] a poor earner, ill
> educated, & with no conception of her [his wife's] quality or
> of the refinements natural to her from inheritance & long
> convent training. He was generous in rare occasional
> childish ways but normally selfish & greedy.

Mrs Helen Billington had four miscarriages, and was frequently moody and withdrawn. In her daughter's estimation, 'William himself more than anything else in life had been her destroyer.' Through gross insensitivity he had 'crushed or thwarted' his wife's 'wide-ranging mind, her interest in Nature, her love of beauty'. Moreover, through his 'unfaithfulness' he had flaunted 'the invincibility of her moral standards.'[65] It seems likely, however, that Helen Billington's discontent had its locus in experiences that preceded her marriage. She had been educated in a convent school, and was given to what her daughter saw as 'an unhealthy absorption in prayer and meditation':[66]

> She would murmer prayers as she moved to and fro at
> household tasks, there would be a 'holy book' beside her
> into which she would dip as she sat over the household
> mending, she would feel her 'beads' or sing a hymn softly
> at any odd moment of the day . . . at our coming she
> would waken up as it were to join us . . . except when with
> closed eyes she was meditating, when she might remain
> withdrawn for a time long enough to make one feel
> excluded. I hated the meditation periods. To come running
> home to her from school, from errands, or from play &
> meet the gone away withdrawness of that quiet figure was
> to have imposed immediate silence on one to shut one out as
> a stranger, an interloper, to be cut off. I hated it.

That William Billington might have hated it too, or that her

---

* Blackman Papers, undated holograph notes. Most of the autobiographical notes of Mrs Teresa Billington-Greig were deposited in the Fawcett Library, but those notes dealing with her girlhood remained in the hands of her niece, Mrs Mary Beatrice Blackman, of Chettle, Dorset. When I read them, the papers were not organized, so no folio references can be given.

mother's withdrawnness might have had its sexual analogue, apparently did not occur to Teresa Billington. She saw her father as guilty of 'pretence of the religion which had so deep a root in her, but which he observed in the most meagre & minor way that the rules of the Church permitted. With her opinions & her convent upbringing this was a major tragedy to Helen.'*

As a result of her parents' manifest incompatibility, Teresa Billington acquired a jaundiced view of marriage at an early age:[67]

> It was an odd sort of puzzle to me to see the sort of marriage award, that is of husband, my mother's manifest virtues & grace had won for her. . . . Revering my mother as I did, how could I believe in the happy marriage myth of the poets or story writers or hope to understand why girls married at all.
>
> But what else was there to do? . . . I brooded a lot about the cruel life choices open to women while still in my early teens.

After leaving home, Teresa Billington became an elementary school teacher, and, later, secretary of the Manchester Teachers' Equal Pay League. She also did social work, becoming secretary of the Ancoats University Settlement. By 1903, she was attending meetings of the Central Manchester ILP, and at one of those meetings she met Mrs Pankhurst. When she joined the WSPU at the end of 1903, Teresa Billington was twenty-six and unmarried, a large, aggressive woman, with firmly held beliefs in Socialism and agnosticism, and a fondness for argument.

The three most important early supporters of the WSPU – aside from the Pankhursts themselves – had, then, a good deal in common. Hannah Mitchell, Annie Kenney, and Teresa Billington all regarded their fathers as pleasant but ineffectual men, who lacked both earning-power and strength of character. The mothers of Hannah Mitchell and Annie Kenney had dominated their respective families, and Mrs Helen Billington was withdrawn and inaccessible – none of the three mothers much resembled the ineffectual angels of Victorian poets and essayists.

* Blackman Papers, undated holograph notes. This judgment is curious in that after leaving home Teresa Billington became a militant agnostic and refused to teach religion in state schools.

C

By becoming a seamstress, cotton operative, and school teacher, respectively, Hannah Mitchell, Annie Kenney, and Teresa Billington had all taken jobs that offered neither the reality nor the prospect of either intellectual challenge or substantial monetary reward. Yet, none of the three had been able to find some degree of fulfilment in marriage – on joining the WSPU, Annie Kenney and Teresa Billington were both twenty-six and unmarried, and Hannah Mitchell (who was thirty-three) was deeply dissatisfied with married life as she experienced it. Finally, prior to joining the WSPU, all three had become members of both the ILP and trade unions, and Hannah Mitchell and Teresa Billington had both acquired some experience of public speaking.

During the summer of 1905, WSPU speakers – of which there were now six – addressed far more meetings than ever before. Now, for the first time, women's suffrage became a heatedly discussed topic within the world of northern radical politics. Ranging as far afield as Leicester, Grimsby, Stockton, and Hartlepool, WSPU speakers addressed between five and ten meetings each week, the six regular speakers being helped by other women from time to time. In addition, when WSPU speakers addressed ILP meetings, male members of the ILP often spoke on behalf of women's suffrage. One of the WSPU's male supporters was the youthful, erratic, Victor Grayson, already well known for the fervour of his Socialism and the carrying-power of his deep rich voice.

WSPU speeches in urban centres were usually given at meetings held under the aegis of the ILP. The weekly meetings held on Sunday evenings at Tib Street in Manchester, under the sponsorship of the Manchester Central Branch of the ILP, showed traces of the street-corner preaching of the Primitive Methodism in which so many ILP members had acquired their first public speaking experience: the portable platform which was assembled on the spot by volunteers was referred to as a 'preacher's platform',[68] and WSPU speakers were known as 'Mrs Pankhurst's suffrage missioners'.[69] Meetings at Tib Street often included a brass band or choir – on 21 May 1905, the Pontycymmer Miners' Choir appeared three times before 'record crowds', and on 6 August the Salford Clarion Choir sang glees.[70] Meetings devoted to women's suffrage usually closed with the passing by acclamation of a resolution 'demanding the Parliamentary vote for women'.[71] After such meetings, collections were taken, Keir Hardie's pamphlet 'The Citizenship of Women' was sold, and women who wished to do so could join the WSPU. WSPU meetings held under ILP auspices in other cities varied only in size and detail.

The WSPU's own efforts were less elaborate: a courageous WSPU member would simply start speaking on a street-corner or village green, without outside aid or sponsorship – Hannah Mitchell worked the Colne Valley from end to end, holding street meetings after first going 'from door to door, to ask the women to listen.'[72] Following the advice of Annie Kenney, the WSPU also made a particular point of sending speakers to wakes-fairs. These week-long events – originally hiring fairs – were held at different times during the summer in towns like Mossly and Stalybridge. By tradition, temperance orators, the Salvation Army, and others desiring public attention appeared on the fairgrounds where audiences could be easily gathered. The WSPU now appeared on the fairgrounds too.

During the summer of 1905, members of the WSPU did not restrict themselves to work for women's suffrage. On 2 July, Christabel addressed the West Salford ILP on 'What the Labour Party Would Do For Children', and later in July she spoke at several meetings held on behalf of an unemployed relief Bill which had been introduced by Walter Long, the president of the Local Government Board.[73] Meetings in support of the Bill were held in industrial centres throughout England, and on 17 July over 1,000 women marched from the East End to Westminster to try to see Balfour or Campbell-Bannerman. By late July, the Bill appeared doomed by a lack of parliamentary time, though on 26 July the government found time to pass a Bill dealing with a dispute between the Scottish Free Churches and the United Free Church of Scotland. Questioned later by Keir Hardie, Balfour explained that a particular crisis had made the Scottish Bill necessary, whereas it was not absolutely necessary to deal with the unemployed that session.[74]

Five days later, 400 to 500 of the unemployed met in the Albert Square, Manchester. W. E. Skivington, who presided, said 'something should be done to force the hands of the Government, and compel them to pass the Unemployed Bill.' The next speaker, Arthur Smith, said that the Manchester unemployed were 'prepared to fight if necessary'.[75] Skivington and Smith then led a procession of ragged men through the streets of central Manchester, accompanied by a hundred police. Near Piccadilly, the march impeded the passage of a tram, and fighting broke out between the marchers and the police, who used their batons. Four marchers were arrested. The following day, Keir Hardie protested to the Commons: 'Englishmen have been bludgeoned in the streets of Manchester'.[76] One of the leaders of the march said, however, with apparent candour, that the marchers 'were only doing what Mr. Balfour had told them to do – to create a crisis'.[77]

The government, though denying that it was acting in response to the Manchester 'riot', now somehow found time for the unemployed relief Bill, which was passed in ten days. Mrs Pankhurst and the other leaders of the Manchester ILP were convinced that the government had acted only because a 'crisis' had been created. On 13 August, the Labour group on the city council and an emergency committee of the ILP met at the Pankhursts' home in Nelson Street to initiate a campaign to take advantage of the new measure.[78]

4 Militancy Begins

During the last two weeks of September 1905 Christabel lectured in the Durham district, one of her topics being 'The Unemployed Act'.[1] She then returned to Manchester to resume her legal studies. Feeling that the WSPU was 'making no headway . . . our work was not counting',[2] and aware of the results of the recent unemployed 'riot' and of the tactics used by the ILP during the fight for the use of Boggart Hole Clough, Christabel now developed a plan. On 13 October, the Liberal Party, generally expected to be voted into office shortly, was to hold a major meeting in the Free Trade Hall at which Grey and Churchill would speak. She and Annie Kenney would attend the meeting, and would attempt to question the men on the platform regarding the future Liberal Government's willingness to enfranchise women. (Christabel, mindful of the chronic ineffi- cacy of private members' suffrage Bills, was coming to believe that only a government measure was likely to bring women the vote.)[3] The questions would not, of course, be answered in the affirmative. After refusal, she and Annie would take steps to create a disturbance sufficient to get themselves arrested. Later, in court, they would refuse to pay fines, and the resulting brief imprisonment would create a cornucopia of publicity for the cause of women's enfranchisement. Martyrdom, deliberately sought after, would, if the deliberation were not revealed, make women's suffrage *newsworthy*.[4]

Christabel did not disclose her plans to the ordinary members of the WSPU, but she did discuss her intentions with her family and Teresa Billington. It was decided that during the forth- coming imprisonment, Teresa Billington would arrange protest meetings, and that, in general, she would handle correspondence connected with the affair.[5] A few days before the Free Trade Hall meeting, Teresa Billington wrote to Sir Edward Grey and asked him to receive a deputation from the WSPU. No answer was received, but reply had been neither expected nor particularly desired. On the afternoon of 13 October, Christabel and Annie Kenney made a banner which would be used to attract attention if their voices were not plainly heard in the large hall – on a swatch of white calico, they wrote with black floor stain, 'Votes for Women'.[6]

That evening, the two young women were seated towards the back of the Free Trade Hall. Sir Edward Grey was urging the return of the Liberals to office, when Annie Kenney shouted the question, phrased in advance by Christabel, 'Will the Liberal Government give women the vote?'* Christabel repeated the question. Then William Peacock, the chief constable of Manchester, a genial and paternal man, came down from the platform and told the pair that if their question were put into writing he would take it to the platform and an answer would be given during the question period. The offer was accepted, and the paper was taken to Grey, who read it and passed it to his colleagues. During the question period no answer was given.† The chairman was about to adjourn the meeting, when Annie Kenney stood on her chair, unfurled the little banner, and shouted again, 'Will the Liberal Government give women the vote?' An uproar ensued, as Liberal stewards and plain-clothes police tried to remove the women from the hall and Christabel and Annie struggled against their ejection. According to testimony given the following day by an Inspector Mather, the pair were informed, in the anteroom of the Free Trade Hall, that they were in the presence of police officers and that they were free to leave, but Christabel spat in the face of Superintendent Watson, and then spat in Mather's face and struck him in the mouth, saying that she wanted to assault a policeman.[7] The women were then ejected into South Street, where, according to Mather, Christabel again struck him in the mouth. She and Annie Kenney then began to shout excitedly to a crowd that gathered around them, blocking the thoroughfare. Said Mather:[8]

* With regard to the precise wording of the question, which has appeared in different forms in various books, see Christabel's letter to the editor in the *Manchester Guardian*, 25 October 1905.
† Grey subsequently explained that he had not mentioned women's suffrage because it was not a matter likely to become a party question (*Manchester Evening News*, 14 October 1905).

I asked them to go away. They did not go – they said they
would be locked up, both of them. I took hold of Miss
Pankhurst. The other defendent clung to her. On the way to
the Town Hall Miss Kenny [sic] said to Miss Pankhurst:
'Never mind; we have got what we wanted.' Miss Pankhurst
replied: 'Yes, I wanted to assault a policeman.'

At the Town Hall, Christabel and Annie were charged with
disorderly behaviour, and obstructing a footway by causing a
crowd to assemble. In addition, Christabel was charged with
striking Inspector Mather twice and with spitting at Mather and
Watson. Both women were released and ordered to appear in
court the following day.

The next morning, after Mather and Watson had testified,
Christabel, who did not dispute the charges against her, said: *

I want to explain as clearly as I can that at the time I
committed the assault that is complained of I was not aware
that the individuals assaulted were police officers. I thought
they were Liberals – some of those responsible for the
meeting. I am only sorry that one of them was not Sir
Edward Grey himself. The reason I was forced to adopt the
mode of assault that I did was because my arms were firmly
pinned down so that I could not raise them. There was no
other course open. My conduct in the Free Trade Hall and
outside was meant as a protest against the legal position of
women today. We cannot make any orderly protest because
we have not the means whereby citizens may do such a
thing; we have not a vote; and so long as we have not
votes we must be disorderly. There is no other way whereby
we can put forward our claims to political justice. When we
have that you will not see us at the police courts; but so
long as we have not votes this will happen.

* *Manchester Guardian*, 16 October 1905. Christabel later wrote that
she spat at the police while her arms were being held because she knew
from her legal studies that doing so would constitute a technical
assault, which might lead to the desired imprisonment: 'I could not and
dare not explain the entirely technical and symbolic character of the
act, because the magistrate might have discharged me and the political
purpose in view would not have been achieved. Even after I came out of
prison I was afraid of explaining and so seeming to weaken or recant'
(Dame C. Pankhurst, *Unshackled*, p. 52).

The magistrates found the pair guilty, and sentenced Christabel to a fine of 10s. 6d. or seven days' imprisonment for assaulting the police, and 5s. or three days' imprisonment for obstructing the public thoroughfare, the sentences to run concurrently. Annie Kenney was given the choice of a fine of 5s. or three days' imprisonment, for obstructing the thoroughfare. Christabel said, 'I shall pay no fine', and Annie said, 'Hear, hear.'[9] Mrs Pankhurst asked her daughter if she might pay the fine, but Christabel, Mrs Pankhurst later told the press, would not hear of it, and 'even went so far as to say that if I insisted she would not return home.'[10] The two young women were taken by cab to Strangeways Gaol.

Teresa Billington immediately began to write to the press and organize meetings of protest. On the evening of 14 October, despite a cold drizzle, almost a thousand people gathered in Stevenson Square to hear Mrs Pankhurst, Teresa Billington, and Hannah Mitchell. John Harker, who had gone to prison in the dispute over Boggart Hole Clough, proposed a resolution which condemned Sir Edward Grey for refusing to answer a legitimate question and protested against the ejection of the two young women from the meeting. His resolution was carried by acclamation.[11] That same evening, a Councillor Royle went to Strangeways Gaol where, on behalf of Winston Churchill, he offered to pay Christabel's and Annie's fines. They refused to permit payment.[12]

When Annie Kenney was released on the morning of 16 October, a large group of friends awaited her at the prison gates, and that evening she received an ovation from a crowd of 2,000 in Stevenson Square. Christabel was released at 7 a.m. on 20 October. Despite the early hour, a crowd of 200 waited to greet her outside the prison gates, and, that evening, a large meeting in her honour was held in the Free Trade Hall. (Teresa Billington and Sam Robinson, the secretary of the Manchester ILP, had made the necessary arrangements during the previous four days.) The Free Trade Hall was filled to capacity, and many were turned away. Bouquets were presented, and Christabel, Annie, and Keir Hardie all spoke. The *Labour Leader* reported Christabel as saying they 'were going to the Tory meetings also. Mr Balfour wanted a crisis before he would legislate. As far as the

women in England was [sic] concerned, there was a crisis today.'[13]
Keir Hardie condemned the Liberals for 'ignoring the legitimate
question asked by two women', and declared that 'the treatment
which Miss Pankhurst and Miss Kenney received was brutal and
unjustifiable'.[14] Hannah Mitchell later wrote of the evening:[15]

> The two girls who only a week before had been flung out of
> the Hall like criminals were now the central figures on the
> platform, which was filled with sympathisers, while the vast
> audience in both the arena and gallery showed the interest
> evoked by the treatment meted out to the women the
> previous Friday. Twenty years of peaceful propaganda had
> not produced such an effect.

In sum, Christabel's calculations had been correct. Militancy
was news. The sympathetic and the curious would never have
filled the Free Trade Hall without the lengthy newspaper
accounts and resulting spate of letters to the editor that the
imprisonments had evoked. Manchester dailies had, of course,
given the most substantial coverage; on 16 October, the *Manchester Guardian* had printed both a transcript of the trial and a
lengthy exposition of WSPU policy by Teresa Billington. The
Guardian would certainly not have carried such a statement
prior to the events of 13 October. Unlike the *Guardian*, *The
Times* had made no mention of the disturbance in its original
account of the Liberal meeting, but, by 16 October, even *The
Times* deemed the story worthy of print.

In subsequent weeks, WSPU speakers found themselves
attracting large audiences, and, despite a storm of criticism of
Christabel's tactics, the Union's membership began to grow. A
basic pattern had been established, wherein pre-planned militant
tactics led to imprisonment, and thus, martyrdom, which led to
newspaper coverage (i.e. free publicity), which led in turn to
increased membership and funds for the WSPU. This sequence,
repeated again and again, was to form the basis of the militant
feminist campaign. It had the double function of both attracting
members to the WSPU and attempting to win wide public
support for women's suffrage.

Some of Christabel's earliest colleagues did not fully approve of
her new tactics. Teresa Billington later wrote that[16]

c*

when Christabel & Annie Kenney were making their
defensive speeches in the series of meetings we ran in
nearby Lancashire after their release from Strangeways,
Eva Gore-Booth seized me dramatically one evening as we
left the platform & urged upon me that I should tell
Christabel not to vary her defence from one meeting to
another. Now she is out in the open, she said, she cannot
fit her explanation to her audience. She either deliberately
invited imprisonment or she was a victim; she either spat at
the policeman or she did not. She can't tell one tale in
Manchester & another in Oldham. I was in direct touch
with the Gore-Booth-Roper household for some weeks
during that emergency & found first to my surprise that
there was no direct communication then surviving between
the parties, & second that it did not matter whether they
showed their support or not. I was discouraged from
approaching them.

Eva Gore-Booth, a woman of lofty ideals, had apparently failed
to perceive that the success of Christabel's tactics *depended* on
deliberately courted imprisonment being seen as martyrdom.
Christabel was in turn quite prepared to part company with
anyone who made too much of apparent inconsistencies.

The imprisonments of October 1905 were not followed immediately by other imprisonments. Soon after Christabel's release,
Owens College threatened her with expulsion if she were
arrested again and made it an absolute condition of her continuing her legal studies that she agree not to cause further disturbances. Christabel agreed, and for the next few months neither
she nor other WSPU members sought arrest. However, after
Balfour resigned on 4 December 1905, the WSPU did begin to
send hecklers to Liberal meetings, to interrupt speeches with
questions regarding the Liberals' willingness to enfranchise
women. (The WSPU assumed that the Liberals would be elected, and for that reason only sent hecklers to Liberal meetings.)
Heckling was hardly a political novelty – electric loudspeakers
were not yet in use, and a sufficiently determined heckler could,
if not ejected, effectively counter a speaker – but both politicians
and the press viewed heckling by women as a radical departure

from normal mores, particularly as photographs of well-dressed women being thrown out of meetings by burly male stewards were shocking to a public accustomed to Victorian forms of chivalry.

On 21 December 1905, a particularly tumultuous scene occurred at the Albert Hall at a meeting addressed by Campbell-Bannerman. Sylvia Pankhurst, who had become an art student in South Kensington, had persuaded Keir Hardie to obtain seats for the use of the WSPU. Annie Kenney, visiting London, found herself seated in John Burns' box, and, during the Prime Minister's speech, she shouted the usual question and hung a banner (upside down) over the edge of the box. Then, from a balcony near the platform, Teresa Billington released a nine-foot-long banner inscribed, 'Will the Liberal Government give Justice to Working-Women?'[17] An uproar ensued, and the two women were thrown out of the hall, while the organ played loudly to muffle their cries.

The foray at the Albert Hall had no immediate sequel in London; during the election campaign of January 1906, the WSPU's efforts were largely directed at attempting to defeat Winston Churchill, who stood for North-West Manchester. The Union chose Churchill not out of any particular animus against him – he was vaguely in favour of women's suffrage – but because Christabel had decided to oppose prospective Liberal Cabinet Ministers, and Churchill was the only prospective Cabinet Minister within easy reach of Nelson Street. The WSPU issued a manifesto against Churchill, and heckled him repeatedly. *

* The Manifesto was as follows (as printed in Dame C. Pankhurst, *Unshackled*, pp. 57–8):
It has been decided to oppose Mr. Winston Churchill at the General Election, on the ground that he is a member of the Liberal Government which refuses to give Women the Vote.
The Government is anxious to have freedom for the Chinese in South Africa, but will not give political freedom to British Women.
'The Passive Resisters' are to have satisfaction, but women are not to have the votes which they have been demanding for some half a century.
The working women of the country who are earning starvation wages stand in urgent need of the vote. These helpless workers must have political power. It is all very well to promise cheap bread, but good wages are quite as important as cheap food and unless working women get votes, their wages and conditions of

On one occasion, Mrs Drummond 'held up' Churchill for half an hour before being invited to the platform to address the audience herself.[18] WSPU members also mutilated Churchill's election posters. Not surprisingly, he was irritated by the tactics used against him. He wrote that whereas his previous attitude towards women's suffrage had been one of 'growing sympathy', and he had voted in its favour in the Commons, he had [19]

> lately been much discouraged by the action of certain advocates of the movement in persistently disturbing and attempting to break up both my own meetings and those of other Liberal candidates . . . the foolish and disorderly

---

labour cannot be improved. The vote is the worker's best friend. Evidently, the Liberal Government cares nothing about the sufferings of underpaid working women, or else votes for women would have a foremost place on the Government programme.

Now that a Liberal Government is in power, the resolution in favour of Women's Franchise, recently carried by the National Liberal Federation, is ignored. In fact, the resolution was carried simply and solely in order to induce women to canvass for Liberal Candidates.

The Prime Minister, though he says he is personally 'in favour' of Women's Franchise, actually expects women to wait until after the General Election before knowing what the Liberal Government will do for them. Everyone knows what this means. If the Liberal leaders will not promise before the General Election to give votes to women, they will not do it after the Election.

Although Liberals profess to believe in political freedom the Liberal leaders have always been opposed to Women's Franchise. It was a Liberal Government in 1884 which refused to give votes to women when the male agricultural labourer was being enfranchised. The present Cabinet contains many enemies and no real friends of Women's Franchise.

INHABITANTS OF NORTH-WEST MANCHESTER!

If you believe that women ought to have political freedom, better wages, fairer treatment all round,

VOTE AND WORK AGAINST WINSTON CHURCHILL AS A MEMBER OF THE LIBERAL GOVERNMENT

As has been pointed out, the WSPU's belief that extending the existing franchise to women would give working women the vote was grossly unrealistic; the rhetoric of the WSPU manifesto against Churchill had little relation to what would most likely have been the results had the then-existing male franchise been extended to women, the measure consistently advocated by the WSPU (see pp. 34–5).

agitation which is in progress . . . so long as it continues,
must prevent me from taking any further steps in favour of
the cause.

Churchill was not the only Liberal heckled by the WSPU –
Asquith, Lloyd George, and Sir Edward Grey received the same
treatment, and, in Liverpool, Campbell-Bannerman was confronted by a group of ten women, who were, in succession,
thrown out of the Sun Hall. An even larger group accompanied
Mrs Drummond to heckle the Prime Minister in Glasgow. No
precise estimate can be given of the number of women who took
part in such expeditions, but there seem to have been not less
than twenty women who, three months after Christabel and
Annie Kenney had set an example, were willing to risk bruises,
torn clothing, and social opprobrium for the sake of the enfranchisement of their sex. In addition, there were by now a number
of women who could be relied on for aid in various towns,
though the primary loyalties of many of these women were
probably to the ILP rather than to the WSPU, no sharp distinction being drawn between the two at this time. Certainly the
indignation meetings that had followed the jailing of Christabel
and Annie Kenney could not have been held without the support
of the ILP. As of January 1906, the WSPU was still a tiny
provincial movement, dependent upon the ILP for much of its
financial support (Keir Hardie had provided £300 from an
unannounced source, and had made Teresa Billington a salaried
ILP organizer),[20] publicity (via the *Labour Leader* and the *ILP
News*), and audiences (at ILP meetings). Only in the wake of the
great Liberal victory of 1906 did the WSPU begin to take steps
to remove itself from the somewhat parochial world of northern
Labour politics.

5 To London

After the Liberals' famous victory, and the less-heralded triumph of twenty-nine LRC candidates, the WSPU's leaders believed that London, as Parliament's seat, would be more fertile ground than the north for suffragist propaganda. Christabel's final examinations were to be in June, so she could not leave Manchester for an extended period, and Mrs Pankhurst was occupied with her work as Registrar of Births and Deaths, but Annie Kenney had already left her home in Oldham and her job in the cotton factory, and had for several months been a member of the Pankhurst household, so her circumstances did not oblige her to remain in Lancashire. Christabel now asked Annie Kenney to carry the WSPU campaign to London. At the end of January 1906, Annie took up residence with Sylvia Pankhurst at 45 Park Walk in Chelsea. Annie thereafter began to contact groups of poor women in the East End; she was aided in this endeavour by Mrs Dora Montefiore, a London widow interested in women's suffrage, and by Mrs Minnie Baldock, the wife of a fitter in Canning Town.

Annie Kenney had come to London bearing neither funds nor specific instructions, and it was with a certain temerity that she and Sylvia Pankhurst decided that on 19 February, the day of the King's Speech, the WSPU would hold a meeting in Trafalgar Square, followed by a procession to Parliament. Annie made inquiries regarding the use of Trafalgar Square, and the Metropolitan Police informed her that it was not available on 19 February. Subsequently, on the advice of Keir Hardie, the two young women engaged the Caxton Hall, which, standing south of St James's Park near Victoria Street, is less than half a mile from Parliament Square. The WSPU did not have funds with which to pay for the use of the hall, so Keir Hardie helped persuade W. T. Stead and Isabella Ford to lend the Union £50 to pay the rent.* Hardie subsequently helped Sylvia Pankhurst draft leaflets advertising the forthcoming meeting.

Towards the middle of February, Mrs Pankhurst came to visit London. On learning of the ambitious plans that were afoot, she was aghast, fearing that she would 'be made ridiculous by a procession of half a dozen people and an empty hall.'[1] Her qualms were not groundless – the Caxton Hall had 700 seats, and the WSPU had never tried to fill so large a hall without substantial outside aid; the meeting in the Free Trade Hall after Christabel's release the previous October had been co-sponsored by the ILP, and Keir Hardie had been the principal speaker. The meeting in the Caxton Hall had already been widely advertised, however, and Mrs Pankhurst agreed to speak.

The idea of a women's march to Parliament, new as it was to the WSPU, was by no means novel. As has been previously noted, 1,000 women had walked from the East End to Westminster on 17 July 1905 to lobby on behalf of the unemployed relief Bill. Subsequently, in November 1905, a far larger march had taken place, when the wives of the unemployed men of Poplar, Southwark, and West Ham had marched in contingents to the Embankment and there formed a procession 4,000 strong, which, led by a band playing 'The Marseillaise', had walked up Northumberland Avenue and then down Whitehall carrying banners that read 'Food for Our Children', 'Work for Our Men', and 'Workers of the World Unite'.[2] Balfour had met the marchers' representatives at the Local Government Board. Such events having recently taken place, Sylvia Pankhurst and Annie Kenney believed that they could probably organize a march of

* On 18 December 1905, three days before the Liberal meeting in the Albert Hall at which the WSPU had created an uproar, Stead had written to Campbell-Bannerman (Campbell-Bannerman Papers, Brit. Mus. Add. MSS. 41238, W. T. Stead to Sir H. Campbell-Bannerman, Holly Bush, Hayling Island, Hants, 18 December 1905):

> I am hoping to hear you on Thursday night at the Albert Hall. . . . I sincerely hope you may see your way to utter some encouraging word to the Women. . . . Our rank & file are all right, but there are some horribly antiquated old fogies on this question in your Cabinet, & I should dearly love to hear you give them to understand that they are not to bar the path of progress on this question. The women will strike some day if we refuse to recognize their citizenship. . . .

groups with which Annie was in contact, such as the 'Unemployed Women of South West Ham'.[3] On inquiry, Annie found that the East End women were by no means adverse to marching under the aegis of the WSPU. She realized, however, that women so poor would have to be transported and fed, so she arranged for fares to be paid for three hundred women to travel from East End stations to the St James's Park District Railway Station, just north of the Caxton Hall, and for food to be served to the women on their arrival at the hall. During the days before 19 February, Annie Kenney went repeatedly to Canning Town, Poplar, and Limehouse to raise support for the impending meeting.

On 19 February, three hundred East End women arrived as planned at St James's Station, and walked to the Caxton Hall carrying red banners which had been made in Canning Town. After tea and buns in a back room, the women were 'stage managed' to seats in various parts of the hall, which soon filled with women of all social classes.[4] Lady Carlisle was among those who came, and some wealthy ladies were later said to have arrived dressed in their maids' clothing to avoid recognition. Before the proceedings began, the East End women sang 'The Red Flag'. The meeting had been planned to coincide with the reading of the King's Speech, and after Mrs Pankhurst, Annie Kenney, and Mrs Montefiore had all spoken, there was a lengthy wait to hear whether the new Government had included women's enfranchisement in its programme. When the news came that such was not the case, there were hisses and cries of 'shame', and Mrs Pankhurst proclaimed: 'We have risked our reputations, our limbs, and even our lives in the cause. But there is nothing.'[5] Mrs Pankhurst then moved that the meeting resolve itself into a lobbying committee, and march to the House of Commons. The women, a few of whom carried banners, walked through cold rain to Parliament Square, where, at the Strangers' Entrance, they were informed that only twenty women at a time would be admitted to the inner hall. For almost two hours, those women permitted inside lobbied indifferent MPs, while the rest stood outside in the rain.

The fruits of the march of 19 February 1906 lay not within the gates of St Stephen's Hall, but in the publicity and new members brought to the WSPU. Many newspapers found the march newsworthy, and the *Daily Mirror* printed a photograph of women carrying a large banner inscribed 'Votes for Women'.[6] During the weeks after the march, a number of unaffiliated women, such as Irene Fenwick Miller, joined the WSPU, and on 27 February the 'Unemployed Women of South West Ham' voted to become the Canning Town Branch of the WSPU.[7] The Canning Town Branch was the Union's first London branch and had forty members at its inception.[8] The last week of February also saw new recruits to the inner councils of the WSPU, by far the most important of these being Emmeline Pethick-Lawrence, who became the Union's Treasurer.

Emmeline Pethick had been born in the West Country on 21 October 1867. She was the second of thirteen children, five of whom died in infancy. She received little attention from her mother, who was a quasi-invalid much of the time because of her almost yearly childbearing. Her earliest years were spent under the care of a 'changing succession of ignorant and inefficient nursemaids who cared neither for their job nor for their charges.'[9] The girl did not, it seems, model herself on her mother. Her father, however, a passionate and rather impulsive man, was a 'born rebel', and from him Emmeline Pethick acquired a lifelong hatred of social injustice.[10]

At the age of eight, Emmeline Pethick was sent to a boarding school called Greystone House, at which she stayed for two years. Discipline at the school was extremely harsh; an unjust accusation brought the girl an entire school term in Coventry, and before the end of the term she developed a 'rheumatic fever' which she later believed to have been psychosomatic in origin.[11] A Quaker boarding school which she attended later also had its repressive facets; when Emmeline Pethick displayed some curiosity about birth, she found herself chastised for corrupting the mind of a younger girl, and 'the result was that for many years I tried to put the whole subject of sex completely out of my mind.'[12] Regarding sexuality, she later referred to 'the tangle of emotion which I and many others of my generation have had with much difficulty to unwind.'[13]

As an adult, Emmeline Pethick took up settlement work at the West London Mission, under the mentorship of Mary Neal. She concerned herself primarily with working-class girls, and, in

1895, she and Mary Neal left the mission to establish the
Esperance Girls' Club. Emmeline Pethick had by then acquired
that combination of deep concern for social reform and uninterest
in marriage which was not uncommon among early leaders of the
WSPU: 'Marriage as an abstract proposition held no attraction for
me. . . . Possibly the absence of desire for marriage was connected with a vague feeling that I was not the kind of girl to
attract a mate.'[14]

In 1899, Emmeline Pethick met Frederick William Lawrence,
a wealthy graduate of Eton and Cambridge, who, while reading
for the bar, was giving free legal advice and acting as treasurer
at Mansfield House, Canning Town, the settlement with which
Emmeline Pethick was then connected. Lawrence had been born
in 1871 to a wealthy Unitarian family. His father died when he
was three, and he was brought up by his mother. At Eton, his
aloofness caused him to be regarded as something of an oddity,
but he met with academic success, and became captain of the
Oppidans. At Trinity College, Cambridge, his reserved mathe-
matical intelligence earned him a Double First in mathematics
and natural sciences, and he became president of the Union.
Between 1897 and 1899 he travelled around the world. His
itinerary included crossing the United States, and he talked to
Jane Addams in Chicago.

Not long after meeting Emmeline Pethick, Frederick Lawrence proposed marriage. She, however, at thirty-two, regarded
herself as wholly dedicated to social service, and feared that a
conventional marriage would not permit to both partners independence sufficient for self-fulfilment, particularly as she was a
Socialist whereas he was a Liberal-Unionist with political
ambitions.[15] They separated for a time, he going to South Africa,
becoming pro-Boer, and beginning to move leftwards in politics.
In 1901, Lawrence took over financial responsibility for the *Echo*,
a London evening newspaper. Emmeline Pethick was among
those invited to sit on the committee that met each week to
discuss the paper's editorial policies. Lawrence soon proposed
once again, and they were married in the town hall of Canning
Town, on 2 October 1901, three weeks before her thirty-fourth
birthday. They had no children.

Frederick Lawrence was deeply aware of his new wife's
desire to maintain her own identity, and shortly after marrying

he added her patronymic to his own – they became the Pethick-Lawrences. The couple leased a large apartment in the building off Fleet Street called Clement's Inn. On their first anniversary, F. W. Pethick-Lawrence gave his wife the key to a garden flat on the roof of Clement's Inn, and told her that the flat would be her private retreat – no one else would have a key.[16] The Pethick-Lawrences also maintained a country home, designed by Sir Edwin Lutyens, near Holmewood in Surrey.

In 1903 F. W. Pethick-Lawrence took over editorial responsibility for the *Echo*. Under his editorship Ramsay MacDonald wrote Labour notes, and H. N. Brailsford contributed leading articles. The *Echo* was not a commercial success, however, and ceased publication early in 1905. Pethick-Lawrence had already taken on the joint editorship of an annual, *The Reformer's Year Book*, and he now also became the publisher and editor of a small monthly magazine, *The Labour Record and Review*.

During the autumn of 1905, the Pethick-Lawrences visited South Africa, where they read of the arrest of Christabel and Annie Kenney outside the Free Trade Hall. They returned to London in January 1906. Keir Hardie had a high regard for Mrs Pethick-Lawrence's executive capabilities, and towards the end of February he persuaded Mrs Pankhurst to offer Mrs Pethick-Lawrence the treasurership of the WSPU. After some initial hesitation, she accepted. Teresa Billington later wrote:[17]

> The inner circle were (at the coming of the P.L.'s) hopeful – because of their earlier reformist work – that they would be a balancing democratic power in the inner councils – the Pankhurst absolutism being already obvious – & feared.

The WSPU now formed a Central London Committee, with Sylvia Pankhurst (who had been Acting Secretary) as Secretary, Mrs Pethick-Lawrence as Treasurer, and Annie Kenney as a paid organizer with a salary of £2 a week. The other members of the new committee were Mrs Pankhurst and Mrs Drummond (who were both returning to Manchester), Mary Neal, Mrs Lucy Roe (Sylvia Pankhurst's landlady), Mrs Mary Clarke (Mrs Pankhurst's sister), Mrs Nellie Martel, and Irene Fenwick Miller. The committee was not given specific powers, and in subsequent practice it had little authority; the WSPU's basic policies continued to be set by the Pankhursts, and then, on occasion, ratified by informal votes of the committee.

Of the committee members who were not Pankhursts, only Mrs Pethick-Lawrence acquired clearly demarcated authority, through the treasurership. Within a week after assuming office, she began to bring order to the vexed financial affairs of the WSPU. Her husband and Keir Hardie donated enough money to pay off the Union's outstanding debts, and in accordance with a stipulation which she had placed on accepting the office, her friend Alfred Sayers, a chartered accountant, became the auditor of WSPU finances. The first recorded fiscal year of the WSPU began on 1 March 1906.

Late in February 1906, the WSPU had written to Campbell-Bannerman, asking for an interview. The Prime Minister refused, and on 2 March a small group of women deposited themselves on the doorstep of 10 Downing Street, having informed the press in advance that they would do so. The women sat on the steps for some time, displaying a banner, and pictures were taken. Then, after speaking to Campbell-Bannerman's private secretary, they departed peaceably.

A second attempt to interview 'C.-B.' was planned for 9 March. On 4 March, Annie Kenney wrote to a Mrs Rowe:[18]

We have decided to go on a deputation to the Prime
Minister on Friday morning . . . there are women coming
from various places and we expect a great number. . . .
Will you write to the women who came before and I
think there are a few more anxious to come, some of their
friends. Bring as many as possible Mrs. Rowe it is quite
right for us to do this as time will prove tell the women not
to be afraid, and to follow us, I may try and address a
meeting in front of his house if he will not see us. You will
tell Mrs. Montefiore will you, if they say it is too soon tell
them we have thought it out carefully and we know it is the
best thing to do. The women will not get in any trouble so
they have no occasion to be nervous. We are meeting at
Westminster Bridge Station on Friday morning at 10–15.

As the letter clearly indicated, ordinary WSPU members did not take part in the formulation of strategy; they were expected to have faith in the wisdom of the Union's leaders.

On 9 March, about thirty women went to 10 Downing Street and asked to see Campbell-Bannerman. After remaining for almost an hour, they were asked to leave. Irene Fenwick Miller thereupon rapped on the door, and Mrs Drummond managed to open it and rush inside. They were both arrested. Annie Kenney then jumped on to the Prime Minister's car, and began to address the crowd. After refusing to descend, she too was arrested. At Cannon Row police station, the three women were released without charge, for Campbell-Bannerman's private secretary had informed the police that the Prime Minister requested[19]

that the women might not be charged on this occasion, as he thought they were only seeking notoriety, which would be successful if they appeared before a Magistrate . . . he would receive a deputation if application was made in a proper manner.

Campbell-Bannerman was not completely successful in fore-stalling 'notoriety', for on the following day the *Daily Mirror* devoted its entire front page to photographs of 'suffragettes' calling on 10 Downing Street.[20] (The word 'suffragette' had first been used by the *Daily Mail* on 10 January 1906. By March 1906 the new word was beginning to come into general currency. It served the legitimate and valuable function of distinguishing between militant feminists – suffragettes – and those suffragists of both sexes who sought the vote by entirely legal means.)

In early April, Mrs Pankhurst returned to London with the idea of making a speech from the Ladies' Gallery of the House of Commons. Keir Hardie and Sylvia Pankhurst persuaded her to delay, as on 25 April Hardie was to present a Resolution (not a Bill, but a Resolution expressing the sentiment of the House) 'That, in the opinion of this House, it is desirable that sex should cease to be a bar to the exercise of the Parliamentary franchise.'[21] Mrs Pankhurst and Christabel were convinced that the Resolution would be talked out by anti-suffragist MPs, and they decided to stage a protest. On 25 April, twelve WSPU members obtained seats in the Ladies' Gallery. As predicted, an anti-suffragist, Samuel Evans, began to talk out Hardie's Resolution, using all the old familiar arguments ('sensible men . . . did not deem it fitting that women should come down into the arena of politics and engage generally in public affairs . . . women had their own honourable position in life . . . accorded to them by nature . . . their proper sphere was the home, where they might exercise their good and noble influence in the sacred circle of the family'.[22] As the end of the time alloted for debate drew near, the women in the gallery, infuriated, shouted 'We will not have this talk any longer', 'Divide, divide', 'Vote, vote, vote', 'We refuse to have our Bill [sic] talked out', and so on.[23] Debate was briefly disrupted, but police soon cleared the gallery, and the Resolution was then talked out. The breach of decorum angered Keir Hardie, who had hoped that the Speaker would allow a division, but F. W. Pethick-Lawrence wrote: 'Surely we of the Labour Party are not going to go so back upon our past as to hold up hands of horror at the breach of antique forms and ceremonies?'[24]

Pethick-Lawrence also opened the *Labour Record* of May 1906 to articles by his wife and by Christabel. Mrs Pethick-Lawrence called for '*Volunteers for the Front*, volunteers for what we call Danger-work', who would carry on[25]

active agitation . . . regardless of the risks or consequences which may be entailed, in the spirit with which they so often sing the well-known song – The Red Flag. . . . This is a people's movement. It is the awakening of the working women of this country to their need of representation.

Such claims notwithstanding, the link between the WSPU's leaders and its working-class members had remained rather tenuous; the women from the East End who were called upon to demonstrate had no representation in the WSPU's inner councils – they were simply asked to follow plans that were made without their being consulted. The minutes of the Canning Town branch of the WSPU for 10 April 1906 reported:[26]

We were sorry to hear Mrs. Lawrence was suffering from a bad cold & could not come. We had a pleasant surprise.
Miss Kenney came unawares as angels do & told us a good many secrets of what the Union intended to do in future. The Meeting then closed with prayer.

Campbell-Bannerman kept his word regarding the receiving of

a deputation, after being asked to do so by a parliamentary Women's Suffrage Committee as well as by the WSPU. On 19 May, at the Foreign Office, he met a group composed of suffragist MPs and representatives of a wide variety of women's organizations, including suffragists, trade unionists, and temperance workers. To his visitors' frustration, the Prime Minister had nothing new to offer. He was in favour of women's enfranchisement, but the Cabinet was divided on the subject, so he could make no pledge or promise – he could only preach 'the virtue of patience'.[27] (This last phrase was received with hisses.) After the interview, the first large open-air women's suffrage meeting ever to take place in London was held in Trafalgar Square. Keir Hardie, Annie Kenney (who dressed as a mill girl, wearing clogs and a shawl), and Teresa Billington were among those who addressed a predominantly male audience of 7,000.

The fruitless meeting with Campbell-Bannerman seemed to confirm Christabel's now frequently reiterated belief that the only way to persuade the Government to espouse women's suffrage was to convert the Cabinet. In June 1906, the WSPU began the regular heckling of anti-suffragist Cabinet Ministers. Asquith, who had become Chancellor of the Exchequer, was known to be the most adamantly anti-suffragist Minister. He was duly heckled, and repeated attempts were made to persuade him to receive a WSPU delegation. The attempts failed, Asquith replying that he would not receive deputations unconnected with his office – to which the WSPU replied that women paid taxes too. On 19 June the WSPU sent eight women to Asquith's home in Cavendish Square. He was said to be out. Two days later, Teresa Billington led a procession of about thirty East End women to the edge of the square, where a line of police ordered the deputation to turn back. Then, according to Mrs Baldock,[28]

> Miss Billington tried to force her way on. A policeman
> struck her in the face, and she retaliated by one slap in his
> face with her open hand. Another policeman . . . caught
> her by the throat until her face became purple and an
> official standing by said 'don't maul them.' I followed to
> the police court.

The Metropolitan Police Report stated that Teresa Billington had 'slapped P.C. Warman three times in the face & kicked him twice on the leg & was taken into custody.'[29] Annie Kenney and two other women were also arrested.

In court, Teresa Billington refused to testify, saying: 'I do not recognize the authority of the Police, of this Court, or any other Court or law made by man'.[30] She was convicted of assaulting the police, and, given the choice of a £10 fine or two months' imprisonment, she chose imprisonment. The cases of Annie Kenney and the two other women were adjourned until 4 July. * On 22 June, Asquith wrote to Herbert Gladstone, the Home Secretary, that he had 'nothing to do with the prosecution of these silly women', and asked that the sentence be mitigated or annulled.[31] Gladstone had the sentence reduced to one month in prison or £5. Teresa Billington was soon released, when, against her will, an anonymous reader of the *Daily Mail* paid her fine.

Two days after the struggle in Cavendish Square, WSPU hecklers in Manchester systematically held up a meeting addressed by Churchill and Lloyd George. The women were ejected with considerable violence, and were prosecuted for 'obstruction' and interfering with the police. After refusing to pay nominal fines, Adela Pankhurst was imprisoned for a week and Hannah Mitchell for three days.[32]

Towards the end of June 1906, Sylvia Pankhurst resigned as secretary of the WSPU. She wanted some degree of independence, and had come to feel that her duties had so increased that a full-time secretary was needed. (On 25 June Mrs Pethick-Lawrence wrote to George Lansbury, 'Endless clerical work. We have sent round thousands of resolutions & letters. There are thousands still to send. The whole country is going to be roused.')[33] Mrs Edith How Martyn and Mrs Charlotte Despard now became the joint honorary secretaries of the WSPU. They were both women of substantial personal achievement, and Mrs Pankhurst feared that their being appointed without Christabel's approval would eventually lead to divided counsels in the WSPU.† She

---

* On 4 July, Annie Kenney and two other defendants were sentenced to six weeks' imprisonment. Theirs was the first trial at which F. W. Pethick-Lawrence acted as defence for the WSPU.

† Edith How had been born in 1875. She was educated at the North London Collegiate School for Girls and University College, Aberystwyth. In 1899, she married Herbert Martyn. She received a London BSc in

was angry with Sylvia for having resigned before Christabel could come to London and oversee the selection process.[34] Other new appointments were now also made: in mid-May, Teresa Billington had resigned her post as an ILP organizer to become the WSPU's second paid London organizer, and soon afterwards Mary Gawthorpe and Mrs Martel also became organizers. Elizabeth Wolstenholme Elmy, the distinguished elderly suffragist, Elizabeth Robins, the playwright and Ibsen actress, and Caroline Hodgson now became members of the committee, and Mrs Roe and Mrs Clarke were dropped. The committee, which heretofore had met at Sylvia Pankhurst's flat in Chelsea, now began to meet at the Pethick-Lawrences' apartments in Clement's Inn.

On 30 June, Christabel received her LLB from Victoria University. She received First Class Honours (along with only one other student) and was awarded the prize in international law. She had been the only woman enrolled in law, there being no possibility of a woman's pursuing a legal career. (In 1903, Christabel had applied for admission to Lincoln's Inn, with the goal of being called to the Bar, but she had not been admitted and had been refused a hearing.) Having received her degree in Manchester, Christabel moved to London to become the WSPU's chief organizer, with a salary of £2 10s. per week. She took up residence with the Pethick-Lawrences at Clement's Inn, and continued to live with them for the next six years.

Soon after arriving in London, Christabel departed for Cockermouth, where a by-election was to be held on 3 August. In April, at a by-election at Eye, the WSPU had campaigned against the Liberal candidate and had distributed ILP literature, though no

---

1903, and became an Associate of the Royal College of Science in physics and mathematics. In 1904, she became an assistant lecturer in mathematics at Westfield College. She was a member of the ILP.

Mrs Charlotte Despard had been born Charlotte French in 1844. In 1870 she married Colonel Maximilian Carden Despard, who died in 1890. They had no children. After her husband's death she turned to social work, becoming a Poor Law Guardian and a founder of workmen's clubs and a child welfare centre. She too was a member of the ILP. She was sixty-two when she joined the WSPU. Her appearance was striking – she was a tall slender woman with ascetic features and snow-white hair who usually wore sandals and a black Spanish lace mantilla.

Labour candidate had entered the field. At Cockermouth, however, Christabel announced that the WSPU would henceforth not only oppose all Liberal candidates, regardless of their personal points of view regarding women's suffrage, but would also maintain an impartial attitude towards all other candidates. Christabel was intent on disengaging the WSPU from its connection with Labour. On arriving in London, she had quickly decided that the London WSPU was too dependent on East End women for its demonstrations – she felt that by relying so heavily on working-class women, the WSPU was forfeiting the support of many suffragists who were not Labour sympathizers.[35] Moreover, Keir Hardie's aid aside, the new Labour Party was proving to be of little help in pressing the Government with regard to women's suffrage; Christabel and Teresa Billington wrote in a joint statement: 'Labour M.P.'s tell us candidly that they are sent by the Trade Unionists to the House of Commons to promote reforms which must take precedence of [sic] women's suffrage.'[36]

At Cockermouth, Christabel's new policy gave rise to confusion and resentment. The other three WSPU women who took part in the by-election – Teresa Billington, Mrs Marion Coates Hansen, and Mary Gawthorpe – were all members of the ILP. When Mary Gawthorpe, who had been Vice-President of the Leeds ILP, insisted on speaking on behalf of the Labour candidate, Smillie, she found herself excluded from WSPU platforms.[37] Smillie himself complained that Christabel had written to the secretary of the local ILP asking that arrangements be made for her coming, and had stayed at the home of a prominent member of the local ILP, both men being 'under the impression before she came that she was coming down to help the Labour Candidate'.[38] The Labour forces also complained that Christabel and Teresa Billington 'held rival meetings to those of the Labour Party on the same ground, and, when asked if Mr Smillie was not in favour of the Women's Franchise they replied "Yes, but so is Sir John Randles." '[39] (Smillie's support of women's enfranchisement was, in fact, rather tepid; an adult suffragist, he had not even mentioned women's suffrage in his election pamphlets.)

Randles, the Conservative, won the by-election with 4,593 votes. Fred Guest, the Liberal, received 3,903 votes and Smillie was a poor third with 1,436. Three weeks later, the Manchester and Salford ILP voted by ninety to three to expel Christabel and Teresa Billington. The vote had no effect, for the two women were members of the Manchester Central Branch of the ILP, which, on 4 September, permitted them to remain members, by a vote of nineteen to eight, on the grounds that their object, the enfranchisement of women, was one of the ILP's objects.[40]

Aside from the short-lived apostacy of Mary Gawthorpe, there seems to have been no serious opposition within the WSPU to Christabel's decision to cease supporting Labour. (The lack of opposition is curious since all the WSPU organizers and the majority of the committee were members of the ILP.) That Christabel had the *right* to be the architect of WSPU strategy was, it seems, assumed. Her primacy was certainly confirmed by arrangements made in September 1906, when the WSPU established a London headquarters in two adjoining rooms on the ground floor of Clement's Inn: whereas the larger of the two rooms became used as a general office, the smaller room became Christabel's private office, and she began to receive the services of a private secretary.

With the establishment of a London office, conveniently adjacent to Fleet Street, WSPU affairs began to be conducted with more regularity. The large room soon became used for weekly At Homes, held on Monday afternoons, at which members and prospective members gathered to hear demonstrations announced and strategy explained. On these occasions, funds were subscribed, new members were enrolled, and literature was sold. WSPU staff work became regulated too, when at the suggestion of F. W. Pethick-Lawrence, Miss Harriet Kerr, who owned a secretarial agency, gave up her business to become office manager for the WSPU, a position she held for the next eight years.

Though the WSPU was in general becoming a more systematically run organization, the process through which its policies were determined remained informal. Committee meetings were held on a more or less *ad hoc* basis, and attendance was irregular.[41] The minutes of committee meetings do not, alas, survive, but Teresa Billington later wrote:[42]

A certain routine/semblance [sic] of democracy was observed but it had no *guts* –

'It was decided' in the minutes might mean Mrs. P. announced it as decided or no one objected – or there was a vote in favour.

Shortly after the opening of the new offices in Clement's Inn, the WSPU held a general meeting to discuss plans for a demonstration to be held on 23 October, the day of the opening of Parliament. For some time, Teresa Billington had desired that the Union's affairs be conducted on a more democratic basis, and on the night before the meeting she drafted a constitution for the WSPU.* Whereas those clauses subsumed under 'Objects',

---

* The Constitution drafted by Teresa Billington was as follows (WSPU [Women's Freedom League] *Programme for Second Annual Conference, October 12, 1907*):

CONSTITUTION

NAME
The Women's Social and Political Union

OBJECTS
To secure for Women the Parliamentary Vote as it is or may be granted to men; to use the power thus obtained to establish equality of rights and opportunities between the sexes, and to promote the social and industrial well-being of the community.

METHODS
The objects of the Union shall be promoted by –
1. Action entirely independent of all political parties.
2. Opposition to whatever Government is in power until such time as the franchise is granted.
3. Participation in Parliamentary Elections in opposition to the Government candidate and independently of all other candidates.
4. Vigorous agitation upon lines justified by the position of outlawry to which women are at present condemned.
5. The organising of women all over the country to enable them to give adequate expression to their desire for political freedom.
6. Education of public opinion by all the usual methods, such as public meetings, demonstrations, debates, distribution of literature, newspapers, correspondence, and deputations to public representatives.

MEMBERSHIP
Women of all shades of political opinion who approve the objects and methods of the Union, and who are prepared to act independently of party, are eligible for membership.

ORGANIZATION
1. The National Officials shall be an Honorary Secretary and an Honorary Treasurer, and such Organizers as are from time to

'Methods', and 'Membership' involved just a codification of policies already in practice, the clauses subsumed under 'Organization' represented an attempt to democratize the Union.

The constitution was adopted at the general meeting, with Mrs Pankhurst in the chair. The Pankhursts and the Pethick-Lawrences later alleged that the constitution was accepted only as an 'experiment', but there is no way of knowing if this was the case.[43] Regardless of the conditions under which the constitution was accepted, it is clear that the clauses subsumed under 'Organization' were never put into effect: the National Executive Council was never established, contributions were not systematically collected, and control of the decision-making processes of the WSPU continued to be dominated by the Pankhursts, the Pethick-Lawrences, and the organizers – save for the idea of an annual conference of delegates, the clauses in the constitution relating to 'Organization' were simply ignored.

In mid-October, 1906, the major concern of the WSPU was not the newly-ratified constitution, but the demonstration planned for 23 October, the day of the opening of Parliament. A deputation of women would arrive at the House of Commons; those admitted would ask the Chief Liberal Whip to obtain a promise from the Prime Minister that women's suffrage would be considered before the end of the session; if the request were refused, certain members of the delegation would mount seats in the lobby and make speeches of protest, while others would link arms and close around the speakers to protect them.[44]

---

time appointed by the Emergency Committee with the approval of the National Council.

2. The National Executive Council of the Union shall consist of the Officers and one Delegate from every Branch, making due contribution to the Central Fund.
3. The contribution required shall be not less than 2*d*. per month per member.
4. The Branches shall pay their Delegate's expenses to the Council Meetings.
5. The Council shall meet every quarter in London.
6. The EMERGENCY COMMITTEE shall consist of the Officers and Organizers, and two additional National Representatives appointed by the Annual Conference.
7. The Annual Conference of Delegates shall be in October of each year.

At 3 p.m. on 23 October, groups of suffragettes began to arrive at the Commons. Only about thirty well-dressed women were admitted to the lobby – a separate contingent of working-class women was forbidden entrance. As news of the suffragettes' arrival spread, the lobby became filled with curious MPs. After the request for an assurance had been refused, Mary Gawthorpe mounted a settee beside Lord Northcote's statue and began a speech, while other women gathered around her. Tumult followed. Mary Gawthorpe was seized by the police, and, as other speakers took her place, they too were arrested, amidst shouting and scuffling. Those arrested were Mary Gawthorpe, Mrs Pethick-Lawrence, Annie Kenney, Mrs Montefiore, Adela Pankhurst, Teresa Billington, Mrs How Martyn, Irene Fenwick Miller, Mrs Baldock, and Mrs Anne Cobden Sanderson, a daughter of Richard Cobden.[45]

At Westminster police court the following day, the ten women were charged with 'using threatening and abusive words and behaviour with intent to provoke a breach of the peace'.[46] The women refused to recognize the jurisdiction of the court, on the grounds that it carried out solely man-made laws, and during their trial they neither cross-examined the police nor called witnesses in their own defence. They were found guilty, and ordered to agree to keep the peace for six months, or be imprisoned for two months in the Second Division, that is, imprisoned as common felons. All chose imprisonment.

The imprisoning of ten women, several of whom were widely known well outside suffrage circles, for demonstrating noisily for women's enfranchisement in the lobby of Parliament, brought the WSPU more sympathy, funds, and new members than any previous imprisonment. Immediately after the trial Mrs Pankhurst presided over a meeting at the Caxton Hall at which money quickly flowed into WSPU coffers. Lady Cook, Mrs Cobden Unwin, and Mr Cobden Sanderson each gave £100, and F. W. Pethick-Lawrence promised to give £10 a day for each day his wife stayed in prison, a proposal some journalists found humorous.

The following day, at least two London newspapers supported the WSPU: the *Daily News* claimed: 'No class has ever got the vote except at the risk of something like revolution.'[47] The *Daily Mirror* asked: 'By what means, but by screaming, knocking, and rioting, did men themselves ever gain what they were pleased to call their rights?'[48] For the first time, support was also received from Mrs Fawcett, the president of the National Union of Women's Suffrage Societies, who wrote:[49]

> I hope the more old-fashioned suffragists will stand by them . . . in my opinion, far from having injured the movement, they have done more during the last 12 months to bring it within the region of practical politics than we have been able to accomplish in the same number of years.

The feeling that an injustice had been committed was kindled above all by the fact that a daughter of Richard Cobden had been imprisoned.* *The Times* printed many letters of protest. In one such letter, the veteran suffragist Mrs Florence Fenwick Miller wrote:†

> You have taken, and are treating as a felon, a daughter of the great Cobden, the man who gave you the cheap loaf. . . .
>   Charles Stewart Parnell, Charles Bradlaugh, Leigh Hunt, Edmund Yates, and other men in like case – that is, who were not criminals, though imprisoned under the laws – were treated differently. They had books and the use of writing materials, they lived in decent rooms, and were allowed to receive letters and occasional callers. But your women political prisoners are being treated like the commonest of criminals, merely for protesting in the hearing of your legislators against the inequality of men and women under our Constitution.

A concerted effort by Keir Hardie and others to secure an amelioration of the conditions of imprisonment followed, and on 31 October Herbert Gladstone announced that the women would be placed in the First Division. The prisoners now no longer had

---

* Anne Cobden Sanderson had been a friend of William Morris, and was a member of the ILP. She had joined the WSPU in the spring of 1906. George Bernard Shaw wrote in *The Times*, on 31 October 1906, that she was 'one of the nicest women in England.'
† *The Times*, 29 October 1906, letter to the editor from F. Fenwick Miller. Mrs Fenwick Miller, the mother of Irene Fenwick Miller, had been a leading member of the Women's Franchise League (see pp. 17–18) and, as editor of the *Woman's Signal*, a pioneer woman journalist.

to live in vermin-infested cells, could wear their own clothes rather than prison dress, and had access to writing materials. On 24 November, on Gladstone's advice, all the women were released, though only half of the currency of their sentences had expired. Mrs Fawcett had visited Mrs Cobden Sanderson in Holloway, and, moved by what she had seen and heard, held a testimonial banquet at the Savoy Hotel in honour of the newly released suffragettes.

The events of October and November 1906 had important results for the WSPU. During his wife's imprisonment, F. W. Pethick-Lawrence had taken over her duties as treasurer. Mrs Pethick-Lawrence was unable to withstand confinement, and on 28 October, on the verge of a nervous breakdown, she gave an undertaking to keep the peace for six months, and was released from Holloway.* Her release was followed by a period of recuperation in Italy, during which her husband continued to act as treasurer of the WSPU. Henceforward, F. W. Pethick-Lawrence devoted himself fully to the legal and financial affairs of the Union. He held no official post, but for the next six years he and his wife were, after Christabel and Mrs Pankhurst, the Union's two most influential leaders. He was the only man ever to be in a high position in the councils of the WSPU.

The demonstration of 23 October 1906 was also significant in that it marked the end of the WSPU's almost exclusive dependence on working-class women for deputations. Of the ten women imprisoned, only one – Mrs Baldock – was of the working class. In contrast with the reaction to the imprisonment of Christabel and Annie Kenney in October 1905, the groundswell of support that the WSPU received in the autumn of 1906 came from the educated and well-to-do, rather than from the rank and file of the Labour movement. The women of Canning Town and East

* Mrs Montefiore procured release on the same terms, after her head had become infested with lice due to the filthy condition of the prison. On 6 November, Mrs Baldock wrote to her husband from Holloway, 'Also give my love to Mrs. Lawrence & Mrs. Montefiore I was glad when I knew they had left I could see by their faces that they could not bear any more they did look so very ill' (M. Baldock to H. Baldock, Holloway Prison, London, 6 November 1906, in album formed by Mrs Baldock, vol. 1, London Museum 60.15/1–2).

1 Mrs Pankhurst departs for the provinces, *circa* 1910

2 Mrs Pethick-Lawrence speaks in Trafalgar Square, 12 December 1908

3 Christabel Pankhurst in her office at Clement's Inn

4 Mrs Drummond invites MPs sitting on the terrace of the House of Commons to come to Hyde Park on 21 June 1908

5 The women's suffrage demonstration held in Hyde Park on 21 June 1908. The conning tower can be seen in the background

Ham were not apt to write letters acceptable to *The Times*, nor could they sign cheques for a hundred pounds. Alice Milne, the secretary of the Manchester branch of the WSPU, visited London late in October 1906, and wrote in her diary:[50]

> arrived at the office we found the place full of fashionable ladies in silks & satins. Tea & cakes were handed round & then the organizers each made a speech. . . . The ladies were much impressed & promised to return the following Monday with friends.
>
> It struck me then that if our Adult Suffrage Socialist friend [probably Snowden] could have looked in that room he would have said more than ever that ours was a movement for the middle & upper classes. What a fever our Union Members in Manchester would have been in if such ladies made a decent [sic] on us.

The unsung death of the pretence that the WSPU was an organization of 'working women' greatly facilitated the subsequent growth of the Union's membership, for after October 1906 women of all political sympathies and social classes were made equally welcome. The way was now paved for the accession of wealthy donors who would not have supported a Labour organization. Concomitantly, the WSPU ceased to envisage votes for women as a measure desirable primarily because it would benefit working-class women. (Given the limited franchise advocated by the Union, this claim had always been dubious, at best.) Women's enfranchisement was no longer tied to any particular set of political goals – the WSPU never committed itself to a specific set of legislative priorities to be pushed for after the vote had been won. WSPU members could and did write as individuals on a multitude of issues, including equal pay, revised divorce laws, open entry to professions, and so on, but the Union itself set no priorities in such matters. To the WSPU, 'votes for women' became virtually an end in itself.*

---

* On 1 August 1913, Christabel wrote to H. D. Harben, 'Another mistake that people make is to suppose that we want the vote only or chiefly because of its political value. We want [it] far more because of its symbolic value – the recognition of our human equality that it will involve' (Pankhurst Papers, in the author's possession, C. Pankhurst to H. D. Harben, Les Abeilles, Deauville, 1 August 1913).

D

Finally, the public applause, new members, and handsome donations which resulted from the imprisonments of October and November 1906 confirmed the WSPU in the pattern of militant action initially adopted by Christabel and Annie Kenney in October 1905, when the deliberately sought out martyrdom of imprisonment had led directly to increased membership and funds. Teresa Billington later wrote of the events of the autumn of 1906:[51]

> The chorus of approval and excuse . . . confirmed in us the pose of martyrdom of which we had been rather ashamed until then, and it strengthened that curious mental and moral duplicity which allowed us to engineer an outbreak and then lay the burden of its results upon the authorities. . . .
>
> The feeling within the Union against this double shuffle, this game of quick change from the garments of the rebel to those of the innocent martyr, was swamped by the public approval and extenuation of our protests. . . . We were accepted into respectable circles not as rebels but as innocent victims, and as innocent victims we were led to pose. If we had frankly and strongly stated that we had set out to make the Government imprison us, that we had deliberately chosen just those lines of protest and disorder that would irritate those in authority into foolish retaliation, if we had told the truth, the very proper persons who became our champions would have spent many weary months and years in condemning us before they had finally realized the value and intention of our efforts.

6   Rapid Growth

During the remainder of 1906 and the whole of 1907 there was little change in the form of WSPU demonstrations, but there was a marked increase in their frequency and size. In November and December 1906, four more forays were made into Parliament Square and another twenty women received prison sentences, almost all of two weeks' duration. The largest demonstration occurred on 20 December, when Mrs Drummond, who had moved to London, led a group into the lobby of Parliament and tried to dash on to the floor of the Commons. This abortive effort resulted in eleven women being imprisoned for a fortnight.

After the eleven women were released, the Pethick-Lawrences held a dinner in their honour at the Holborn Restaurant. The next batch of newly-released prisoners was given a breakfast of welcome at Anderton's Hotel, and such breakfasts thereafter became customary. The breakfasts served a double function – to laud the women who had gone to prison, and to wrest as much publicity as possible from their incarcerations.

The effectiveness of the WSPU's tactics in garnering publicity now inspired the flattery of imitation: on 7 February 1907, the National Union of Women's Suffrage Societies held its first outdoor procession, as some 3,000 women walked in a downpour from Hyde Park Corner to the Exeter Hall. The procession was subsequently dubbed 'the mud march'. Inside the Exeter Hall, Israel Zangwill informed the assembled constitutional suffragists that he endorsed militancy. The NUWSS did not agree with that endorsement, but it was by no means unwilling to reap the harvest sown by others' use of militant tactics. Mrs Fawcett later wrote, regarding militancy:[1]

Those who thought that these unusual proceedings would strike the Women's Suffrage Movement dead were soon proved to be wrong. The very reverse was the case. The secretaries and other active members of the older Suffrage Societies were worked off their feet; every post brought applications for information and membership. . . . Money rolled in in an unexpected way; where we were formerly receiving half-crowns and shillings, we were now getting £5 and £10 notes.

During the same week as the mud march, the WSPU completed plans to march from the Caxton Hall to Parliament on 13 February, the day after the King's Speech. In the north of England, WSPU organizers sought out women willing to go to prison, and arrangements were made for their brief stay in the homes of London suffragettes. Two days before the demonstration the WSPU held secret meetings at which 200 delegates were divided into fourteen groups, and each group was provided with a leader.[2]

On 13 February the 'Women's Parliament' met at 3 p.m. Tickets for the Caxton Hall had been sold out well in advance, and the Exeter Hall, which the NUWSS had barely filled the previous week, had been hired to seat the overflow.* Amidst great excitement, a resolution condemning the omission of women's suffrage from the King's Speech was passed, as was a motion that the resolution be taken to the Prime Minister. Then Mrs Pankhurst's cry 'Rise up, women!' was answered by shouts of 'Now!' and a procession of about 400 women was formed. Mrs Despard led the marchers out into bright sunshine, and some of them sang, to the tune of 'John Brown':[3]

Rise up, women! for the fight is hard and long;
Rise in thousands, singing loud a battle song.
Right is might, and in its strength we shall be strong,
And the cause goes marching on.

When the first contingents reached the green beside Westminster Abbey, the police announced that the procession could continue no further. The women refused to halt. As they went forward, mounted policemen began to ride through their ranks, in an attempt to break up the march, and constables on foot

* The sale of tickets for meetings was one of the WSPU's numerous fund-raising devices.

seized women and shoved them down side streets and alleys. The struggle continued for several hours, as bedraggled women hurled themselves again and again against the police. Fifteen women managed to reach the lobby, where they were promptly arrested.

By 10 p.m. the mêlée had ended. For the first time, arrests had not been confined to a handful of WSPU leaders – fifty-one women had been arrested in addition to Mrs Despard, Sylvia, and Christabel. * Most of the women arrested were under the age of forty, the ages of forty-nine of those arrested being published as in table 6.1.[4]

Table 6.1

Ages of forty-nine women arrested on 13 February 1907

Number of women	Age
16	under 30
24	30–9
5	40–9
4	50 and over

The women in custody were informed that overnight bail would be arranged only if they found a person of standing who would vouchsafe their appearance in court the next day. F. W. Pethick-Lawrence was called, and he proceeded to arrange bail and explain police-court proceedings. On the following day, most of the defendants received fourteen-day sentences.

On 2 March 1907, Mrs Pankhurst wrote to Sam Robinson, the secretary of the Manchester ILP, 'We are doing very well all over the country & demand for meetings & speakers greatly exceeds power to comply'.[5] The WSPU was indeed doing well. On 8 March, a private member's suffrage Bill sponsored by W. H. Dickinson, a Liberal, reached its Second Reading in the Com-

---

* Sylvia Pankhurst later wrote that Christabel 'told me later that she thought it would be necessary to go to prison in London, and on the spur of the moment she had decided to take this opportunity while sentences were short. She feared that if her absence were protracted, her influence might be undermined' (*The Suffragette Movement*, p. 253).

mons. Philip Snowden later wrote of the occasion: 'Enormous interest had been aroused both in and out of Parliament, and I cannot remember there having been in my time such a large attendance of members on a Friday afternoon.'[6] Several of the speakers observed that the debate was far more serious than debates on the subject had been for many years. Militant feminism had created this new seriousness. The WSPU was not, however, able to influence the fate of the measure, which was, like its forbears, talked out, on the following day. Throughout the debate, the Ladies' Gallery was kept closed as a precaution against any militant outbreak.

In response to the defeat of Dickinson's Bill, the WSPU marched again from Caxton Hall to Parliament. Among the hundreds of marchers were about forty Lancashire mill girls, who had been recruited by Annie Kenney and Adela Pankhurst and sent to London with funds raised by local WSPUs. On 20 March, the day of the procession, the mill girls dressed (by instruction) in clogs and shawls, and Annie Kenney herself came to the Caxton Hall dressed as the mill girl she had once been. Mrs Pankhurst chose Viscountess Harberton to lead the procession.

The marchers found the House of Commons defended by over 500 constables. During the late afternoon and evening, the women rushed repeatedly at police lines, without success. The Caxton Hall was used as a sanctuary at which first aid and the repair of clothing could be obtained, and Christabel told a gathering there to 'get inside the Lobby, inside the House itself, sit down next to Sir Henry Campbell-Bannerman; if you can, seize the mace.'[7] Perhaps, to Christabel, the mace, symbol of the authority of the House, embodied the concept of masculinity itself. By the end of the evening, seventy-four women had been arrested. They were charged with 'disorderly conduct' and 'resisting the police in the execution of their duty.'[8] As before, F. W. Pethick-Lawrence spent many hours arranging bail and giving legal advice. Most of the women arrested were again under forty. The ages of forty-three of the women arrested were published, as in table 6.2.[9]

On 21 March, sixty-five women were sent to prison – fifty-five for two weeks, and ten for a month.[10]

Shortly after the demonstration of 20 March 1907, the WSPU

Table 6.2

Ages of forty-three women arrested on 20 March 1907

Number of women	Age
22	under 30
14	30–9
3	40–9
4	50 and over

released its *First Annual Report,* which covered the period from 1 March 1906 to 28 February 1907.* Membership figures were not divulged, but other indexes made it clear that the Union had expanded rapidly. Forty-seven branches had been established by 28 February 1907, and the Union now employed nine paid organizers.† Moreover, £2,959 had been collected during the fiscal year, and expenditure had risen steadily as shown in table 6.3.

Table 6.3

WSPU expenditure, 1 March 1906–28 February 1907

March–May 1906	£124
June–August 1906	£350
September–November 1906	£768
December–February, 1906–7	£1,252

* *First Annual Report, Women's Social and Political Union,* 1 March 1906–28 February 1907, London, 1907. For the historian, the issuing of this report marks the first point at which the growth of the WSPU can be quantified.

† Teresa Billington-Greig wrote of organizing activities in the provinces during the summer of 1906, 'We tried to leave a "cell" or group or at least one worker' (Billington-Greig Papers, Fawcett Library, box: A.K./W.S.P.U./P.). It is not possible to ascertain when such nuclei became WSPU branches. There seems to have been no minimum membership necessary for the establishment of a branch, and specific connections between the branches and the national headquarters were as yet not well defined. The branches were in many respects autonomous. They were urged to donate funds to Clement's Inn, but were under no obligation to contribute regularly or to donate a fixed amount. In general, they were free to run their own affairs as long as the basic policies formulated by Christabel were followed. In the rare event that a branch failed to comply with those policies, it could be disaffiliated. At

£644 had been spent on literature, £560 on salaries to organizers and office staff, £424 on travelling expenses, and £202 on the hiring of halls. By early 1907, 100 to 200 people were attending the weekly At Homes at Clement's Inn, and, in February, four more rooms had been leased in the building for additional office space. *

The *First Annual Report* had reprinted the first section of the 1906 constitution, in which 'participation in Parliamentary Elections in opposition to the Government candidate and independently of all other candidates' had been called for.[11] During the eight months that had passed since Christabel's declaration of independence at the Cockermouth by-election, this policy had not been opposed within the Union. On 1 April 1907, however, at the ILP's annual conference at Derby, Mrs Despard and Mrs Cobden Sanderson somewhat belatedly announced their rejection of the policy: the ILP conference was presented with a message, which stated: 'We pledge ourselves never to go down to any constituency or take part in an election unless we go to help the Labour party.'† The message was greeted with loud applause. Mrs Pankhurst, who was seated in the audience, sprang to her feet and with lively gesticulations proclaimed:[12]

> We are not going to wait until the Labour Party can give
> us a vote. It is by putting pressure on the present Govern-
> ment that we shall get it. We have opposed nobody but
> Government nominees, and in that we have followed the
> tactics of the Irish Party; but if I were a man I would

the beginning of December 1906, Mrs Pankhurst objected to a Mrs J. M. Robertson's being secretary of the Westminster branch of the WSPU on the grounds that Mrs Robertson's husband was a prominent Liberal MP. On 6 December, the Westminster branch was informed that it was no longer part of the WSPU (D. Montefiore, *From a Victorian*, p. 111).

* *First Annual Report, Women's Social and Political Union*, 1 March 1906–28 February 1907, pp. 3–9. All sums have been rounded to the nearest £.

† Independent Labour Party, *Report of the Fifteenth Annual Conference*, Derby, 1 and 2 April 1907, p. 48. The message was signed by Mrs Despard, Mrs Cobden Sanderson, Mrs Snowden, and Isabella Ford. The latter two women were not members of the WSPU.

condemn what we women are doing. If you think my conduct inconsistent with my membership I will resign.

Some weeks later, without further ado, Mrs Pankhurst and Christabel resigned from the ILP.* Save among old friends like Keir Hardie and Isabella Ford, their resignation was little noted, for it merely completed the process, initiated by Christabel at Cockermouth, of disinvolving the WSPU from its once pervasive connections with the Labour movement. During its political infancy the WSPU had been dependent upon the ILP for platforms, publicity, and financial support, but the Union was by now well past needing such aid, and Mrs Pankhurst's and Christabel's remaining members of the ILP would have served no tangible purpose, given the independence to which the WSPU was by now firmly committed.

* After the Labour Party's annual conference in Belfast in January 1907, loyalty to both Labour and the WSPU had become doubly difficult, since at that conference the party adopted by a majority of 605,000 to 268,000 an amendment which stated that 'to extend the franchise on a property qualification to a section only is a retrograde step and should be opposed' (*Proceedings, Annual Conference of the Labour Party*, Belfast, January 1907, p. 43). With this amendment, the Labour Party had specifically rejected the measure of enfranchisement sought by the WSPU.

7 The Split

During the summer of 1907, Mrs Pankhurst and Christabel did not openly press their differences with Mrs Despard and Mrs Cobden Sanderson, but it became increasingly clear that the Union was no longer united. Lack of unity stemmed from several factors. For one thing, the WSPU's estrangement from its original ideals was becoming increasingly evident in the management of its financial affairs. On 30 May, at the Exeter Hall, the WSPU launched a drive to raise £20,000. Mrs Pethick-Lawrence said to the audience, seeking support and donations, 'If you have an influential position, socially or professionally, we want you . . . if you are a working woman . . . we want you'.[1] No WSPU official would have openly courted the rich during the Union's Manchester years. On 11 July, Mrs Pethick-Lawrence wrote privately to the wealthy suffragist Mrs Maud Arncliffe-Sennett that the Union would spend at least £6,000 during 1907, and added:[2]

> This sum of £6000 . . . can only be raised by persistent organization; by getting as many people as possible on this particular business of raising money and by widening our circle of supporters . . . in any canvass such as that being undertaken in Paddington, a list should be made of every woman of good position. Her name and address should be tabulated and notes should be placed against her name, which would make it easy to write a letter from Headquarters. The first letter of course should not be an appeal for money, but in this way she could be roped in and made a responsible member of the Union. Will you undertake to see that this is done during the remaining part of the Paddington canvass.

Whereas Clement's Inn was now actively seeking the support of well-to-do London women, many of whom had Tory connections, in Lancashire and Yorkshire by-elections the distinction between opposing the Liberal and actively supporting Labour was not always stressed. One of the several by-elections to which the WSPU sent workers during the summer of 1907 was a contest in the Colne Valley in which Victor Grayson, the Pankhursts' erstwhile ally on Manchester street-corners, stood as an independent Socialist. Mrs Pankhurst, who was charmed by the youthful Grayson, was among the WSPU speakers who came north to support him. Grayson, a strong suffragist, won the election by a small margin, and the *Daily Mirror* wrote of his campaign:[3]

> One of the most remarkable features of the Colne Valley
> election . . . was the great interest taken in the election by
> the young mill girls of the constituency. Not only made
> suffragettes by Mrs. Pankhurst's eloquence, many of them
> wore the Socialist colours and helped the Labour candidate to
> win the seat.

The non-support of Labour could hardly be stressed under such circumstances; indeed, the Union's leaders were themselves enthusiastic about the victory of an old friend.* Mrs Pankhurst

---

* Mrs Mabel Tuke wrote privately to Mrs Arncliffe-Sennett (Arncliffe-Sennett Collection, Brit. Mus., Vol. 1, M. Tuke to M. Arncliffe-Sennett, 23 July 1907):

> I was at the Colne Valley By Election & can truthfully say I
> have never spent a more interesting week in my life, & of course
> the result for us may be beyond our wildest expectations.
>   Grayson is only 25, with youth & tremendous enthusiasm on
> his side. He goes to the House pledged to fight for the women.

Christabel, who took great delight in the rough-and-tumble of street-corner politics, was also jubilant at Grayson's victory, writing (*Women's Franchise*, 25 July 1907):

> By the defeat of the Government at Colne Valley our movement
> is brought a stage nearer to success. The only question now is how
> long the Government can afford to have the Women's Social and
> Political Union turning the scale against them at by-elections. . . .
> We have only to pursue with unflagging energy our by-election
> policy, and victory is certain.

On the other hand, W. W. Hadley of the *Observer*, Rochdale, wrote to Mrs Arncliffe-Sennett on 27 July (Arncliffe-Sennett Collection, Brit.

and Christabel were, however, becoming increasingly concerned by the rapid accretion of newly-formed northern and Scottish WSPU branches, not all of which were tightly bound to the policies established at Clement's Inn. Whereas the WSPU had 47 branches on 28 February 1907, by 10 May 1907 it had 58, and by 31 August there were 70.[4] The majority of these branches were in Lancashire, Yorkshire, and Scotland. The Pankhursts' fears were largely caused by the influx of new WSPU members who had never laid eyes on the Pankhursts or become bound to their policies, and, thus, could not be relied upon to follow Christabel's decisions without question.

During the summer of 1907, as the number of new branches mounted rapidly, a sharp conflict developed between the Pankhursts and Mrs Billington-Greig, who was actively engaged in furthering the establishment of new branches.* The origins of this quarrel are obscure.† It is clear, however, that during the

---

Mus., vol. 1, W. W. Hadley, the *Observer*, Rochdale, to M. Arncliffe-Sennett, 27 July 1907):

> I do not agree with you as to the result of the women's efforts in the Colne Valley. The average male politician is just now in such a mood that I don't think the action of the suffragists would injure any candidate they oppose.

There would seem to be no way of seriously assessing the influence of the WSPU on by-elections. It does seem clear that Christabel grossly exaggerated the influence of by-election losses on Liberal thinking, as there does not seem to be evidence that Liberal leaders believed that women's suffrage was a decisive factor in determining the outcome of by-elections. The WSPU was, after all, appealing to an exclusively male electorate.

* Teresa Billington had married Frederick Greig in February 1907. Like Mrs Pethick-Lawrence, Mrs Cobden Sanderson, and other prominent feminists, Teresa Billington added her maiden name to her husband's patronymic.

† Several letters survive, which allude to sharp personal friction as early as June 1907, but these letters do not make clear the point then at issue. On 19 June 1907, Christabel wrote to her sister Sylvia (E. S. Pankhurst Papers, Internationaal Instituut, 33d, C. Pankhurst to E. S. Pankhurst, in train to Portsmouth, 19 June 1907):

> I feel as tho' some of us wd have to round upon the enemy. . .
> T. B. is a wrecker . . . we have just to face her & put her in her place. She has gone too far this time.

On 22 June, Mrs Pankhurst wrote to Sylvia (E. S. Pankhurst Papers,

summer of 1907 Mrs Billington-Greig sought to further the autonomy of the new provincial branches, in the cause of organizational democracy, and that, in turn, the Pankhursts and the Pethick-Lawrences sought to counter what they saw as a challenge to their authority. In April or May, Mrs Billington-Greig had worked out a scheme for provincial organization, the details of which have not survived. Her plan was ignored by Clement's Inn, but it was put into effect in Scotland, and by the end of the summer the Scottish branches formed a semi-autonomous Scottish Council with a treasury of its own.[5] During the course of the summer, other evidence that a spirit of independence was stirring in the branches also came to the attention of Clement's Inn: one Scottish branch balked at not being allowed to support the Labour Party, and several other branches sent in resolutions seeking to limit the number of paid organizers who could sit on the WSPU committee – a move made because Mrs Pankhurst, Christabel, Mrs Pethick-Lawrence, and the paid organizers appointed by them dominated the committee.* The court was being challenged by the country.

By the end of August, the Pankhursts and the Pethick-Lawrences had reason to believe that if the annual conference planned for 12 October was allowed to take place, their joint control of the WSPU might be seriously weakened through the election of new committee members representing the provincial branches.† Such representation might well infringe upon

---

Internationaal Instituut, 33d, E. Pankhurst to E. S. Pankhurst, County Hotel, Jarrow, 22 June 1907):

> I have just written to J. K. H. [J. Keir Hardie] about Teresa
> B. G. He promised me he would help with Mrs. C. S. [Cobden
> Sanderson] if it became necessary & judging from what I hear the
> time has come to act. I wish we had done it long ago.

* See undated statement, Women's Freedom League, in folder: Constitution-Organization, London Museum. For Mrs Billington-Greig's side of the dispute, see 'Points of personal attack', a statement by Mrs Billington-Greig written during the autumn of 1907, in the same folder.

† Their fears were apparently not without grounds; Teresa Billington-Greig later wrote that as a result of 'feelings of resentment' at control of WSPU committee meetings by the paid organizers, 'preparations for seeking a remedy at the [annual] Conference were redoubled' (T. Billington-Greig, *Militant Suffrage Movement*, p. 82).

Christabel's heretofore unchallenged power to formulate strategy. Mrs Pethick-Lawrence later wrote:[6]

> New-comers were pouring into the Union. Many of them were quite ill-informed as far as the realities of the political situation were concerned. Christabel, who possessed in a high degree a flair for the intricacies of a complex political situation, had conceived the militant campaign as a whole. . . . She never doubted that the tactics she had evolved would succeed in winning a cause which, as far as argument or reason were concerned, was intellectually won already. She dreaded all the old plausible evasions and she feared the ingrained inferiority complex in the majority of women. Thus she could not trust her mental offspring to the mercies of politically untrained minds.

Mrs Pankhurst, Christabel, and the Pethick-Lawrences therefore decided to cancel the annual conference, and end any pretence of democracy in the Union's affairs. Plans to do so were made in secret over a period of several weeks.[7] At the end of August, Christabel informed the London members of the WSPU – but not the provincial members – that a meeting at which 'important business' was to be discussed would take place in the Essex Hall on 10 September.[8]

Two meetings were held on 10 September. During the afternoon, Mrs Pankhurst, Mrs Pethick-Lawrence, Mrs Despard, Caroline Hodgson, and five paid organizers held a meeting of the WSPU committee. At this meeting, Mrs Pankhurst announced that the annual conference, planned for 12 October in accordance with the 1906 constitution, would not take place, that those sections of the constitution relating to organization were annulled, and that a new committee would be elected immediately by those present. Mrs Despard asked on whose authority it was proposed that such changes be made. Mrs Pankhurst answered that she was responsible, and that in future she would have no one on the committee who was not in absolute accord with her. Mrs Pankhurst then read aloud the names of those who were to sit on the new Committee: it would be composed of herself and Mrs Tuke as joint secretaries, Mrs Pethick-Lawrence as treasurer, Christabel as organizing secretary, and Annie Kenney, Mary Gawthorpe, Mary Neal, Elizabeth Robins, and Elizabeth

Wolstenholme Elmy. The WSPU would become the National Women's Social and Political Union, and all members would be required to sign a pledge:[9]

> I endorse the objects and methods of the N.W.S.P.U., and I hereby undertake not to support the candidate of any political party at Parliamentary elections until women have obtained the Parliamentary vote.

Mrs Pankhurst put her edicts in the form of resolutions, and these were passed by herself, Mrs Pethick-Lawrence, and the five organizers who were present. The new pledge was passed around for signatures. Mrs Despard and Caroline Hodgson refused to sign.[10]

That evening, in the Essex Hall, the announcements made during the afternoon were repeated to the London members of the WSPU. Cries of 'We want the Constitution!' were heard, but no vote was taken – Mrs Pankhurst simply presented the London members with a *fait accompli*. It was, however, immediately clear that Mrs Despard, Mrs How Martyn, Caroline Hodgson, and Mrs Billington-Greig refused to accept the authority of the afternoon meeting. On 14 September, they and about seventy other WSPU members held a meeting, and called on Mrs Pankhurst to honour the constitution by holding the annual conference on 12 October, as originally planned.[11] Claiming that the name 'Women's Social and Political Union' was rightfully theirs, they formed a provisional committee to arrange for the holding of the conference. The provisional committee included Mrs How Martyn, Mrs Despard, Mrs Billington-Greig, and Irene Fenwick Miller. In a letter dated 17 September, the provisional committee stated that 'the members of the branches are the ultimate power in the Union', and that by forming a new 'basis', the WSPU committee 'lost all claim to the title W.S.P.U. and has constituted itself a new society' in which 'the branches will have no share in the Government of the Union, and will have to submit to dictation on all vital points from Clement's Inn.'[12]

In the meanwhile, the Pankhurst–Pethick-Lawrence faction moved quickly to consolidate its claims. On about 15 September, Mrs Pankhurst had letters sent to all local WSPU branches asking that their members become members of the National Women's Social and Political Union, and on 17 September

Clement's Inn sent packets of members' pledge cards to the branches.* By signing these cards, members of the branches would accept the pledge announced on 10 September and become members of the NWSPU. No dues were required.

By 20 September, it was clear to all concerned that the original WSPU had become irrevocably split into two separate organizations, each of which claimed to be the true Union. The provisional committee did not, however, press legal claims to the funds held by Mrs Pethick-Lawrence, nor was any serious attempt made to acquire use of the offices at Clement's Inn, a move that would have been awkward at best, inasmuch as the Pethick-Lawrences and Christabel lived on the second floor. On 12 October 1907, the provisional committee held what it called the Second Annual Conference of the WSPU. Mrs Despard was elected president.[13] A few weeks later, not wishing to promote further friction between two organizations fighting for the same cause, the provisional committee ceased claiming to be the WSPU and became the Women's Freedom League. The League had fourteen branches at its inception.[14] Precise membership figures are not available, but the small number of branches (as compared with the WSPU) and the limited size of subsequent WFL demonstrations suggest that the organization did not carry with it more than 20 per cent of the WSPU's membership. †

The events of September and October 1907 – subsequently

* London Museum, Mrs Pankhurst to Miss Thompson, Clement's Inn, 17 September 1907. Though the organization led by the Pankhursts was now officially named the National Women's Social and Political Union, the word National, while printed henceforward on pledge cards and stationery, never came into common use – in general, the Union continued to be referred to as the WSPU. For the sake of simplicity, and in keeping with the general practice of both the Union's leaders and members, the organization will herein be referred to throughout as the WSPU, save with regard to the formal citation of annual reports, where NWSPU will be used.

† The subsequent history of the WFL must remain outside the purview of this book. For the next several years, the WFL carried on activities essentially similar to those of the WSPU, but on a much smaller scale. The WFL did not, however, follow the WSPU into the extreme militancy of 1913–14. Although the WFL did not associate itself with any political party, individual members like Mrs Despard were not hindered from personal involvement with political parties.

known as 'the split' – had a profound effect on the WSPU.
Henceforward, the hegemony of Mrs Pankhurst, Christabel, and
the Pethick-Lawrences was unchallenged. (It was, of course, an
irony that an organization devoted to securing the vote for
women had itself become strikingly undemocratic.) Mrs Pankhurst was the Union's founder, star orator, and spiritual leader,
but she had no taste for day-to-day administration, and for the
next five years she spent much of her time lecturing in the
provinces, while Christabel and the Pethick-Lawrences admini-
stered the Union's affairs. Acting as a triumvirate, they alone
determined WSPU policy – the committee named at the 10 September meeting never actually met, though the names of its
members were printed on the letterheads of WSPU stationery.

With their hegemony secure, Mrs Pankhurst, Christabel, and
the Pethick-Lawrences became increasingly fond of describing
the Union in military similes and metaphors. Clement's Inn
became 'headquarters', members the 'rank and file', marches on
Parliament 'raids', and so on. In October 1907, F. W. Pethick-
Lawrence began to publish a monthly, *Votes for Women*,
which was to be the official organ of the WSPU.* The leader in
the first issue – probably written by Christabel – stated:[15]

> If you have any pettiness or personal ambition you must
> leave that behind before you come into this movement.
> There must be no conspiracies, no double dealing in our
> ranks. Everyone must fill her part. The founders and
> leaders of the movement must lead, the non-commissioned
> officers must carry out their instructions, the rank and file
> must loyally share the burdens of the fight. For there is no
> compulsion to come into our ranks, but those who come
> must come as soldiers ready to march onwards in battle
> array.

After September 1907, positions of lieutenancy could only be
held by women willing to place uncritical faith in the political
judgment of Christabel and the Pethick-Lawrences. The
reliability of new appointees was carefully scrutinized. Mrs
Pethick-Lawrence later wrote:[16]

* *Votes for Women* was inaugurated as a threepenny monthly. The
Pethick-Lawrences were its joint editors. Its initial circulation was
2000 copies (see *Votes for Women*, Supplement, 24 September 1909).

Every would-be organiser has to undergo a training and testing of three months, and during that time a sum to cover board and lodging expenses is paid to her. At the end of that time she will discover whether the work suits her. If she is fitted for the work she will become one of the staff organizers. We must have women of the right spirit and the right temperament. The method and routine of the organization we can teach them.

Under such careful control, the WSPU became increasingly polarized into leaders and followers. Whereas the most prominent of the women who left the Union in September 1907 had come to the organization with substantial previous experience in the Labour movement, experience which had given them ample basis for independent judgment, most of the women who came into prominent positions after the split had little or no political experience prior to joining the WSPU, and could not have easily challenged the Union's leaders even if they had wished to do so. In any case, after the split, effective criticism of Christabel's policies became virtually impossible, since Christabel and the Pethick-Lawrences controlled WSPU appointments, finances, and publications, including *Votes for Women*. The effects of the loss of those women best able to bring a critical judgment to bear on the Union's policies was not immediately apparent – the WSPU and the WFL did not pursue radically dissimilar paths between 1907 and 1909 – but was to be of decisive importance during 1913 and 1914.

8 To Hyde Park!

During the rest of the autumn of 1907, the members of the WSPU carried out much proselytizing and heckling, but put on no sizeable demonstrations. The only large demonstration was held in Edinburgh on 5 October, when the major women's suffrage societies jointly sponsored a peaceful parade down Princes Street. The WSPU did, however, hold hundreds of indoor meetings throughout Scotland, the North, and the Midlands. By now, the Union could fill the largest halls available, and at least fifty WSPU meetings drew audiences of over 1,000 persons. By September 1907, the Monday afternoon At Homes at Clement's Inn were attracting from 100 to 150 women each week, and the Union began to hold a second At Home on Thursday evenings.

In the late autumn, the Union's leaders became involved in considerable correspondence and forward planning: on 6 October, Christabel initiated a private correspondence with A. J. Balfour, who had become the Conservative leader in the House of Commons. She asked Balfour if he would meet a WSPU deputation in Birmingham, on 9 November, and make a 'favourable declaration' concerning his intentions regarding Government sponsorship of women's suffrage legislation when he was next in office.[1] Balfour replied, on 23 October, in a letter marked 'Not for Publication':[2]

> I do not approach any of these Suffrage questions from the point of view of abstract rights. If I did, I should, of course, be a strong supporter of the movement to which you are devoting yourself. . . . The main object, in my view, at which we should aim when we modify the Constitution of a free country is to obviate the danger of any important class feeling that they are excluded from their legitimate share of influence, and that, through this exclusion, Government ceases in any true sense to be 'government by consent'. . . .

It is because I am not as yet at all convinced that the exclusion of women at the present moment does really cause, among the mass of women themselves, a feeling that by an arbitrary distinction they are deprived of a privilege which they desire, that I hesitate to recommend a change which is certainly of great magnitude, and may possibly produce quite unexpected consequences.

. . . whereas it is certain, I think, that, could we have polled the unenfranchised town and country populations in '67 and '85, we should have found an immense majority anxious to obtain a vote, I think most observers would hesitate to prophesy a similar result of a poll taken among the women.

On general grounds, therefore, I should be in no hurry (I am speaking only for myself) to make any change in the present electoral arrangements of the country. They seem to work fairly well. . . .

. . . if it can be shown either that women as a class seriously desire the franchise, or that serious legislative injustices are being done them, which the extension of the franchise would obviate, I think the change should be made.

Christabel replied to Balfour that his answer was not 'favourable enough to make its public expression expedient', and she went on to say:[3]

The demand for the vote on the part of women is far stronger than people imagine. If only you would say what you would regard as a proof that a demand exists! I know that we can fulfil any condition that you may lay down, but at present we are working in the dark.

I wish I could put into words the desire that the women of my generation have for this thing. It is very hard and such a waste of energy to spend the best years of one's life in working for what ought to be ours by right.

Of course . . . we have to make this question ripe before it is possible for you to act. But I do hope that you will come to our rescue as soon as you reasonably can.

Balfour was not, of course, in office. By the autumn of 1907 it was widely rumoured that H. H. Asquith would be the next

Prime Minister. Asquith had long opposed women's enfranchisement. On 27 April 1892, in his first major speech on the subject,
he had expressed what subsequently became his most frequently
reiterated objections: most women were uninterested in the vote –
the 'great mass of the sex' were 'watching with languid and
imperturbable indifference the struggle for their own emancipation'.[4] It was not a question, he continued, of 'whether the
average woman is fit for the franchise', but 'whether the franchise is fit for her' – women were innately endowed with
characteristics peculiar to themselves, and they contributed to
political life [5]

> through their own appropriate agencies . . . imagination,
> insight, sympathy, a host of moral and intellectual qualities
> . . . all of which have this common property – that they
> operate by personal influence, and not by associated or
> representative action . . . their natural sphere is not the
> turmoil and dust of politics, but the circle of social and
> domestic life. . . . The inequalities which democracy
> requires that we should fight against and remove are the
> unearned privileges and the artificial distinction which
> man has made, and which man can unmake. They are not
> those indelible differences of faculty and function by which
> Nature herself has given diversity and richness to human
> society.

Asquith's use of the words 'natural' and 'indelible' may well
provide a key to his view of the matter. His objection to women's
enfranchisement was based on a belief that, as far as women were
concerned, existing social arrangements were *natural* arrangements; there was no pressing reason to tamper with them. Roy
Jenkins has referred to Asquith's 'failure of imagination'[6]
concerning women's suffrage, and Asquith does indeed seem to
have been unable to conceive of ordinary women – about whose
lives he knew very little – benefiting substantially from the
wider horizons which the vote might bring. As to women of his
own class, Asquith liked them the way they were far too much to
be interested in their potential for 'serious' endeavours – the
qualities of frivolity and sympathy, on which he depended for
respite from politics, might be eroded by women's involving
themselves in 'masculine' pursuits and concerns.

In December 1907, Asquith expressed views not completely
unlike the views vouchsafed by Balfour to Christabel, two
months earlier: on 19 December, at Aberdeen, he said:*

> I am prepared to withdraw my opposition, which is a very
> unimportant factor in the case, to what is called female
> enfranchisement . . . the moment that I am satisfied of two
> things, but not before, namely, first, that the majority of
> women desire to have a Parliamentary vote, and next, that
> the conferring of a vote upon them would be advantageous
> to their sex and the community at large.

Both Balfour and Asquith had asked for proof that women
really wanted the vote. In response, Christabel formulated a
'comprehensive plan of campaign' designed to demonstrate the
existence of wide support for women's suffrage.[7] The plan was
announced in the January 1908 issue of *Votes for Women*:
Women's Parliament would meet in the Caxton Hall on 11, 12
and 13 February. Then, on 19 March, the WSPU would sponsor
the first women's suffrage demonstration ever held in the Albert
Hall. Finally, on 21 June the Union would hold a mass meeting
in Hyde Park. Christabel also announced that the WSPU had
rented six more rooms at Clement's Inn – the Union now occupied thirteen rooms in the building – and that, as the At Homes
had become seriously overcrowded, from 3 February they would
be held in the Portman Rooms, which could seat about 400
people.[8]

While large public meetings were now to be emphasized,
militant acts had not been precluded. On 17 January 1908, Mrs
Drummond and four other women padlocked themselves to the
railings in front of 10 Downing Street, where the Cabinet was in
session. The act was predictably newsworthy: on the following
day, the *Daily Graphic* devoted its entire front page to photographs of Mrs Drummond and her followers.[9] As a result of the
episode, the five women subsequently received three weeks in the
Second Division – treatment of suffragettes as political prisoners,
entitled to First Division treatment, had been ended, chaining
oneself to the railings outside the Prime Minister's residence

* *Votes for Women*, January 1908. On 30 January, Asquith reiterated
substantially the same view to an NUWSS delegation (see *The Times*,
31 January 1908).

being judicially regarded, it seems, as an act of mere common criminality.

The day after the call on Campbell-Bannerman, Mrs Pankhurst was physically attacked at a by-election in Newton Abbot. Following a Conservative victory, young Liberals rioted, and Mrs Pankhurst and Mrs Martel, who had opposed the Liberal candidate, were shoved fifty yards down a street, and then pushed down and rolled in mud. Mrs Pankhurst's ankle was injured to the extent that she was unable to walk. The violence apparently did not stem from animosity directed at the WSPU as such – during the morning, the body of a prominent local Conservative had been found in a nearby millstream, and some local citizens mistakenly believed that he had been murdered in connection with the by-election. The result was that a day of rioting ensued, during which several persons were injured and fourteen windows were smashed in the local Conservative club.[10]

Like several previous meetings, the Women's Parliament of 11–13 February 1908 was timed to take place just after the King's Speech; once again, the Government's failure to include women's suffrage in its programme would be followed by a march from the Caxton Hall to Parliament. The march which took place on 11 February was much like previous marches, save that the WSPU hired two furniture vans and had them driven to the public entrance of the House of Commons; upon arrival, twenty-one women concealed inside the vans threw open the doors and rushed into the lobby, from which they were speedily ejected. By the end of the day, fifty-four women had been arrested. Forty-eight of them subsequently received two months in the Second Division.

Mrs Pankhurst had not marched on 11 February, being at a by-election in Leeds, but on 13 February, though still lame from the attack at Newton Abbot, she marched to Parliament with twelve other women. The size of the deputation had been set at thirteen, because at the trial of the women arrested two days before, the prosecuting solicitor had cited an Act of Charles II in which petitioning of Parliament by processions of more than twelve persons had been forbidden. Mrs Pankhurst and eight of the twelve women who marched with her were arrested. After refusing to be bound over, they were sentenced to six weeks in the Second Division. This was Mrs Pankhurst's first imprisonment.

The WSPU had continued to grow rapidly. In the *Second Annual Report*, which covered the fiscal year 1 March 1907 to 29 February 1908, the Union claimed that during the year it had held 'upwards of 5,000 meetings', 400 of which had drawn audiences of over 1,000 people.[11] Though in January 1908 the WSPU had begun to use the small Portman Rooms for At Homes, the receptions were so overcrowded that in February they were moved to the large Portman Rooms in Baker Street, where they immediately began to draw over 600 men and women. Revenue had risen in proportion to the burgeoning interest in the WSPU. Gross receipts were £7,546 compared with £2,959 the previous year.* Expenditure had risen accordingly – £714 was spent on the hiring of halls, compared with £202 the previous year, and £1,472 was allocated for the salaries of office staff and organizers, compared with £560 the previous year. By the end of February 1908, the WSPU employed eighteen paid office staff, and fourteen salaried organizers. One year earlier, it had employed seven organizers. Finally, the aggregate weeks of imprisonment served by WSPU members – 191 weeks in 1906–7 – totalled 350 weeks in 1907–8.[12]

In order to raise funds, Mrs Pethick-Lawrence had designated 15–22 February 1908 as self-denial week. During this week, WSPU members were to do without luxuries such as cocoa, coffee, and tea, perform extra work, or use other means to raise funds for the Union. John Galsworthy, H. W. Nevinson, and E. V. Lucas all donated autographed copies of their books to be sold. The total amount raised would be announced at the meeting to be held on 19 March in the Albert Hall.

On the appointed evening, over 7,000 people filled the Albert Hall, in what the WSPU claimed was the largest meeting of women ever held under one roof. Mrs Pankhurst was not expected to appear on the platform, for her sentence was to run until 20 March. Herbert Gladstone decided, however, to release Mrs Pankhurst and her fellow-prisoners one day early 'so that they could take part in a large and legitimate demonstration', and,

---

* In accordance with normal WSPU accounting practice, money carried over from the previous year was included in the gross receipts. £465 had been carried over from 1906–7, so the net receipts for 1907–8, excluding money brought forward from the preceding year, were £7,081.

somewhat late, Mrs Pankhurst walked on stage, to her followers' great delight.[13] During the course of the evening, F. W. Pethick-Lawrence manipulated a large scoring clock, which registered the sums donated to the WSPU. Mrs Pethick-Lawrence announced that £2,382 had been raised during self-denial week, and that one woman had promised to give £1,000 a year until women could vote. Twelve other women, including Mrs Bernard Shaw, gave sums of £100. Money and pledge cards poured in from various parts of the hall, accompanied by cheering and applause, and by the end of the evening over £7,000 had been raised.[14] The Pethick-Lawrences themselves had promised to donate £1,000 a year to the Union.

At Easter, Campbell-Bannerman finally resigned, and both prospective Cabinet Ministers and Ministers changing posts within the Cabinet were obliged to seek re-election. The WSPU took part in all of the nine contests thus engendered, but evinced a particular interest in the campaign of Winston Churchill in North-West Manchester. Christabel settled in Manchester to lead the Union's forces, which comprised about forty women. An average of twelve WSPU meetings were held daily, theatres being rented for the larger meetings.

Churchill lost to Joynson-Hicks, the Conservative, 5,417 to 4,998.* The WSPU promptly proclaimed itself responsible for Churchill's defeat, and when Christabel returned to London Mrs Pethick-Lawrence presented her with a statuette of the Victory of Samothrace. As is generally the case with the WSPU's role in by-elections, it is difficult to assess the Union's claims. In North-West Manchester the candidates had certainly campaigned on issues other than women's suffrage – the most hotly debated issues had been tariff reform and the future of the House of Lords.† The *Manchester Guardian* pointed out that Churchill had been opposed by 'a dozen outside organizations', each with 'its own little army, its own committee-rooms, its own special methods of appeal'. The *Guardian* also claimed that 'the great brewers' monopoly' had worked 'desperately' against Churchill, and that an SDF candidate, who had garnered 276 votes, had

* Churchill was subsequently re-elected for the safe seat of Dundee.
† For a full account of the issues debated in this by-election, see R. S. Churchill, *Winston S. Churchill*, vol. 2, pp. 252–60.

been put up for the seat to draw away Liberal voters.[15] Anyway, from its formation in 1885 until 1906, the seat had been exclusively a Tory one – so much so that the Liberals had left it uncontested in 1892 and 1900 – and the *Daily News* observed, reasonably enough, that 'what was surprising was not Churchill's defeat, now, but his *victory* in the seat in 1906.'[16] Finally, on 27 April, Churchill himself wrote to Clementine Hozier, his future wife, that 'but for those sulky Irish Catholics changing sides at the last moment under priestly pressure, the result would have been different.'[17]

It was Christabel's opinion, however, that 'without our opposition Mr. Churchill would certainly have been reelected.'* *Votes for Women* stated, similarly, 'we know, and Manchester knows, that the women turned the scale against him.'[18] The validity of such claims is open to question, and it is certainly clear that the WSPU was inordinately optimistic regarding the effects of by-election defeats on the Liberals' attitudes towards women's suffrage: regarding a Conservative victory at Peckham, in early April, *Votes for Women* had gone so far as to claim: 'It only requires a few such defeats to force the Cabinet to give way.'[19] Regardless of the validity of the Union's claims to have defeated Liberal candidates, what really mattered was whether Liberal candidates *thought* they were being defeated by the WSPU. There does not seem to be evidence that this was the case.

By late April, 1908, the WSPU was engrossed in preparations for the enormous meeting to be held in Hyde Park on 21 June. The reason for holding the meeting was stated repeatedly:[20]

> We have been frequently asked to produce numbers to show that there are a great many women who are demanding the vote. . . . It will be remembered that on the famous occasion in Hyde Park, when the men pulled down the railings, 67,000 men demonstrated . . . we are confident of being able to double this figure.

---

* *Votes for Women*, 30 April 1908. With the issue of 30 April 1908, *Votes for Women*, heretofore a threepenny monthly, became a weekly costing a penny. Its circulation, estimated at 2,000 at its inception, was now 5,000.

And, again:[21]

> Members of the Government, when called upon to grant
> votes to women, have said that proof is lacking that women
> demand the vote, and have told women to hold demon-
> strations like those organized in the past by men. The
> Women's Demonstration . . . will give the final answer to
> this argument, and will prove that there is a national
> demand for women's enfranchisement.

The Pethick-Lawrences were placed in charge of all arrangements for the meeting, which, under their guidance, was
modelled on the demonstrations of 1867. On Sunday, 21 June,
there were to be seven processions – from Euston Station,
Trafalgar Square, the Victoria embankment, the Chelsea
embankment, Kensington High Street, Paddington, and Maryle-
bone Road – and these processions were to converge on Hyde
Park, where the public would assemble. (Sunday had been chosen
as the day of the demonstration because it was the only day on
which processions could easily be marshalled in the London
streets, as well as being the only day of leisure for many working-
class women.) Each of the seven processions was to be organized
by a chief marshal, and there would also be group marshals,
banner marshals, marshals in charge of railway stations, and so
on. In supreme control of the march would be Mrs Drummond,
who was now dubbed General Drummond.* Under her leadership, the marchers were to be 'an army', which would 'march as
to certain victory with bands playing, colours flying, and trumpets sounding'.[22]

Aware of the impact of costume and pageantry, Mrs Pethick-
Lawrence invented WSPU colours – purple, white, and green –
and asked marchers to wear white dresses with favours of purple
or green.† White, Mrs Pethick-Lawrence later wrote, stood for
'purity in public as well as private life', green stood for 'hope', for

---

* See *Votes for Women*, 18 June 1908. Mrs Flora Drummond was
known as 'General Drummond' or 'the General' for the rest of the
militant campaign. A rather squat woman with a face like a good-
natured bulldog, her bluff hearty manner made her well beloved as a
leader of parades and other quasi-martial affairs.
† As Anna Davin has pointed out to me, few working-class women
could have afforded the costume Mrs Pethick-Lawrence suggested.

'the "green fire" of a new spring tide' that had 'kindled life in a movement apparently dead', and purple stood for 'dignity', for 'that self-reverence and self-respect which renders acquiescence to political subjection impossible'.[23] At the direction of Mrs Pethick-Lawrence, 700 purple, white and green banners were made, each eight feet by three feet. Each banner would be borne on two six-feet-long poles. There would also be ten silk banners, each eight feet by ten, and thousands of flags. Each item was paid for by a donor, and the price and the donor's name were listed in *Votes for Women*.

As the day of the great demonstration drew near, the Union sponsored much advertising. Enormous posters were manufactured, on which were printed life-size portraits of the twenty women who would be the chairmen at twenty different platforms in Hyde Park. (Loudspeakers not yet being in use, twenty platforms were necessary to ensure audibility.) Shop windows carried displays, buses were covered with posters, and a steam launch, covered with bunting and filled with suffragettes, called at the terrace of the House of Commons at 4 p.m., while MPs were taking tea. Mrs Drummond, who stood on the cabin roof, invited the MPs to attend the demonstration, and assured them that there would be no arrests.

Other arrangements were also made. Approached by Mrs Drummond, the police agreed to take up a quarter mile of railings around Hyde Park, and to escort each of the seven processions. Transport for the marchers was provided for too – thirty special trains would arrive from seventy provincial cities.

On 21 June, 30,000 marchers wended their way to Hyde Park.* Keir Hardie, Bernard Shaw, Israel Zangwill, Mrs Thomas Hardy, and Mrs H. G. Wells were among those who rode in four-in-hand coaches at the heads of processions. The march also included forty bands. An immense throng gathered in the park – the *Daily Chronicle* estimated there were over 300,000 people, *The Times* thought there were from 250,000 to 500,000, and *Votes for Women* claimed: 'it is no exaggeration to say that the

* The demonstration had been preceded, on 13 June, by a march sponsored by the National Union of Women's Suffrage Societies, in which 10,000 women walked from the embankment to the Albert Hall.

number of people present was the largest ever gathered together on one spot at one time in the history of the world.'[24]

In order to accommodate the crowd, the twenty platforms had been placed about 100 yards apart. In the centre of the demonstration area was a large furniture van. The roof of the van served as a conning tower, from which the proceedings were directed by the blowing of bugles. The crowd, which was tightly wedged around each platform, was fairly orderly, but there were disturbances at three platforms. Helen Fraser, a WSPU organizer in Scotland, and one of the platform chairmen, later wrote privately:[25]

> the 21st was very wonderful. It was successful and yet not entirely satisfactory – the crowd was about half a million . . . at three platforms there was much rowdyism – Christabel's, Mrs. P.'s, & Mrs. Martel's. At mine, we had a splendid hearing. . . . It seemed to me, however, that the vast mass of people were simply curious – not sympathetic – not opposed. Simply indifferent.

The newspapers took the same point of view: the *Daily Chronicle* believed that the majority of those present had been 'drawn by curiosity, as well as by interest in the remarkable personalities of the movement.'[26] *The Times* claimed that 'the great majority were there simply from curiosity and love of diversion.'[27]

At the close of events in Hyde Park, a resolution was carried (by acclamation) 'that this meeting calls upon the Government to grant votes to women without delay.'[28] Immediately afterwards, Christabel rushed to Clement's Inn and dispatched to Asquith, by special messenger, both the resolution and a note in which she asked what action the Government intended to take. Two weeks earlier, Christabel had written:[29]

> It remains to be seen what effect that [the demonstration] will have. If the Government still refuse to act, then we shall know that great meetings, though they are indispensable for rousing public interest, fail as a means of directly influencing the action of the Government. We shall then be obliged to rely more than ever on militant methods.

On 23 June, Christabel received a reply from Asquith's private secretary: the Prime Minister desired to inform her that he had nothing to add to the statement he had made on 20 May.* Christabel immediately announced that militancy would be resumed. On the evening of 23 June, H. W. Nevinson visited the Pethick-Lawrences, and 'found them obdurate in every way & determined to renew violence.'[30]

Militancy was resumed not only because the Hyde Park demonstration had failed to sway Asquith, but also because it simply did not seem feasible to attempt to hold demonstrations of any greater magnitude. Christabel wrote, 'no larger meeting is conceivable . . . if the holding of public meetings were our last resource, our case would indeed be helpless.'[31] Mrs Pethick-Lawrence wrote:[32]

> The possibilities of constitutional agitation culminated on June 21 of this year. It would be impossible to have a greater demonstration than was then held. . . . We have touched the limit of public demonstration. . . . Nothing but militant action is left to us now.

The WSPU planned that on the afternoon of 30 June, a small deputation would attempt to interview Asquith at the House of Commons, and that in the evening a militant demonstration would be held in Parliament Square; the public was invited to assemble there to show sympathy with the demonstrators. On the

* V. Nash to Dear Madam, 10 Downing Street, 22 June 1908, as quoted in *Votes for Women*, 25 June 1908.
On 20 May, Asquith had stated that the Government would introduce an electoral reform Bill before the end of the present Parliament. Women's suffrage would not be included in the original Bill, but he would not object to its being proposed in a private amendment, provided the amendment were on democratic lines, and 'had behind it the overwhelming support of the women of the country, no less than the support of men' (*The Times*, 21 May 1908). Christabel saw clearly (and realistically) that Asquith had allowed himself room to object to any amendment unless it were so broad as to stand no chance of passing a free vote of the House of Commons, let alone the Lords, and she rejected his statement as being of 'too negative and vague a character to be of any value' (*ibid.*, letter to the editor from C. Pankhurst). On 26 May, in the House of Commons, when asked if a women's suffrage amendment, if carried, would become part of the Government-sponsored legislation, Asquith replied: 'My honourable friend asks me a contingent question in regard to a remote and speculative future' (*H. C. Deb.* 4s. vol. 189, 26 May 1908, c. 962).

afternoon of 30 June, a group of thirteen women, including Mrs Pankhurst, left the Caxton Hall to carry a women's suffrage resolution to Asquith. Neither Asquith nor his private secretary would receive the delegation, which returned to the hall. That evening, a dense crowd filled Parliament Square. Many of its members were, however, far from sympathetic to the WSPU – indeed, a number of men seemed to have come expressly to bait and bully the suffragettes. During the evening, women who tried to speak from the steps of buildings or while clinging to the railings around Palace Yard were repeatedly flung back into the crowd, both by the police and by gangs of roughs. A cordon of police barred access to Palace Yard, and, in trying to penetrate the cordon, twenty-five women were arrested. *The Times* remarked that the arrests evoked 'the intense joy of the crowd . . . it was the spectacle of the arrest and of the taking to Cannon-row Police-station that pleased the multitude; not the cause for which the martyrdom was undergone.'[33]

Exasperated by Asquith's unwillingness to receive a deputation, and by the brutality with which women were being treated in Parliament Square, two WSPU members, Edith New and Mary Leigh, filled a bag with stones, took a cab to 10 Downing Street, and smashed two of Asquith's windows.* They were arrested immediately. At the station house, Mary Leigh, a small fiery-tempered woman, said, 'It will be a bomb next time'.[34] On 1 July, the two women were sentenced to two months in the Third Division. The other twenty-five women arrested on 30 June received sentences of from one to three months.

At the time, the leaders of the WSPU attached no special importance to the breaking of two windows – window-breaking had not been sponsored by the Union, and Mrs Pankhurst later told a police superintendent, 'We cannot always control our women. It was no part of our programme to break windows in Downing-street. It was not prearranged. It was done by individuals on their own initiative.'[35] Frustration at the failure of both large peaceful demonstrations and mild forms of militancy alike to achieve tangible progress towards women's enfranchisement, when that frustration was exacerbated by brutal treatment at the hands of men, had set off resentment strong enough to lead

* Edith New had joined the WSPU in 1906. She had been the chief marshal of one of the processions on 21 June.

to acts of militancy beyond the pale of existing WSPU policy. On 16 July, Christabel wrote, with some prescience:[36]

> As for the stone-throwing, that caused a very trifling damage to property, and was of importance only as an indication that the patience of women Suffragists may in future prove to have its limits.

6 The WSPU uniformed fife and drum band. Mary Leigh, drum major, stands at right

7 General Drummond

8 One of the WSPU's innumerable processions through the streets of central London—in this case the procession of 23 July 1910

9 The funeral of Emily Wilding Davison, 14 June 1913. A WSPU guard of honour salutes as the coffin is carried into St George's Church, Bloomsbury

9 Frustration Mounts

Soon after the great demonstration in Hyde Park, Mrs Pankhurst announced that the WSPU would hold similar demonstrations throughout the country. On 15 July 1908, the Union attracted a crowd of 20,000 to Clapham Common, on 19 July 150,000 came to Heaton Park, Manchester, and on 26 July 100,000 were present on Woodhouse Moor in Leeds, where women spoke from ten different platforms.[1]

Edith New and Mary Leigh were released from Holloway on 23 August. Before their release, a crowd that included Mrs Pankhurst and Christabel gathered at the prison gates. When the prisoners appeared, a brass band struck up the 'Marseillaise', and Edith New and Mary Leigh were conducted to a landau, in which they were drawn by a team of women to the ceremonial breakfast of welcome accorded to all newly-freed suffragettes. Such festivities were by no means merely ornamental. On 1 July, when twenty-seven women had been sentenced to terms of varying lengths, Mrs Pethick-Lawrence had remarked that 'every prisoner means a harvest of converts.'[2] Four of the women imprisoned on 1 July were due to be released on 16 September, and one week before their release, Mrs Pethick-Lawrence issued the following instructions:[3]

> At eight o'clock next Wednesday morning every member of
> this Union not absolutely prevented by imperative duty
> should be waiting outside the gates of Holloway. They
> should come, if possible in full uniform . . . a white dress
> with belt and regalia in the colours.
>   The horses will again be taken out of the traces, and the
> released prisoners will be drawn to Queen's Hall by a team
> of Suffragettes. . . . Names of volunteers must be sent in at
> once to Mrs. Drummond at 4, Clement's Inn, so that
> every one may have her own special place alloted to her,
> and be definitely instructed in a letter as to her precise duty.

E

One of our great banners will be carried. . . . Names of those who will volunteer to assist in carrying it must be sent in at once, as a little practice would be desirable, and a rehearsal in one of the unfrequented squares near Clement's Inn can be arranged. Mrs. Drummond would like names of those who will sell the paper to the people in the crowd. . . .

A very great effort should be made by every one of the members to push the sale of breakfast tickets amongst their friends, for no better opportunity could possibly be afforded for making converts and enthusiastic adherents to our cause. Of all our meetings the breakfast party is the most significant. The sight of the women who have suffered so bravely, and their words of greeting to the world as they come back to it, must go straight to the heart of everyone present, whether previously friend or foe to the women's movement. It is incumbent upon all our members to bring, if possible, at least one stranger with them.

Well before all of the women imprisoned on 1 July had been released, plans had been completed for the next raid on Parliament, to be held on 13 October. This time, Mrs Pankhurst said, a deputation would 'enter the House, and, if possible, the Chamber itself'.[4] To advertise the event, Christabel had thousands of handbills printed, as follows:[5]

Women's Social and Political Union

VOTES FOR WOMEN

Men & Women

HELP THE SUFFRAGETTES
TO RUSH
THE HOUSE OF COMMONS
ON
TUESDAY EVENING, 13th October, 1908
at 7:30

What Christabel meant by 'rush' was not clear. Asked to explain, she said, 'By rushing the House of Commons, the suffragettes mean going through the doors, pushing their way in, and confronting the Prime Minister.'[6] Apropos entering the floor of the Commons, Mrs Pankhurst said that the women 'meant to get there if they possibly could.'[7]

On 8 October, in the WSPU offices, Christabel gaily showed the new flyers ('Have you seen our new bills?') to an Inspector Jarvis.[8] The police also procured some copies being handed out in Trafalgar Square. Four days later, summonses were issued against Mrs Pankhurst, Christabel, and Mrs Drummond, alleging that they were 'guilty of conduct likely to provoke a breach of the peace in circulating . . . a certain handbill calling upon and inciting the public to do a certain wrongful and illegal act, namely, to rush the House of Commons'.[9] On 13 October, after eluding the police for a day, the three women presented themselves for arrest at 6 p.m., just before the demonstration. (They had spent most of the day sitting in the Pethick-Lawrences' roof-garden, reading newspapers.)

That evening, about 60,000 people gathered in the vicinity of Parliament Square. Five thousand constables had been placed on special duty, and they completely cordoned off the square. As on previous occasions, groups of suffragettes tried to force their way past police lines, and were arrested for trying to do so. During the course of the evening, twenty-four women and thirteen men were arrested, and ten persons were taken to hospital. Haldane, Burns, and Lloyd George, who was accompanied by his six-year-old daughter Megan, saw parts of the struggle. One woman – Keir Hardie's secretary, Mrs Travers Symons – managed to enter the floor of the House while debate was in progress. Mrs Symons said a few words before being taken out.

On the following day, Mrs Pankhurst, Mrs Drummond, and Christabel went on trial for circulating the handbill which advocated rushing the Commons. The proceedings were soon recessed until 21 October so that the defence could gather evidence and procure witnesses. Subsequently, at the defendants' request, Gladstone and Lloyd George were subpoenaed. The procuring of two Cabinet ministers as witnesses was no mean *coup* for the WSPU, and it gained the Union much publicity: *The Times* and the *Manchester Guardian* devoted many columns to the trial, and photographs covered the front pages of the *Daily Mirror* and *Daily Graphic*.[10] The three accused did not employ counsel; Christabel examined Lloyd George and Gladstone, and gave what amounted to a summing up for the defence. The gist of

Christabel's argument was that 'rush' did not imply violence or the destruction of property. In her final speech, which lasted two hours, she said, mockingly, that if the WSPU had used the expression 'storm the House', she[11]

> could have understood a little fear creeping into the mind of Mr. Herbert Gladstone, because they knew he was rather a timid person. . . . With regard to the events of October 13, they had shown that the crowd was the most orderly that had ever been known to assemble in the streets of London. Lloyd George thought so little of the danger that he actually took his little daughter out with him, and Mr. Gladstone said he was not afraid that night. If there had been a shadow of a danger, he would have been afraid. No one thought for a moment that the women could rush the House of Commons. They went there under escort to show their indignation against the Government. . . . The only woman who actually succeeded in rushing the House had been allowed to go scot free, and nobody seemed to mind. If the 60,000 people who assembled in the streets had really meant to rush the House, the 6,000 police would have been powerless.

The magistrate found the defendants guilty, and bound them over to keep the peace; in default of agreeing to do so, Mrs Pankhurst and Mrs Drummond were to serve three months' imprisonment and Christabel ten weeks'. Mrs Pethick-Lawrence later wrote: 'We could not but realize that the proceedings for two days in Bow Street Police-Court had been like a suffrage meeting attended by millions. In fact, the whole newspaper-reading world had been presented with our case.'[12]

On 29 October 1908, the Union held its second meeting in the Albert Hall. £3,000 was raised, including jewellery, valuables, and donations promised in advance by wealthy supporters. That evening, Mrs Pethick-Lawrence said: 'So far as the power lies in us, we do not intend to allow a single Cabinet Minister to speak in public.'[13] During the next two months, the Union indeed made prodigious efforts to halt Cabinet Ministers' speeches. Birrell was severely heckled at Bristol on 14 November, and his tormentors were ejected with violence. Lloyd George was to speak in the

Albert Hall on 5 December at a women's suffrage meeting
sponsored by the Women's Liberal Federation, and before the
meeting, correspondence passed between him and the WSPU,
the Union offering not to heckle if Lloyd George pledged Government action or else offered to resign from the Cabinet over
women's suffrage.[14] Inclined to do neither, Lloyd George wrote
to Gladstone on 9 November:[15]

> As to the Pankhurst business I quite agree with you. Let
> them break up the meeting – a meeting specially convened
> to support the suffrage movement. That would be the
> [unreadable] of their folly.
>
>   I have no desire to speak by Gracious permission of
> Queen Christabel.

On 5 December, in the Albert Hall, about seventy WSPU
members heckled Lloyd George. Some of the women had managed
to procure front row seats, and removed their cloaks to reveal
mock prison garb. The first heckler, Helen Ogston, had come
armed with a dogwhip, to ward off handling of the sort meted out
by stewards at previous meetings. As stewards forced her out of
the hall, she flicked at them with the whip. (Her actions went
beyond the purview of existing WSPU policy, and were received
rather coolly by Christabel and F. W. Pethick-Lawrence.) During
the rest of the evening, the heckling was so persistent that it took
Lloyd George two hours to deliver a twenty-minute speech. *
Many of the hecklers were ejected roughly, emerging with cuts,
bruises, and torn clothing. In his speech, Lloyd George had
nothing new to offer; he merely endorsed Asquith's circumscribed
pledge of 20 May.†

Two weeks after Lloyd George's speech, Mrs Pankhurst and
Christabel were released from Holloway, on orders from the
Home Secretary. On the following morning, 350 people attended
a breakfast held in their honour. They were then driven through
central London to Clement's Inn in a carriage escorted by two
bands, nine women riding white horses, and 200 women in
white dresses. The parade was led by a young woman carrying a

---

* *The Times*, 7 December 1908. Helen Ogston held a BSc from St
Andrews, and was the daughter of a professor at the University of
Aberdeen.
† See fn. *, p. 106.

tricolour. That evening, in the Queen's Hall, Christabel claimed
that the protests at Cabinet Ministers' meetings had been very
effective and that the members of the Government were 'simply
terrified'.[16]

Christabel's rhetoric notwithstanding, the first five months of
1909 were marked by the virtual ossification of militancy into
forms that had become predictable through familiarity. Asquith's
position too seemed frozen. In January and early February, he
twice refused to receive WSPU deputations; he was repelled by
the clamour now surrounding women's suffrage, and he had no
inclination to meet deputations which, he believed, represented a
rather small minority of British women. On 24 February, the
WSPU once again marched to Parliament, with the avowed
intention of seeing Asquith. The usual rushes at police lines
occurred, and many of the women were treated roughly by
constables who seized them and hurled them into the crowd.
Mrs Pethick-Lawrence, who led the deputation, and Lady
Constance Lytton, a recent recruit to the WSPU, were among the
twenty-eight women who were arrested and subsequently
sentenced to from one to two months in prison.

28 February was the last day of the 1908–9 fiscal year. The
WSPU's *Third Annual Report*, covering the period 1 March 1908
to 28 February 1909, indicated that during the fiscal year the
income of the Union had virtually tripled, being £21,214
compared with £7,546 the previous year.* Expenditure in
1908–9 had included £2,896 for salaries of staff and organizers,
£3,401 for the hiring of halls, and £4,314 for the expenses of the
Hyde Park demonstration, including special trains, bands,
ambulances, and advertising. During the year, the number of
paid organizers had doubled, going from 14 to 30, and the
number of paid London office staff had increased from 18 to 45,
including the staff of *Votes for Women* and the Women's Press.
The Union now occupied 19 rooms in Clement's Inn, compared
with 13 rooms a year earlier. In addition, 11 regional WSPU
offices had been established in eight provincial districts. (Local
Unions maintained separate premises, if they maintained

* The gross income for 1908–9, £21,214, included £981 carried over
from the previous year.

premises at all.) The Union's newly established regional offices
were as in table 9.1.*

Table 9.1   Regional offices of the WSPU in February 1909

Region	Organizer
West of England (offices in Bristol and Torquay)	Miss Annie Kenney
Lancashire (headquarters in Manchester and offices in Preston and Rochdale)	Miss Mary Gawthorpe
Birmingham	Miss Gladice Keevil
Leeds and Bradford	Miss Charlotte Marsh
Newcastle	Miss Edith New
Glasgow	Miss Conolan
Edinburgh	Miss Macauley
Aberdeen	Miss Ada Flatman

As usual, the Union did not divulge its membership, but the
rapidity with which its support was rising was suggested both by
the tripling of its income and by two other factors: first, by
February 1908, attendance at the Monday afternoon At Homes,
which had been moved to the Queen's Hall in July 1908, had
risen to about 1,000 people each week. Second, *Votes for Women*
had greatly expanded both its circulation and its number of
pages per issue – established in October 1907 as a twelve-page
monthly with a circulation of 2,000, by May 1908 it had become a
sixteen-page weekly with a circulation of 5,000, and, by the end
of February 1909 it had twenty-four pages per issue and a
circulation of 16,000.[17]

On 16 April 1909, Mrs Pethick-Lawrence, who had been jailed
at the end of February, was released from prison. She was greeted
by a gala parade from Marble Arch to the Aldwych Theatre,
where an audience of 400 awaited her. The parade, which took
place in sparkling sunshine, was led by Elsie Howey dressed in

* Although none of the regional organizers was married, married
women were not, apparently, absolutely excluded, for two married (or
widowed) regional organizers were listed in the 1909–10 annual
report (see fn. †, p. 133).

armour as Joan of Arc and riding a large white horse. The procession also included the newly formed WSPU uniformed women's fife and drum band. Mrs Pethick-Lawrence was presented with a motor car for the use of the Union, a fifteen horsepower Austin painted purple, white, and green.

One month later, the Union held a Women's Exhibition at the Princess Skating Rink in Knightsbridge. The exhibition, which was held from 13 to 26 May, included a photographic history of feminism, a full-size reproduction of a prison cell, suffragist plays put on by members of the Actresses' Franchise League, and lessons in ju-jitsu. The exhibition was advertised by a parade of the fife and drum band, with Mary Leigh, who was apt to have a rather military bearing, acting as drum major. According to *Votes for Women*, 'the twenty-nine members of the band went through a course of drill and physical exercises under the direction of military noncommissioned officers.'[18] At the Princess Skating Rink exhibition, over 200 women were enrolled as new WSPU members and £5,664 was raised.[19]

By June 1909, almost a year had passed since the enormous meeting in Hyde Park. During the latter half of that year, the tactics used by the WSPU had more and more often met with resistance, or else had simply been ignored: women who heckled Cabinet ministers found themselves ejected with dispatch, and often with violence. Moreover, women were increasingly being admitted to Liberal meetings by signed tickets only, if not excluded altogether. In marches on Parliament, WSPU members now had to endure much buffeting by the police before arrests could be secured, as the police were not anxious to make arrests they knew were desired for the sake of martyrdom and publicity. Finally, for all of Christabel's insistence on the efficacy of the WSPU's anti-Liberal campaigns at by-elections, the Liberals seemed disinclined to connect by-election defeats with the suffrage agitation.

In short, the WSPU had succeeded in making women's suffrage a heatedly debated issue, but seemed to be making no tangible progress towards persuading the Government to sponsor women's suffrage legislation. The Union could not, after all, point to any conversions among 'anti' Cabinet Ministers, let alone any change in Asquith's attitude. Moreover, the parliamentary outlook was now particularly unpropitious, as there was to be no autumn sitting. On 10 June 1909, Mrs Fawcett wrote privately to Mrs Arncliffe-Sennett: 'I agree with you in thinking the immediate outlook for our cause gloomy in the extreme'.[20] It was under such circumstances that the WSPU began laying plans for yet another march to the House of Commons.

10 Violence Begins

The march to Parliament on 29 June 1909 was to be larger than any of its twelve forebears. In publicizing the march, the WSPU stressed that the right to petition had been guaranteed by the Bill of Rights of 1689. Leaflets were issued that quoted the Bill: *

> 'It is the right of the subjects to petition the King, and all committments and prosecutions for such petitioning are illegal.' Mr. Asquith, as the King's representative, is bound, therefore, to receive the deputation and hear their petition. If he refuses to do so, and calls out the police to prevent women from using their right to present a petition, he will be guilty of illegal and unconstitutional action.

On 22 June, Marion Wallace Dunlop, a sculptress, attempted to print the extract from the Bill of Rights on the wall of St Stephen's Hall of the House of Commons. Ejected without being arrested, she returned on 24 June and used indelible ink to stamp the quotation on the wall. This time she was arrested.

On 29 June, the usual meeting in the Caxton Hall began with martial music played by the new fife and drum band; the musicians wore purple uniforms, adorned by green sashes and white braid. Subsequently, a small initial deputation set out, led by Mrs Pankhurst and composed of eight women, two of whom were elderly. The police conducted the little group to the door of the Commons, where Chief Inspector Scantlebury, the stout, red-faced head of the police attached to Parliament, gave Mrs Pankhurst a large envelope. The envelope contained a letter

---

* *Votes for Women*, 25 June 1909. The WSPU's emphasis on the right to petition seems to have been rather fatuous, in that the organization's right to petition was not in question. It was, after all, the *manner* of petitioning that had been alleged to take illegal forms. That the rules of the game had been set by men alone would seem to have been a stronger point than that the thwarting of rushes at the House of Commons involved a denial of the right to petition.

from Asquith's private secretary, stating that the Prime Minister would not receive the deputation. Mrs Pankhurst threw the letter to the ground, saying that she would not accept it – she and the ladies accompanying her were subjects of the King and had come in the assertion of a right.[1] As the police began to push the women away, Mrs Pankhurst lightly struck Inspector Jarvis in the face three times. He told her she was striking him for a purpose, and that he would not be perturbed. (She was in fact attempting to secure immediate arrest, so that the elderly women accompanying her – one of whom was seventy-six – would not be pushed about before being arrested.) After Mrs Pankhurst gave Inspector Jarvis two stronger blows and another woman knocked off his hat, arrests were obtained.

A prolonged mêlée followed in which 3,000 police were engaged, and 108 women and 14 men were arrested.* (The largest number of women arrested in any previous demonstration had been 74, on 20 March 1907.) The scrimmage was watched by a number of MPs, some of whom climbed the railings of Palace Yard to obtain a better view. According to the *Daily Telegraph*: 'One well-known peeress was assisted up a lamp-post by her husband, whence she surveyed the surging scene.'[2]

At nine o'clock, a group of thirteen women, using small stones wrapped in brown paper, began to break windows at the Privy Council, Treasury, and Home Offices. To avoid injuring anyone within, pieces of string had been tied to the stones, which were swung against the windows while held by the string, and then dropped through the holes. The window-breakers were arrested immediately.

Window-breaking had not been authorized by the Union's leaders, and apparently was undertaken without their fore-knowledge.† A Mrs Bouvier, one of the window-breakers, subsequently testified:[3]

---

* The marital status of 106 of these women was indicated in a list compiled by *Votes for Women*, 2 July 1909. Eighty of the women arrested were listed as 'Miss', and twenty-six as 'Mrs'. The number of widows listed as 'Mrs' cannot be ascertained.

† See *Votes for Women*, 2 July 1909. Sylvia Pankhurst's later claim that this was the first 'official' window-breaking (*The Suffragette Movement*, p. 309) was incorrect – the WSPU leaders' approval was retroactive in nature: on 1 July Christabel spoke of the window-breaking as 'essentially right, appropriate, and fitting' (*Votes for Women*, 9 July 1909),

we had decided that the time for political arguments was thoroughly exhausted, and we made up our minds that the time for militant action had arrived. We decided to wait till nine o'clock, when we could be sure that the peaceful deputation headed by Mrs. Pankhurst had been arrested, then we determined to show by our action what we thought of the Prime Minister in refusing these ladies admission to the House of Commons. That was our motive for throwing the stones at the windows.

Though the breaking of windows involved destruction of property, the act was obviously circumscribed and symbolic in nature: only Government panes had been attacked, the damage had been slight, and the perpetrators had made no attempt to evade arrest. Their trial was set for 12 July.*

On 2 July, Marion Wallace Dunlop was sentenced to one month in prison for defacing the wall of St Stephen's Hall on 24 June. She asked to be treated as a political prisoner, and placed in the First Division. Her request was denied. Three days later, without the foreknowledge of the Union's leaders, she began a hunger strike.† After refusing all food for ninety-one hours, she was released from prison. On 9 July, F. W. Pethick-Lawrence wrote to her: 'Nothing has moved me so much – stirred me to the depths of my being – as your heroic action.'⁴

The stone-throwers were convicted on 12 July. Offered the choice of £5 fines or prison terms of one month for breakers of small panes and six weeks for breakers of large plate-glass windows, the stone-throwers chose imprisonment. Before going to Holloway, the women informed the officers of the WSPU that unless they were treated as political prisoners, they would

---

and on 15 July she referred to the stones thrown through Government windows as 'precious stones' and 'jewels in the Suffragettes' crown' (*Votes for Women*, 23 July 1909).

* The window-breakers were largely unmarried women, eleven of the thirteen being single (see *Votes for Women*, 23 July 1909).

† *Votes for Women*, 16 July 1909. See also Gladstone Papers, Brit. Mus. Add. MSS. 46067, E. Hobhouse to H. Gladstone, Westminster, 17 November 1909. In this letter Emily Hobhouse cited Mrs Pethick-Lawrence as saying that Marion Wallace Dunlop began her hunger strike strictly on her own initiative and without the knowledge of the WSPU leaders.

refuse to wear prison dress (prison dress was not required of First Division prisoners), refuse to be put into Second Division cells, and refuse to obey the rule of silence.[5] Later, when the women indeed refused to don prison dress, they were stripped by force. They subsequently complained of poor ventilation, broke windows in their cells, and shouted to Union members outside, who responded through a megaphone. On 14 July, visiting justices ordered the women to be held in solitary cells. That same afternoon, the prisoners began a hunger strike, and six days later they were all released.

Christabel was jubilant. She wrote to Balfour, privately:[6]

> We are feeling proud of having destroyed the Government's weapon of coercion. They will never in future be able to keep us in prison more than a few days, for we have now learnt our power to starve ourselves out of prison, and this power we shall use – unless, of course, the Government prefer to let us die. I hardly think, however, that even they will adopt so extreme a course, if only for the reason that it would not pay them politically to do so.

Christabel's Achilles' heel as a politician was that she consistently exaggerated the potential effectiveness of policies to which she gave her approval.

By August 1909, hunger-striking had become the normal practice of imprisoned suffragettes. Hunger-striking was not made mandatory by the Union's leaders, but it was welcomed and lauded. As far as the members of the WSPU were concerned, hunger-striking created a martyrdom of far greater magnitude than the martyrdom incurred by imprisonment alone. The knowledge that women were starving themselves in lonely prison cells fostered a fierceness which had not existed before, and violent incidents now became common. Many of these incidents took place just outside large halls, because the Liberals had taken to either excluding all women from meetings or else admitting only known women under close scrutiny. The conditions of admission to a meeting addressed by Asquith at Bletchley on 13 August 1909 were:[7]

> Tickets are not transferable. They are sold only upon

condition that the holder agrees not to disturb the meeting.
Should any person break this contract the audience is
requested to remain seated and silent, and thus assist those
responsible for the conduct of the meeting.

Ladies' tickets can be purchased only through recognized
Liberal officials, when the applicant is prepared to accept
the conditions. They are non-transferable, must be ordered
beforehand, and the lady's name must be written on the
face of the ticket. No ladies' tickets will be supplied until the
day before the meeting.

Such safeguards led the suffragettes to find new means of
harassing the Liberals. Only the most serious of the many
incidents of the late summer and autumn of 1909 need be
described here. Knowing that Haldane was to speak in the Sun
Hall in Liverpool on 20 August, the WSPU rented a house
adjoining the hall, and during Haldane's speech suffragettes in
the house threw bricks at the hall's windows. * On 5 September,
as Asquith was leaving Lympne Church, he was accosted by
three WSPU members, Jessie Kenney, Elsie Howey, and Vera
Wentworth. One of the three struck him repeatedly. Later that
day, the same trio approached the Prime Minister's party on a
golf course, and, timid or no, Herbert Gladstone rose to the
defence and had his cap knocked off. That evening two stones
were thrown through one of the windows of the house in which
Asquith was dining.[8]

On 17 September, Asquith spoke in the Bingley Hall in
Birmingham. The hall was surrounded by police, and no women
were admitted to the meeting. Earlier that day, Mary Leigh and
Charlotte Marsh, the WSPU's regional organizer for Yorkshire,
had equipped themselves with axes and climbed on to the roof of
a house near the hall. During the meeting they chopped slates
from the roof and threw them down at the police and at Asquith's
motor car. A policeman standing in the crowd below was badly
cut by a slate, and a detective who climbed on to the roof had
slates thrown at him and was knocked down to a lower building.

* *The Times*, 22, 23 and 25 August 1909. At least six of the seven
women involved were unmarried. Rugged exploits were usually
carried out by younger unmarried women, who were helped both by
youthful agility and, during prison terms, by not having children to
care for.

When a hose was turned on the women, they called out, holding fast: 'Will you see that Mr. Asquith receives us if we surrender?'[9] The police eventually climbed on to the roof and arrests were made. In the meantime, a suffragette in the crowd below, Mary Edwards, assaulted several policemen. Subsequently, at the police station, she broke every pane of glass in her cell.[10] Later that day, as Asquith returned to London by train, two WSPU members threw a metal object at the train and broke the window of a compartment in which passengers were seated.[11] That evening, two other WSPU members entered the Birmingham Liberal Club armed with an axe and did £5 worth of damage to the windows.

At her trial on 20 September, Mary Edwards admitted that she had assaulted policemen outside the Bingley Hall, and added:[12]

> I had the opportunity, had I chosen to take it, of seriously injuring Mr. Asquith. I am now sorry I did not do it. As he will not listen to words I think it is time that blows should be struck. . . . I was two yards from him.

On 22 September, Mary Leigh was sentenced to three months in prison with hard labour, Charlotte Marsh was given two months with hard labour, and the other defendants received shorter sentences. The seven women arrested on 17 September were all imprisoned in Winson Green Gaol, in Birmingham.

During the previous two and a half months, thirty-seven women had managed to terminate imprisonment by hunger-striking. On 13 August 1909, Herbert Gladstone had received word from Marienbad that 'His Majesty would be glad to know why the existing methods which must obviously exist for dealing with prisoners who refuse nourishment, should not be adopted.'[13] When, six weeks later, the seven women in Winson Green began hunger strikes, a new policy was instituted: under orders from the Home Secretary, the medical officers of the prison began to use force to feed women who refused food. While still in prison, Mary Leigh wrote:[14]

> I was . . . surrounded, forced back on the chair, which was tilted backwards. There were about ten of them. The doctor then forced my mouth so as to form a pouch, and held me while one of the wardresses poured some liquid from

a spoon; it was milk and brandy . . . on Saturday afternoon, the Wardresses forced me on to the bed and the two doctors came in with them, and while I was held down a nasal tube was inserted. It is two yards long with a funnel at the end – there is a glass junction in the middle to see if the liquid is passing. The end is put up the nostril, one one day, and the other nostril, the other. Great pain is experienced during the process . . . the drums of the ear seem to be bursting, a horrible pain in the throat and the breast. The tube is pushed down 20 inches. I have to lie on the bed, pinned down by Wardresses, one doctor stands up on a chair holding the funnel at arms length, so as to have the funnel end above the level, and then the other doctor, who is behind, forces the other end up the nostrils.

The one holding the funnel end pours the liquid down; about a pint of milk, sometimes egg and milk are used. . . . Before and after use, they test my heart and make a lot of examination. The after effects are a feeling of faintness, a sense of great pain in the diaphragm or breast bone, in the nose and the ears. . . .

I was very sick on the first occasion after the tube was withdrawn.

Other prisoners had similar stories of mouths prised open, lacerations, phlegm, vomiting, pain in various organs, loss of weight, and so on.[15]

The WSPU responded bitterly: forced feeding was a 'horrible outrage' and its victims had 'violated bodies'.[16] Mrs Pankhurst claimed that the Government had 'resorted to torture', and the Union began legal proceedings against the Home Secretary and the officials of Winson Green on the grounds that an assault was being committed.* The WSPU was not without allies. One

* *Votes for Women*, 1 October 1909. The case, involving Mary Leigh, was decided in early December. The defence argued that forced feeding was necessary to save the plaintiff's life, and that the minimum of force necessary was used. The Lord Chief Justice ruled that, as a matter of law, it was the duty of prison officials to preserve the health of the prisoners and, *a fortiori*, their lives, and he asked the jury to decide whether the means adopted were proper for the purpose. After two minutes, the jury returned a verdict in favour of the defendants (*The Times*, 10 December 1909).

hundred and sixteen doctors, some distinguished, signed a memorial against forced feeding, and in early October, H. W. Nevinson and H. N. Brailsford, both ardent suffragists, resigned as leader-writers for the *Daily News* in protest against that newspaper's support of forced feeding, writing: 'We cannot denounce torture in Russia and support it in England'.[17] Gladstone, they wrote, could release the prisoners after five or six days of starvation, or else transfer them to the First Division.

Shortly after her husband's resignation, Mrs Jane Brailsford resolved to go to prison. On 8 October, she, Lady Constance Lytton, and Christabel travelled together to Newcastle, where Lloyd George was to speak. That evening in Newcastle, twelve WSPU members met to concert their plans, and on the following afternoon, women broke windows at a theatre and two post offices, Lady Constance Lytton threw a stone at the radiator of a motor car in which Sir Walter Runciman was riding, and Mrs Brailsford, carrying an axe festooned with chrysanthemums, removed the garland and chopped at a barricade. Lady Constance Lytton and Mrs Brailsford were sentenced to one month in prison, and placed in the Second Division. The other women were placed in the Third Division, reserved for the most common criminals. All of the imprisoned women began hunger strikes, but Lady Constance Lytton and Mrs Brailsford alone were not forcibly fed, and were released on 13 October on medical grounds. The WSPU alleged that as the daughter of a peer and the wife of an important Liberal journalist they had received preferential treatment.*

A few weeks later, prison treatment of a different kind was accorded to a less prominent suffragette. Emily Wilding Davison, a tall, slender, red-haired girl, with a London BA, attempted to forestall further forced feeding – she had already fasted for five days and been forcibly fed for three – by barricading herself into her cell in Strangeways Prison. Visiting magistrates voted that she be dislodged by water shot into the cell from the nozzle of a hose. She stood her ground, and the authorities eventually had to break into the cell. Herbert Gladstone subsequently ordered her release, and admitted that a 'grave error of judgment' had been made.[18]

* *Votes for Women*, 22 October 1909. Lady Constance Lytton suffered from a serious heart condition, which led to heart attacks and an incapacitating stroke in 1912.

The most serious incident of the late autumn of 1909 took place on 13 November in the Great Western Station in Bristol, when Winston Churchill, who had just alighted from a railway carriage, was attacked by a suffragette wielding a riding-switch. Theresa Garnett, a member of the WSPU, broke through the cordon of private detectives surrounding Churchill, gripped his coat, and hit him in the face with her hand. For a moment, Churchill grappled with her as she shouted, 'Take that, you brute! You brute! I will show you what English women can do.'[19] Charged with assaulting Churchill with a whip, she said, 'Has it hurt him much?' * Churchill, not hurt, refused to prefer the charge, probably because he did not wish to have to appear in court. Theresa Garnett was sent to prison for a month for disturbing the peace.

The proliferation of violent incidents weighed heavily on Herbert Gladstone, who as Home Secretary was in the extremely uncomfortable position of being an apologist for women's suffrage yet responsible both for the introduction of forced feeding and for the safety of the Prime Minister and the Cabinet. On 27 September Gladstone had been sent copies of a police report which stated that, off and on for the past six weeks, two members of the Women's Freedom League had been practising with revolvers at a miniature shooting range at 92 Tottenham Court Road.[20] E. T. Troup, the Commissioner of the Metropolitan Police, wrote to Gladstone:[21]

> The annexed report seems to me to show that there is now definite ground for fearing the possibility of the P.M.'s being fired at by one of the pickets [of the WFL] at the entrance to the House. . . . It seems to me that we have in fact prima facie grounds for believing, though of course not evidence, that there is something nearly amounting to a conspiracy to murder.

Two weeks later, Gladstone wrote to his fellow Cabinet member, and fellow suffragist, Sir Edward Grey:[22]

---

* *Votes for Women*, 19 November 1909. Christabel justified the assault, writing, 'Moved by the spirit of pure chivalry, Miss Garnett took what she thought to be the best available means of avenging the insult done to womanhood by the Government to which Mr. Churchill belongs' (*ibid.*).

As things are I am in a state of constant anxiety touching
the safety of the P.M. We know that women have been
practising shooting. Some of them are half crazy, or wholly
hysterical. The most stringent precautions have to be taken.
The Lympne affair & resulting investigation [unreadable]
that but for an accident, violent & dangerous action wd.
have been taken. Thereupon I gave directions to Scot^d Yard
that a division of what we call the Special Branch in the
C.I.D. shd be immediately formed & that the whole affair
shd be treated as a dangerous conspiracy . . . this stage may
be passed safely. It will be different at a Gen. El.

There will first be the question of personal safety: &
secondly the position of the Gov^t relatively [sic] to the
Franchise. I am concerned about both.

1. In the rough & tumble of a British election, it will be
most difficult to take effective precautions. . . . The proba-
bility is that if things go on as they are, something very bad
will happen. Attempts at violence will be made & there may
be reprisals. I speak in no language of exaggeration. In
these matters I am responsible now & I have much anxiety.
I have put them before Asquith & he fully realises the
situation. I thought I ought to put it up to the Cabinet but
he did not wish it. . . .

. . . don't let us acquiesce in the idea that we can muddle
through. The position of the P.M. and of 2 or 3 of our
colleagues is wholly adverse to the suffrage. Months ago I
went to the P.M. I pressed him to receive a deputation of
all the women's organizations. The abominable way in wh.
he had been treated made him refuse – absolutely. The
recent refusal to receive the Fawcett non-militant deputation
seems for the present at any rate to preclude the possibility
of arriving at an understanding with or through them. Are
we then to go back on the main justice because of militant
violence. . . ?

Gladstone's discomfort did not make him any the less an
apologist for forced feeding. He wrote to Emily Hobhouse on
9 November:[23]

My duty is as clear as that of a policeman in the street. . . .
If the spirit of any movement is exemplified by actions of

incredible folly wh. exasperate reasonable & friendly
opinion, it can only be the worse for the movement. On
different occasions in recent years I have spoken as strongly
as I could for enfranchisement. But for three years I have
been pursued by the militant section with venom & false-
hood simply because I have been discharging a public duty.
These persons choose to organize disturbances & to commit
assaults. . . . They refuse to find sureties for good behaviour,
& to pay fines. They elect to go to prison. They elect to
refuse food. They elect to resist forcible feeding. They
demand to be released after 2 or 3 days in order to create
fresh disturbances. They wish to have it all ways – to put
the authorities to great trouble and expense – to break the
law – & time after time practically to collapse its penalties.
. . . My duty is unpleasant & distasteful enough, but that is
no reason why I sh^d shirk it.

. . . forcible feeding is not punishment. To let women
starve w^d not only be inhuman but in the event of death w^d
expose all concerned to a charge of manslaughter. As
regards allowing them to starve for 100 hours, I know by
experience that is both cruel & dangerous & I cannot be a
party to it.

While continuing to equate forced feeding with assault, the
WSPU was by no means unaware that the very severity of
forced feeding was helping to attract support. On 2 December,
Josephine Gonne wrote to Kitty Marion, who had been forcibly
fed in Newcastle:[24]

If you have nothing better to do on Wed. 8th Dec. at 3 o'c.
will you come here to a small Suff. drawing room meeting?
& help with yr. experiences to put our case before some
people. . . . These drawing room meetings are sometimes
very useful – & you are a splendid card to play – !!. . . .

The Countess Russell – who is forwarding this letter – is
anxious to meet you – & hear your experiences of forcible
feeding while you were in Newcastle Gaol.

In the meanwhile, the controversy over the House of Lords' veto
of Lloyd George's budget was bringing Parliament to a prema-
ture close. In response to pressure from the Women's Liberal
Federation, Asquith stated, on 10 December 1909:[25]

Nearly two years ago I declared on behalf of the present
Government that in the event, which we then contemplated,
of our bringing in a Reform Bill we should make the insertion of a suffragist amendment an open question for the
House of Commons to decide. Through no intention and
through no fault of ours the opportunity for raising the
matter has been taken away . . . my declaration survives the
expiring Parliament, and will hold good in its successor. . . .
The Government . . . has no disposition or desire to burke
this question. It is clearly one on which a new House of
Commons ought to be given the opportunity to express its
views.

On 15 December, Parliament was dissolved.

The WSPU denounced Asquith's pledge as worthless. During
the ensuing election campaign, however, Herbert Gladstone's
worst fears were not realized, for though some WSPU members
carried out militant acts, the Union in general emphasized the
use of public meetings to attempt to draw votes away from the
Liberals. The two most notable exceptions to this policy involved
controversies which resulted from the treatment accorded to
imprisoned suffragettes. On 20 December, in Liverpool, two
working-class women, Selina Martin and Leslie Hall, threw a
ginger beer bottle into Asquith's empty car, just after the Prime
Minister had stepped out. No damage was done, but the two
women were arrested, denied bail, and imprisoned before trial.
Selina Martin broke the windows in her cell and refused all food.
According to *Votes for Women*, she was subsequently 'pummelled
by the wardresses, handcuffed, frog-marched so that her head
banged from step to step, and finally, after having been fed by
force . . . thrown down the steps handcuffed.'[26] Selina Martin and
Leslie Hall were not brought to trial until 27 December, and
remained in prison until 3 February.

Horrified by the treatment meted out to the two working-
class women, Lady Constance Lytton disguised herself as a
seamstress, and on 14 January joined a protest meeting outside
Walton Gaol in Liverpool. As 'Jane Warton', she was arrested for
leading the crowd to the Governor's house and throwing a stone
wrapped in brown paper. Sentenced to fourteen days in the
Third Division with hard labour, she refused to wear prison

dress, work, or eat. On the fourth day of her hunger strike, forcible feeding was begun. A cursory medical examination on the following day failed to reveal heart disease, the existence of which she had not vouchsafed to the prison authorities. She was forcibly fed eight times. On 23 January, she was released in a state of exhaustion. The treatment accorded to 'Jane Warton', a working-class woman, in January 1910, and that accorded to Lady Constance Lytton, a peeress with a heart murmur, in October 1909, were obviously dissimilar. Much controversy was engendered.[27]

At its dissolution in December 1909, Parliament had been composed of 373 Liberals, 168 Conservatives, 83 Irish Nationalists, and 46 Labour MPs.[28] After the election of January 1910, the Liberals held 275 seats, the Conservatives 273, the Irish Nationalists 82, and Labour 40.[29] The WSPU proclaimed itself responsible for Liberal losses in many constituencies:[30]

> These results reveal the power of the Women's Social and Political Union in striking a blow at the Government. All over the country the influence of the women's agitation has been felt; no one who has studied carefully the facts on the spot can doubt that the defeat of Liberal candidates has been largely due to the attitude which the Liberal Government has taken up towards women.

Even the Union's best friends were dubious: H. W. Nevinson wrote in his diary: 'Jan. 18 . . . *Nation* lunch, all rather jubilant over elections. Refused to believe in WSPU influence.'[31]

As the Liberals had lost their overall majority in the Commons, the success of any legislation was now dependent on the support of more than one party. Perceiving this new fact of political life, H. N. Brailsford began to talk of founding a new committee that would compose and promote an agreed suffrage Bill. He wrote to Mrs Fawcett, on 18 January 1910:[32]

> I have some thought of attempting to found a Conciliation Committee for Woman's Suffrage. My idea is that it should undertake the necessary diplomatic work of promoting an early settlement. It should not be large, and should consist of both men & women – the women in touch with the

existing societies but not their more prominent leaders, the men also as far as possible not identified officially with either party.

On 25 January, Brailsford wrote to Mrs Fawcett, with regard to his 'scheme', that 'The W.S.P.U. was doubtful about it, though it ultimately gave its consent.'[33] It is not clear whether the WSPU's leaders initially agreed to support a committee of the sort outlined by Brailsford in his letter of 18 January, or a committee more nearly resembling the all-male committee, with fifty-four suffragist MPs of all parties as members, that eventually came into being. Be that as it may, on 31 January 1910, in the Queen's Hall, Mrs Pankhurst announced that until further orders, militant tactics would cease – only peaceful and consti-tutional methods would be used. The anti-Government policy would continue at by-elections, but in non-militant form. Many years later, Christabel wrote in her autobiography:[34]

My own strongest, but unspoken, reason for welcoming the Conciliation movement was that it might avert the need for stronger militancy and would at least postpone the use thereof. Mild militancy was more or less played out. The Government had, as far as they could, closed every door to it, especially by excluding Suffragette questioners from their meetings. Cabinet Ministers had shown their contempt for the mildness of our protests and had publically taunted us on that score. And neutral onlookers had warned us that these milder acts would, by their 'monotony', grow futile, because they would cease to impress anybody, and therefore would cease to embarrass the Government. . . . Strategically, then, a pause in militancy would be valuable, for it would give time for familiarity to fade, so that the same methods could be used again with freshness and effect. Much depen-ded in militancy, as it depends in other things, upon timing and placing, upon the dramatic arrangement and sequence of acts and events. . . .

Another reason why mild militancy could not avail much longer was that our women were beginning to revolt against the one-sided violence which they experienced in the course of their attempts to petition the King's Prime Minister. It was being said among them that they would prefer to break a window than be themselves thrown about and hurt. They were arguing that the W.S.P.U. respect for human safety ought to apply to themselves as well as to everyone else. They were questioning whether, for the sake of others dear to them, or even for their own sake, they had any right to risk personal injury, if a little damage to panes of glass would have the same, and indeed more, effect.

11 The Truce

Save during one week in November 1910, militancy remained suspended until 21 November 1911. It is probably best to begin an account of the period during which militancy was suspended with the Union's annual report for 1 March 1909 to 28 February 1910, since the report largely dealt with fiscal trends prevailing before the truce was declared. In 1909–10, the WSPU's income had continued to grow rapidly, the total income being £33,027 compared with £21,214 the previous year.* Expenditure had included £4,939 for the salaries of staff and organizers and £3,473 for the hiring of halls. Twenty-three more salaried employees had been taken on at Clement's Inn, the total paid staff there now numbering 98. The Union's national organization had expanded too – by the end of the fiscal year 26 salaried organizers were in charge of 23 separate districts.† Three of these districts were in Scotland, but none was in Ireland or Wales. Finally, by the end of February 1910, the circulation of *Votes for Women*, 16,000 copies a year earlier, was 'between 30,000 and 40,000'.[1]

When the new Government took office in February 1910, Winston Churchill became Home Secretary. (Herbert Gladstone was made Governor of South Africa.) On 15 March, Churchill laid on the table rule 243a, an addition to the rules for prisons framed with the suffragettes specifically in mind. The new regulation was as follows:[2]

In the case of any offender of the second or third division

* The gross income of £33,027 included £1,340 brought forward from the previous fiscal year, whereas £981 had been brought forward the previous year.
† In three districts, two women were in charge. Virtually all of the twenty-six organizers were unmarried women, twenty-four organizers being listed as 'Miss' in the annual report (see pp. 5–6 of *Fourth Annual Report*).

whose previous character is good, and who has been convicted of, or committed to prison for, an offence not involving dishonesty, cruelty, indecency, or serious violence, the Prison Commissioners may allow such ameliorations of the conditions prescribed in the foregoing rules as the Secretary of State may approve in respect of the wearing of prison clothing, bathing, hair-cutting, cleaning of cells, employment, exercise, books, and otherwise. Provided that no such amelioration shall be greater than that granted under the rules for offenders of the first division.

Under rule 243a, prison conditions for suffragettes would be less onerous, should militancy be resumed, and the WSPU welcomed Churchill's reform as 'a step in the right direction'.[3]

In the meanwhile, during the early spring Lord Lytton and H. N. Brailsford quietly gathered support for the proposed Conciliation Committee. The committee came into being with Lytton as Chairman, Brailsford as Secretary, and a membership composed of 25 Liberal MPs, 17 Conservative MPs, 6 Irish Nationalist MPs, and 6 Labour MPs. The committee decided to sponsor a private member's Bill, so framed that it could receive support from MPs of all parties. The Bill was as follows:[4]

A Bill to Extend the Parliamentary Franchise to Women Occupiers

1. Every woman possessed of a household qualification, or of a ten-pound occupation qualification, within the meaning of the Representation of the People Act 1884, shall be entitled to be registered as a voter, and, when registered, to vote for the county or borough in which the qualifying premises are situate.

2. For the purposes of this Act, a woman shall not be disqualified by marriage for being registered as a voter, provided that a husband and wife shall not both be qualified in respect of the same property.

The Bill had been deliberately made narrow in order to obtain Tory support. Only about a million women – one woman in thirteen – would be enfranchised under its terms. Relatively few married women would be enfranchised, since husband and wife could not qualify with respect to the same property (though, under existing law, two men could qualify as joint occupiers), and relatively few working-class women would be enfranchised, due to the property restrictions. At least two suffragist Cabinet Ministers, Churchill and Lloyd George, believed that the majority of the women enfranchised by the Bill would be propertied elderly spinsters and widows, who would on balance vote Tory.*

In private, Mrs Pankhurst held that the Bill was too narrow. On 14 April, Nevinson wrote in his diary:[5]

> To me she [Mrs Pankhurst] lamented policy of Conciliation Com[ee] that proposes municipal Franchise. thus excluding lodgers & some forms of property. Said she had spoken of objection to HNB. [Brailsford] but he had for the moment overborne her.

In public, however, the WSPU joined other suffrage societies in supporting the measure. The Bill's very narrowness would, its projectors claimed, placate the Tories. Indeed, with regard to the Bill's prospects, Lord Lytton was optimistic to the point of effusiveness, writing:[6]

> The publication of the proposals of the Conciliation Committee has aroused in every direction a degree of unanimity and a spirit of hopefulness even exceeding the most sanguine expectations of the members of the committee. Every section of suffragist opinion has agreed to support the proposed Bill as a satisfactory instalment of justice to the disenfranchised women of this country, and all the conditions of a non-party settlement have been fulfilled. Politicians who, six months ago, despaired of any solution during the present Session of Parliament now admit that the omens are favourable and that victory is in sight.

Christabel too was highly hopeful. She wrote, on 3 June, that the prospects of the Bill seemed 'very bright',[7] and nine days later she wrote to Balfour, with an optimism so marked as to be almost out of character:[8]

> I am so happy in the thought that we have your support for the plan of carrying a suffrage bill this year. It means that our troublous times are over. Of course we should be ready

* See p. 137.

to go through hard fighting again, but it is much better that it should all be peacefully settled here and now.

When you so kindly saw me a few weeks ago you made me realise how easy, from the practical, House of Commons point of view it would be to carry the bill this year. Since then everything has moved forward so smoothly and well. With your help, we shall in a few days have the assurance of enfranchisement.

Christabel had not, it seems, taken full measure of her chief adversary. Asquith was determined not to allow the Conciliation Bill to pass beyond its Second Reading. At a Cabinet meeting on 23 June it was agreed that the Bill would be allowed a Second Reading Debate and Division, but that no further facilities would be granted during the Session.[9] When Asquith announced the decision in Parliament, Christabel immediately wrote to Balfour:[10]

I should greatly like to see you if I may. Mr. Asquith's statement with regard to the suffrage bill has greatly dissatisfied us, but before taking any action I want your advice if you will be so very kind as to give it to me.

Balfour replied:[11]

You want my 'advice': but I am afraid you are very unlikely to take it!

The situation, as I understand it, is that, partly for Parliamentary, but still more for other reasons, the Government do not propose to give time this Session for the *agreed* Bill. They hope, I understand, to find time next year for a Bill. What Bill I do not know. . . .

If rumour is to be believed, the Government is not only divided on the question of Suffrage, but those who are in favour of Suffrage are divided as to the *kind* of measure which they will consent to support. . . .

I have frankly to admit that, in these untoward circumstances, I have no advice to offer but patience. . . .

I need hardly say that this letter is 'private'.

The Second Reading of the Conciliation Bill took place on 11 and 12 July. On 11 July, Lloyd George asked the Speaker, as a point of order, whether, if the Bill passed its Second Reading, it could be amended in the Committee or the Report stages either so as to omit the provision in the second clause, or so as to extend the franchise to women whose husbands possessed the household qualification, regardless of the value of the house. The Speaker declined to give a definitive ruling immediately, but said that the Bill was so framed as to apply only to 'women occupiers', and that amendments probably would not be possible.[12] On the following day, Lloyd George voted against the Bill, as did Churchill, who had described it as 'anti-democratic' and said it would give an 'entirely unfair representation to property', and 'electoral advantage' to the Unionists.[13] The Bill passed its Second Reading by a vote of 299 to 189, but the vote was essentially an affirmation of support for the principle of women's suffrage, rather than for the particular measure, inasmuch as a few minutes later the Commons voted, by 320 to 175, to refer the Bill to a Committee of the whole House, thereby virtually extinguishing its chances.[14] Nevinson wrote in his diary: 'So another hope is killed.'[15] On 20 July, the Speaker ruled firmly that widening amendments would not be permitted, and on 23 July Asquith wrote to Lord Lytton that the Bill would not be granted further time during the session.[16]

During June and July 1910, the WSPU had sponsored several large peaceful demonstrations. A great franchise procession had been scheduled for 28 May, but following the death of Edward VII on 6 May the procession had been postponed until 18 June. The march held that day was organized by the WSPU, but other suffrage societies joined in. The march was composed of about 10,000 women, and included forty bands. That evening the WSPU raised £5,000 in the Albert Hall. On 23 July, another demonstration was held in Hyde Park, again in co-operation with other suffrage societies. At this demonstration there were forty platforms and 150 speakers, and groups of from 100 to 500 persons gathered around each platform.

At the end of July, Parliament was prorogued until November. The WSPU decided to wait until the beginning of the autumn sitting to see if the Government announced the granting of facilities for the Conciliation Bill. If facilities were again refused, Mrs Pankhurst would lead a deputation to Parliament. The deputation would demand that the Bill be made law, and 'refuse to leave until the demand is conceded'.[17] By 27 October, 150 women had been enrolled for the deputation.

During August, September, and October, the WSPU held large meetings in major provincial cities, and on 10 November the Union once again filled the Albert Hall. The Pankhursts had continued to talk of renewing militancy, and on 9 November H. W. Nevinson wrote in his diary:[18]

> Talked long with HNB. [Brailsford] Who has had trouble with the Pankhursts: accuses them of having no means but threats and flattery: says they are wrecking all his diplomacy.

On 12 November, Sir Edward Grey, one of the suffragists in the Cabinet, stated that it would not be possible for the House of Commons to give adequate time this year for the complete passage of a women's suffrage Bill. The WSPU regarded Grey's statement as a definitive refusal of facilities, and announced that a militant demonstration would take place on the day of the opening of Parliament.

When Parliament reconvened on 18 November 1910, Asquith informed the Commons that as the conference with the Lords had broken down he had advised the Crown to dissolve Parliament. Government business would take precedence until the dissolution, which would occur on 28 November. Asquith did not allude to the Conciliation Bill.* While Asquith was speaking, the WSPU was meeting in the Caxton Hall. After it was learned that Asquith had not mentioned the Conciliation Bill, a deputation of over 300 women, divided into detachments of twelve, set out for the House of Commons. As on so many previous occasions, the women tried to rush past the police. On this occasion, however, the police behaved with a brutality the women had not experienced before. Reluctant to make arrests, the police used instead a variety of means to force the women back: women were kicked, their arms were twisted, their noses were punched, their breasts

---

* Later in the day, with a riot going on outside Parliament, Asquith said that the women's suffrage Bill would not receive consideration prior to the dissolution (*H.C. Deb.* 5s. vol. 20, 18 November 1910, cc. 82–135).

were gripped, and knees were thrust between their legs. After six hours of struggle, 115 women and four men had been arrested. On the following day, the charges against most of those arrested were withdrawn after the prosecutor announced that the Home Secretary had decided that 'no public advantage would be gained by proceeding with the prosecution.'[19]

H. N. Brailsford and Dr Jessie Murray soon began systematically to collect depositions from women who said they had been mishandled on 18 November, or Black Friday, as the day was soon referred to by the women of the WSPU. Regarding Black Friday (and smaller demonstrations on 22 and 23 November), fifty women testified that they had been injured to the extent that the effects were 'felt for many days, and in some cases for several weeks'.[20] Many of the fifty women apparently regarded their treatment by the police as particularly grievous not so much because of the relatively minor injuries received as because of the sexual nature of many of the assaults. In a summary of the testimony, Brailsford and Murray stated:[21]

The action of which the most frequent complaint is made is variously described as twisting round, pinching, screwing, nipping, or wringing the breast. This was often done in the most public way so as to inflict the utmost humiliation. Not only was it an offence against decency; it caused in many cases intense pain. . . . The language used by some of the police while performing this action proves that it was consciously sensual.

Some of the supporting testimony was as follows:

A 'young woman' testified:[22]

Several times constables and plain-clothes men who were in the crowd passed their arms round me from the back and clutched hold of my breasts in as public a manner as possible, and men in the crowd followed their example. I was also pummelled on the chest, and my breast was clutched by one constable from the front. As a consequence, three days later I had to receive medical attention from Dr. Ede as my breasts were much discoloured and very painful.

A 'Miss H.' testified:[23]

One policeman . . . put his arm round me and seized my
left breast, nipping it and wringing it very painfully,
saying as he did so, 'You have been wanting this for a long
time, haven't you.'

A Miss Elizabeth Freeman testified:[24]

I saw one policeman deliberately break the bamboo pole of
a bannerette across a woman's shoulder.
. . . Some of the language used by the policemen was beyond
description. One gripped me by the thigh, and I demanded
that he should cease doing such a hateful action to a woman.
He said, 'Oh, my old dear, I can grip you wherever I like
to-day.'

A 'Mrs. S.' stated:[25]

the policeman who tried to move me on did so by pushing
his knees in between me from behind, with the deliberate
intention of attacking my sex.

Finally, a Mary Frances Earl, who had tried to reach the Commons by an underground passage, testified that her nose had been
bloodied, her thumbs had been twisted, she had been kicked, and
that the police[26]

deliberately tore my under-garments, using the most foul
language. . . . They seized me by the hair and forced me up
the steps on my knees. . . . I was then flung into the crowd
outside.

Many more examples could be given. Almost all of the 135
statements collected by Brailsford and Murray described acts of
violence, and twenty-nine of the statements complained of
violence involving indecency.[27]

In the wake of Black Friday, the WSPU's leaders repeatedly
alleged that Churchill had given the police specific orders which
resulted in women being knocked about for hours rather than
arrested with dispatch.* Churchill had not, in fact, done so.

* For examples, see *Votes for Women*, 25 November 1910, and *The
Times*, 2 March 1911. Churchill eventually became so nettled by the
WSPU leaders' repeated accusation that he had given orders which
brought about the brutality of Black Friday that he gave serious

10, 11, 12 Violent treatment of WSPU hecklers, Llanystymdwy, Wales,
21 September 1912

13 The interior of Holloway Prison, London. Emily Wilding Davison first tried to kill herself by throwing herself over these railings

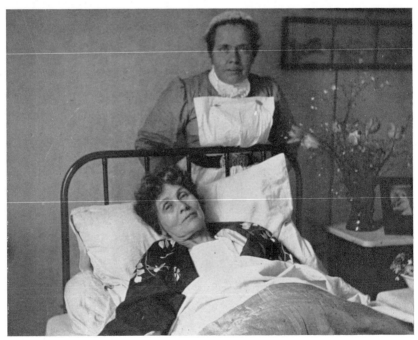

14 Mrs Pankhurst after a hunger strike, attended by Nurse Pine

Four days after Black Friday, he wrote to the Commissioner of the
Metropolitan Police:[28]

> I am hearing from every quarter that my strongly expressed
> wishes conveyed to you on Wed evening & repeated on Fri
> morning that the suffragettes were not to be allowed to
> exhaust themselves but were to be arrested forthwith upon
> any defiance of the law, were not observed by the police on
> Friday last, with the result that vy regrettable scenes
> occurred. It was my desire to avoid this even at some risk;
> to arrest large numbers & then subsequently to prosecute
> only where serious grounds were shown & I am sorry that,
> no doubt through a misunderstanding, another course has
> been adopted.

In the Commons, Churchill later stated that the police had acted
under orders already in effect under Gladstone to avoid arresting
women for 'merely technical obstruction'.[29]

The orders already in force could not in themselves have been
completely responsible for the brutality of Black Friday, for in
WSPU marches to Parliament while Gladstone was Home
Secretary, police efforts to minimize the number of arrests had
also prolonged conflicts, as the same women rushed again and
again, yet the brutality of a Black Friday had not resulted. The
immediate catalyst for the events of 18 November was probably
an administrative decision made by police officials who had no
idea of the possible consequences. At previous WSPU demonstrations, the police called out to guard the Commons had been
constables of the A Division. Over the years, these men had
become accustomed to dealing with militant feminists, and had
acquired some understanding of the women's cause and of the
nature of their marches. Sylvia Pankhurst wrote that, as a
result, the men of the A Division had 'come to treat the women
as far as possible with courtesy and consideration, while still
obeying their orders.'* On Black Friday, however, the police

---

consideration to prosecuting Christabel for libel (see Sir E. Troup to Sir
C. Mathews, Home Office, 4 March 1911, as quoted in R. S. Churchill,
Winston S. Churchill, vol. 2, Companion, Part 3, 1911–1914, pp.
1468–9).
* *Votes for Women*, 25 November 1910. In view of previous instances of
roughness, Sylvia Pankhurst's statement was probably over-generous.

F

guarding Parliament Square had been specially brought in from
Whitechapel and other East End districts.[30] These men had no
previous experience of suffragette demonstrations. They were,
moreover, used to dealing with poor and ill-educated people who
were seldom able to make police brutality a *cause célèbre*. As has
been shown in tables 6.1 and 6.2, the great majority of the
women who took part in militant demonstrations were in their
twenties and thirties.* By attempting to rush through or past
police lines, these women were bringing themselves repeatedly
into abrupt physical contact with the police. That the police
found in the youthful femininity of many of their assailants an invitation to licence, does not seem, all in all, completely surprising.

In the long run, the brutality that occurred on Black Friday
had a significant impact on the form of WSPU militancy. The
origins of that impact emerge from some of the testimony
collected by Murray and Brailsford: a 'Miss B. W.' testified:[31]

> On November 18th I was treated both violently and
> indecently by police officers in uniform. . . . Keen as is my
> desire to help on our cause, my self-respect prevents me from
> voluntarily subjecting myself again to similar treatment. In
> future my protest must be made by stone-throwing or some
> other actionable offence.

And a 'Mrs. J. B.' testified:[32]

> On Wednesday, I saw one nurse with two large bruises on
> her breast where a policeman had pinched her. . . .
> Various girls have been told by their mothers that they
> might break windows but must not go on any more raids.

Black Friday provided the members of the WSPU with a strong
argument against risking injury and public degradation by
going on marches in which physical abuse might take the
place of immediate arrest. To many women, window-breaking –
which resulted in immediate arrest – was beginning to seem a
far safer form of militancy.†

Four days after Black Friday, on 22 November 1910, Asquith

* See pp. 81, 83, and fn. *, p. 119.
† See Mrs Pankhurst's speech at the Old Bailey, 21 May 1912, as
reported in *Votes for Women*, 24 May 1912; see also p. 154.

stated that 'The Government will, if they are still in power, give facilities in the next Parliament for effectively proceeding with a Bill which is so framed as to admit of free amendment.'[33] The WSPU regarded Asquith's emphasis on free amendment as opening the way to a Bill so broad that it would have little chance of passing the Commons, let alone the Lords. To make matters worse, Asquith had pledged facilities in the next Parliament but not necessarily in the next session. In response to Asquith's statement, 200 women marched to Downing Street, where a struggle took place between suffragettes and the police. Windows were broken on Asquith's car and at the Colonial and Home Offices, and by the end of the day 159 women had been arrested.

During the course of 'the Battle of Downing Street', Augustine Birrell, the Chief Secretary for Ireland, was pushed about by a crowd of angry women, and twisted his knee in an effort to escape. He was subsequently confined to bed with a slipped cartilage. C. P. Scott later recorded in his diary that Birrell was 'deeply exasperated against the women who had attacked and injured him – perhaps permanently – and evidently quite prepared to see the suffrage question shelved in this Parliament and indefinitely postponed.'[34] Birrell told Scott that *

a body of about 20 suffragettes on their way to take the Prime Minister's house from the rear . . . swarmed round me. I was not kicked, but they pulled me about and hustled me, 'stroked' my face, knocked off my hat and kicked it about and one whose unpleasant features yet dwell in my memory harangued me with 'Oh! you wicked man; you must be a wicked man not to help us' and so forth. I didn't like to use my fists and I couldn't swing my umbrella. . . . I struggled to get free and in so doing I twisted my knee (pointing to his left knee) and slipped the knee-cap (I had done the same thing before to my right knee). . . .

* C. P. Scott, *Political Diaries*, 2 February 1911, p. 36. Birrell eventually recovered from his injury, and declined to prosecute his alleged assailants, writing to Churchill, 'Let the matter drop but keep your eye on the hags in question' (A. Birrell to W. S. Churchill, Irish Office, Old Queen Street, 21 February 1911, in R. S. Churchill, *Winston S. Churchill*, vol. 2, Companion, Part 3, 1911–14, p. 1468).

There was no attempt to do me any serious physical injury and if I had lain down on the ground I don't suppose they would have jumped upon me but it was a brutal, outrageous and unprovoked assault and it may lame me for life.

On the day after Birrell was injured, a march to Parliament Square resulted in eighteen arrests. Charges were subsequently dropped against those women who had been arrested on 22 and 23 November but not charged with damaging property or with assault, and the result was that of the 177 women arrested on those two days, only seventy-five were convicted. Their sentences varied from two weeks to two months. Under rule 243a, prison conditions had improved, and only two women hunger-struck. The fines of these two women were paid almost immediately by friends outside.

The events of 18 to 23 November 1910 had created a sensation, but the political effects of renewed militancy were probably not great, given Asquith's fundamental intractability. Nevinson did write in his diary on 29 November that Brailsford was[35]

much distressed at the W.S.P.U. distrust of him & their action agst his advice. They have even refused his letter to *Votes* on behalf of the Conciliation Com[ee] & their sudden first raid entirely wrecked his diplomacy with Asquith.

And on 2 January 1911, Nevinson wrote that Brailsford was 'still bitter about the Friday raid as preventing Lytton's meeting with Asquith & the gathering of the Liberal Members.'[36] It does not seem likely, however, that Lytton and Brailsford were about to accomplish much with Asquith anyway.

After 24 November, the struggle between the Commons and Lords and the forthcoming General Election pre-empted the centre of the political stage. During the General Election of December 1910, the WSPU once again laid aside militancy, and used legal means to campaign against Liberal candidates in fifty constituencies. The WSPU's efforts did not, apparently, have a significant effect on the overall results, for the new House of Commons was virtually the same as the old, the division of seats being:[37]

Liberals	272
Conservatives	272
Irish Nationalists	84
Labour	42

Votes for Women claimed, however, that the WSPU was 'probably responsible for some 30 or 40 defeats, and thus for reducing the Government majority by 60 or 80.'[38]

12 The Truce Renewed

During January and early February 1911, there was a lull in the WSPU's activities pending clarification of the status of women's suffrage legislation in the new Parliament. No reference was made to such legislation in the King's Speech on 6 February, but shortly afterwards suffragist MPs managed to secure the first three places in the private members' ballot, and Sir George Kemp, who obtained first place, announced that he would sponsor a Conciliation Bill. 5 May was secured as the date for the Bill's Second Reading.

The title of the Conciliation Bill was now revised, from 'A Bill to Extend the Parliamentary Franchise to Women Occupiers', to 'A Bill to Confer the Parliamentary Franchise on Women' thus making free amendment possible. In addition, the £10 occupation qualification was omitted, leaving only the household qualification.[1]

Christabel wrote:[2]

> Our extraordinary success in the ballot for Parliamentary Bills has generated the feeling of optimism and confidence needed to sweep away all obstacles and to carry the Bill into law . . . it will be perfectly easy in the present Session to spare the time necessary for the full discussion of the Bill.

As usual, the WSPU's fiscal year ended on the last day of February. The *Fifth Annual Report*, which covered the period 1 March 1910 to 28 February 1911, showed that during the first recorded fiscal year in which militancy had been held in abeyance, the Union's income had, for the first time, dropped. The decrease in income was obscured by the WSPU's method of accounting: the Union reported £34,506 in receipts for 1910–11, as opposed to £33,027 the previous year. The receipts for 1910–11 included, however, £5,119 brought forward from the previous fiscal year, whereas only £1,340 had been brought forward the year before. If money brought forward from previous years is excluded in both cases, the Union's income was £29,387 in 1910–11, as compared with £31,687 in 1909–10.

In other respects, the WSPU had expanded. By the end of February 1911, the Union had a salaried staff of 110 London employees (excluding organizers), compared with 98 employees a year earlier. The Union had also enlarged its premises, taking fourteen additional rooms at 156 Charing Cross Road, where the Women's Press was now housed, and two additional rooms at Clement's Inn where the WSPU now occupied twenty-three rooms. The national WSPU now also held premises in nineteen provincial cities, and, in addition, fifteen of the twenty-nine local Unions in greater London by now had premises of their own.[3]

During the early spring of 1911, widespread support for the revised Conciliation Bill was evident well outside suffrage circles: eighty-six city and town councils – with female as well as male constituents – passed resolutions supporting the Bill. Among those doing so were the councils of the five largest provincial cities in England and the three largest cities in Scotland.[4]

On 5 May, the revised Conciliation Bill passed its Second Reading with little difficulty, by a vote of 255 to 88. In contrast with the previous year, the Bill's sponsors moved that the measure be referred to a Committee of the Whole House, thus challenging Asquith to keep his word with regard to the provision of facilities. The WSPU did not regard the Bill's being referred to a Committee of the Whole House as a defeat: on 19 May, *Votes for Women* declared:[5]

> The great victory which we announced last week . . . is
> being turned to good account in the House of Commons,
> and there are grounds for confidence that the year 1911 will
> see the enfranchisement of women an accomplished fact.

When Asquith had pledged, on 22 November 1910, that the Conciliation Bill would be given facilities in the next Parliament, he had avoided pledging facilities in the next session. On 29 May 1911, Lloyd George announced that the Government had decided it could not, without jeopardizing Government measures, allot further time for the Conciliation Bill during the present session. Next session, after the Bill had again been read a second time, the Government would provide a week for its further stages.[6] Nevinson wrote, the following day:[7]

> Ld. George's statement seen to be a mere trap & snare in vain hope of securing peace for this year. . . . Christabel . . . also condemns statement, but was awaiting developments.

The WSPU did not immediately re-institute militancy, because Christabel had been informed, privately, that Sir Edward Grey was to make a statement of clarification.* Those WSPU members who had volunteered for the next militant demonstration were, however, contacted: Christabel wrote to them, on 1 June:[8]

> During the long days of waiting for the Government's answer in regard to giving facilities for the Conciliation Bill, it has been a great strength to us to know that you and the army of others who have volunteered to join the deputation are in readiness to act when the moment for action comes.
>
> As expounded by Mr Lloyd George on Monday, the Government's attitude is very unsatisfactory, and his statement is a warning to members of the Union to be ready to make a vigorous protest at short notice. . . .
>
> In the meantime, we urge you to help by enrolling more members for the deputation. Everything depends upon numbers, and if the deputation is sufficiently large, the authorities will be placed in an insurmountable difficulty.

On the evening of 1 June, Grey made his statement: the week allotted for the Conciliation Bill would be 'elastic', and the opportunity offered for the passage of the Bill would be a real one.[9] According to Nevinson, Grey's speech 'altered the situation & restored hope.'[10] Hope was further restored when, on 16 June, Asquith wrote to Lord Lytton that Grey had accurately expressed the Government's intentions, that the 'week' offered would be 'interpreted with reasonable elasticity', that the Government

* See p. 149.

would not oppose 'proper use of the closure', that if the Bill got through Committee in the time proposed, 'the extra days required for Report and Third Reading would not be refused', and, finally, that the Government (i.e. the Cabinet) had unanimously agreed 'to give effect, not only in the letter but in the spirit, to the promise in regard to facilities which I made on their behalf before the last General Election.'[11]

The WSPU was considerably mollified by Asquith's statement, and a period of high optimism ensued. On 17 June 1911, in co-operation with at least twenty-eight other women's suffrage organizations, the WSPU sponsored a gala march called 'The Women's Coronation Procession'.* Headed by 700 ex-prisoners, a procession of about 40,000 women, five abreast and seven miles long, with banners, floats, and historical costumes, walked from the Embankment to the Albert Hall, where Christabel said: 'we have in any event got an assurance which will place in our hands before the next general election the right to vote.'[12]

Christabel was no less sanguine in private. On the day after the march, Nevinson wrote in his diary:[13]

June 18 Sunday
. . . we all went to Hachette's in Piccadilly to dine – the Lawrences, Vida Goldstein . . . and Christabel. Who was most lovely to me, smiling & indiscreet & trustful. She said they were actually printing a resolution for the Albert Hall telling Mrs. Pankhurst to go with a named deputation to Asquith when Asquith's letter to Lytton arrived. Also that they did not strike after Ld. George's statement because they knew privately that Grey was going to make another. They now accept Asquith's letter as an absolute pledge, chiefly because he promises in spirit and not in letter. They were all full of hope & joy & good spirit, designing the future campaign. . . . They spoke of the

---

* Among the organizations taking part were the Conservative and Unionist Women's Franchise Association, the Actresses' Franchise League, the Free Church League for Woman Suffrage, the Men's Political Union for Women's Enfranchisement, the Women Writers' Suffrage League, the Fabian Women's Group, the Catholic Women's Suffrage Society, and, most important, the National Union of Women's Suffrage Societies, which had never before accepted an invitation from the WSPU.

F*

intense anxiety & strain of the last few weeks while further
pledges were being slowly forced out of Cabinet – forced by
fear of militancy in Coronation time as I believe. All very
sweet & pleasant.

Christabel's optimism was now more marked than ever before:
on 23 June 1911, she went so far as to write of Asquith's letter
to Lytton:[14]

It is a pledge upon which women can base the expectation of
taking part as voters in the election of the next and every
future Parliament.
    The Prime Minister has now assured us that the
Women's Enfranchisement Bill is to be allowed to pass
within the first two Sessions. Consequently the measure
will have the security, afforded by the Parliament Bill, of
becoming law before the next General Election.

On 7 June, Christabel announced a new by-election policy.
For the first time since August 1906, the WSPU would not
oppose Liberal candidates at by-elections, provided that candidates stated that they supported the Conciliation Bill and agreed
not to support widening amendments which would alienate
Conservative supporters of the Bill.[15] During the period in
which this by-election policy was in effect, the WSPU opposed
only two Liberal candidates.

By the end of the summer of 1911, Lloyd George, the Cabinet's
most vocal suffragist, was working behind the scenes against the
Conciliation Bill. On 5 September, he wrote to the Master of
Elibank, his party's Chief Whip:[16]

I am very concerned about our pledges on the Female
Suffrage question. We seem to be playing into the hands of
the enemy. The Conciliation Bill would, on balance, add
hundreds of thousands of votes throughout the country to
the strength of the Tory Party. We would thus lose more
than we could possibly gain out of the Registration Bill.
We have never really faced the situation manfully and
courageously. I think the Liberal Party ought to make up
its mind as a whole that it will either have an extended
franchise which would put working men's wives on to the

Register as well as spinsters and widows, or that it will
have no female franchise at all.

After receiving Lloyd George's note, Elibank asked J. Renwick
Seager, the head of the Registration Department at Liberal
headquarters, to write to the secretaries of the twelve provincial
Liberal federations. Seager asked the secretaries 'to inform
me . . . what are the opinions expressed in the area which you
deal with as to the Women's Conciliation Bill and its prospects?'[17]
Seager subsequently reported to Elibank that[18]

the majority of districts are emphatically adverse to the
Bill . . . it is almost unanimously agreed that the women to
be enfranchised under this Bill, being of the propertied
class, would, by a large majority, be against the Liberal
Party.

Seager appended summaries of the twelve reports he had received.
Only the Northern Federation had reported that passing the
Conciliation Bill would aid the Liberal Party in its area.

Christabel could not have known of Seager's poll, but by
October, if not earlier, she had become well aware of the general
nature of Lloyd George's activities. She wrote:[19]

there exists a conspiracy of wreckers and reactionaries who
are bent upon carrying widening amendments in Committee
in the hope of destroying the majority for the Bill. . . .
   The particular amendment which Mr. Lloyd George
intends to promote is one to give a vote to the wife of
every elector, in virtue of her husband's qualification. This
provision would apply to no less than six millions of women,
so that the Conciliation Bill, instead of enfranchising one
million women . . . would enfranchise *seven* million women.

Such a measure, Christabel continued, could not possibly pass
the Commons without Government aid. Lloyd George's object
was, she concluded, 'not, as he professes, to secure to women a
large measure of enfranchisement, but to prevent women from
having the vote at all.'[20]
   Intent as she was on Lloyd George's machinations, neither
Christabel, nor, for that matter, her colleagues, expected the
statement made by Asquith on 7 November; Asquith announced

that, in the next Session, the Government would introduce a
measure providing manhood suffrage for all *bona fide* residents.
The Bill would be so drafted that it could be amended, if the
House desired, to include the enfranchisement of women.[21]

That evening, Brailsford went to Clement's Inn where,
according to Nevinson, he 'found them livid with rage & deaf
to reason.'[22] Militancy was to be resumed. On the following day,
Mrs Drummond sent letters to the secretaries of the local
WSPUs, stating:[23]

Of course you have seen that the Government intend to
introduce a Manhood Suffrage Bill next Session. In consequence of this our Anti-Government policy will be resumed.
Please at once call upon your members to volunteer to take
part in a deputation to Westminster on Tuesday, November
21st, and send me at the earliest possible moment the name
and address of every volunteer that you secure.
. . . we absolutely refuse to trust to any amendment to
the Government's Manhood Suffrage Bill, and . . . we
regard the proposal that we should do so as insulting to our
intelligence.

Christabel explained, in *Votes for Women*, that the WSPU
regarded supporting a women's suffrage amendment as futile,
because such an amendment could not be carried without
Government support – the suffragist majority in the Commons
was composed of members of all parties, and an amendment so
greatly increasing the electorate would destroy this majority
by alienating Unionists and moderate Liberals. Christabel
concluded, bitterly:[24]

The Government's latest attempt to cheat women of the
vote is, of course, inspired by Mr. Lloyd-George. The whole
crooked and discreditable scheme is characteristic of the
man and of the methods he has from the first employed
against the Suffrage cause.

According to the diary of C. P. Scott, Brailsford said that
Christabel 'envisaged the whole suffrage movement in its
present phase as a gigantic duel between herself and Lloyd
George whom she designed to destroy.'[25] By 13 November, the

WSPU had enrolled 400 women for the deputation to be sent on 22 November.[26]

On 17 November, Asquith received representatives from nine women's suffrage societies. He claimed that introduction of the Reform Bill would not affect the chances of the Conciliation Bill. Even the anti-suffragist *The Times* was dubious, stating:[27]

> We confess to some difficulty in gathering with any certainty what the Government's real intentions are, and experience warns us against interpreting Mr. Asquith's words in their plain and obvious sense.

A day or two later, the WSPU issued the following circular to members of the forthcoming deputation:[28]

FINAL INSTRUCTIONS TO MEMBERS OF DEMONSTRATION, 21ST NOVEMBER, 1911

On Tuesday evening, when coming to the Demonstration, it is advisable not to bring more money than is absolutely necessary, nor to wear jewelry, furs, nor to carry umbrellas.

In the event of arrest, you will be taken to Cannon Row or another police station and charged, when it is advisable *to make no statement*, as anything said to the Police may be used in evidence against you next day. After an interval, you will be bailed out until the following morning, when you will be ordered to appear at Bow Street, or any other police court named on your charge-sheet.

Bring with you to the police court the next morning a HANDBAG containing night things and a change of clothing, brush and comb, etc., also *do not forget to come provided with food sufficient to keep you going for the day*, as the proceedings may be lengthy.

With regard to the policy to be adopted when in prison, you will receive full instructions direct from Mr. Pethick-Lawrence on Wednesday morning. You need not worry, as everything has been foreseen, and fortunately the regulations, issued by the Home Office last year with regard to prison treatment of Suffragists still hold good.

On 18 November, a second letter was sent to selected members of the deputation. The recipient was asked to arrive at the

Women's Press shop at 156 Charing Cross Road at 7 p.m. on 21 November, dressed as quietly as possible, wearing no badge, and bearing an enclosed ticket of admittance to the shop, where full instructions would be given.[29]

On 21 November, Mrs Pethick-Lawrence led the usual deputation from the Caxton Hall to Parliament Square.* The women who met at 7 p.m. at 156 Charing Cross Road did not march with the deputation. Instead, armed with bags of stones and hammers supplied to them at the WSPU shop, the women went singly to break windows at Government offices and business premises.[30] Windows were smashed at the Home Office, Local Government Board, Treasury, Scottish Educational Office, Somerset House, National Liberal Federation, Guards' Club, two hotels, the *Daily Mail* and *Daily News*, Swan and Edgar's, Lyon's, and Dunn's Hat Shop, as well as at a chemist's, a tailor's, a bakery, and other small businesses.[31] Two hundred and twenty women and three men were arrested. The WSPU had never before attacked premises connected with neither the Government nor the Liberal Party. Christabel wrote, a few days later: 'Remembering the injuries and insults done to the Deputation on Black Friday, we say that we prefer a thousand times the window-breaking of the 21st of November.'[32]

The window-breakers did not receive sentences longer than those previously meted out for milder forms of militancy: the majority of those convicted as a result of the events of 21 November received sentences of one month or less. Twenty women who had done more than £5 worth of damage received longer sentences of two months in prison.

Asquith had consistently asserted that the introduction of a manhood suffrage Bill would not affect the chances of the Conciliation Bill. Yet, before 5,000 people at Bath on 24 November, Lloyd George said that the Conciliation Bill 'would have been grossly unfair to Liberalism. Now that Bill has been torpedoed'.[33] Lloyd George appeared to have confirmed the WSPU's worst suspicions of Asquith's intentions. The moderate suffragists, who had accepted Asquith's word, were appalled. Brailsford wrote to Mrs Fawcett on 26 November: 'My con-

* Mrs Pankhurst was not present, having left on 4 October for a three months' tour of Canada and the United States.

fidence in my own judgment (which I am afraid has absurdly misled me) is now so healthily shaken, that I hardly like even to discuss the position with anyone else.'[34]

Enraged at what they regarded as the trickery of Asquith and Lloyd George, WSPU members heckled Asquith severely at the City Temple on 28 November. Women shouted, unfurled banners, and blew police whistles. Unable to continue his speech, Asquith departed. On the following day, Lloyd George wrote to C. P. Scott:[35]

The action of the Militants is ruinous. The feeling amongst sympathisers of the cause in the House is one of panic. Whilst not being despondent, I am frankly not very hopeful of success if these tactics are persisted in.

On 2 December, Lloyd George had breakfast with Scott, who recorded the following conversation in his diary:[36]

'But what can they hope to achieve by attacking him [Asquith]?', he [Lloyd George] asked, 'they can't expect to make him change his mind'. 'Oh! yes, they do; they are quite hopeful of converting him'. (I had this the previous day from Brailsford). 'Then they must be mad'. 'They are mad, Christabel Pankhurst has lost all sense of proportion and of reality'. 'It's just like going to a lunatic asylum' [,] said George, 'and talking to a man who thinks he's God Almighty'. 'Yes, very much like that.'

With Lloyd George's statement of 24 November 1911 that the Conciliation Bill had been 'torpedoed', and the WSPU's angry reaction to that statement, the era of conciliation had completely ended as far as the WSPU was concerned. That the Conciliation Bill was to be read again the next session was no longer of interest, for the Union's leaders now believed that the Bill had no chance; after November 1911, they consistently claimed that only a suffrage Bill sponsored by the Government could possibly succeed. Within the WSPU, the strongest legacy of almost two years of truce and attempted conciliation was the growth of the belief that politicians' promises were not to be trusted; with regard to the probity of male politicians, the WSPU was now in the incipient stage of what was to become a most Manichean outlook.

13 Violence, Flight, and Divided Counsels

The mass window-breaking of 21 November 1911 had not been accepted with equanimity by all of the Union's members. The tactic caused Dr Elizabeth Garrett Anderson, the pioneer woman physician, to resign from the WSPU. Her daughter, Dr Louisa Garrett Anderson, like her mother a Union member, told Nevinson that she was 'now very doubtful about the wisdom of the tactics . . . they take too much explanation.'[1] On 7 December, Nevinson talked with Annie Kenney, 'who also had doubts about the policy, but "would go through fire for Christabel" .'[2]

Although the WSPU had sponsored acts of organized window-breaking, it had not espoused the uncontrolled destruction of property. On 15 December Emily Wilding Davison, one of the Union's more erratic members, set three postboxes ablaze by lighting pieces of linen saturated with paraffin and thrusting them through the letter slots. She said, afterwards: 'I did this entirely on my own responsibility.'[3] The Union was not anxious to foster such independently conceived acts of destruction, and *Votes for Women* gave Emily Wilding Davison's deed brief mention on an inside page, and omitted the eulogy usually accorded to militant deeds.[4] Setting postboxes on fire was not regarded as the precursor of a new form of militancy. Emily Wilding Davison was sentenced to six months in prison.

By January 1912, the WSPU was deeply involved in preparations for its next major militant foray. On 22 January, H. N. Brailsford wrote to Mrs Fawcett:[5]

I saw Mrs. Pankhurst, but clearly I am no longer the person to approach her. She regrets having ever looked at 'that abominable Conciliation Bill', and declares they will never again tolerate anything but a Government measure of full sex equality. She is optimistic & even triumphant. If she fails to force the P.M. to take up Adult suffrage (& for this she still hopes) she is sanguine of destroying this and every succeeding Government. I am not a good emissary, but I doubt if anyone cd have succeeded.

On 16 February, Mrs Pankhurst told the members of the WSPU that 'the argument of the broken pane of glass is the most valuable argument in modern politics'.[6] A week or so later, Mrs Pankhurst practised stone-throwing near the country home of Dr Ethel Smyth, the composer, who found it amusing to act as Mrs Pankhurst's mentor 'in an art hitherto unknown to her'.[7] On 24 February, Mrs Pankhurst wrote to Ethel Smyth that 'On Friday [March 1] there will be an unannounced affair, a sort of skirmish, in which some of our bad, bold ones will take part'.*

The WSPU had always announced militant demonstrations well in advance. On 1 March, for the first time, the Union struck without warning: about 150 women were given hammers, told exactly which windows to break, when to break them, and how to hit panes low so that glass would not fall from above.[8] At 5.45 p.m. in Oxford Street, Regent Street, the Strand, and other prominent thoroughfares, well-dressed women produced hammers from handbags and began to smash windows. The firms whose windows were damaged included Burberry's, Liberty's, Marshall & Snelgrove, and Kodak. Foreign firms were not exempt – windows were broken at the offices of the Canadian Pacific, the Grand Trunk Railway, and Norddeutscher Lloyd. Police arrested 124 women. The damage was estimated at £5,000.[9] Mrs Pankhurst was among those arrested; she and two

---

* E. Pankhurst to E. Smyth, 24 February 1912, from prosecution evidence presented 20 March 1912, as reported in *Votes for Women*, 22 March 1912.

The WSPU's *Sixth Annual Report*, which covered the period 1 March 1911 to 29 February 1912, reported on a fiscal year during the first nine months of which the truce had still prevailed. During 1911–12, the Union's gross income had fallen slightly, to £33,980. Only £3,496 had been brought forward from the previous year, however, so excluding funds carried over from previous years the Union's net income had risen slightly, from £29,387 in 1910–11 to £30,484 in 1911–12. Other expenditure had also remained about the same (*Sixth Annual Report, National Women's Social and Political Union*, London, 1912).

other women had driven by taxi to 10 Downing Street, where they had broken four windows.

In court, the next day, Mrs Pankhurst said that women had failed to gain the vote because they had failed to use the methods previously used by men. She cited a speech made by C. E. Hobhouse, on 16 February, in which Hobhouse had said that the women's suffrage agitation had not created 'the kind of popular sentimental uprising which accounted for Nottingham Castle in 1832, or Hyde Park railings in 1867.'[10]

On the following day, 3 March 1912, Ellen Pitfield, a forty-five-year-old midwife afflicted with incurable cancer, entered the General Post Office and set fire to a basket of wood shavings saturated with paraffin. Her attempt at arson was purely symbolic, for she immediately proceeded to attract attention by throwing a brick through a window of the building. Her actions were not sponsored by the WSPU. On 19 March, she was sentenced to six months in prison, having been carried to court from a bed in the prison hospital. Released in May, she died on 6 August. *

The day after Nurse Pitfield's protest, members of the WSPU again smashed windows of commercial premises, this time in Knightsbridge, Kensington High Street, and the Brompton Road. At Ponting's £400 of damage was done; at Barker's, £250. Harrod's, too, had its windows smashed. About £1,000 worth of plate glass was broken in Knightsbridge and the Brompton Road. Later in the day, the WSPU began to encounter retaliation. At a meeting in the Pavilion Theatre, WSPU speakers were drowned out by the cries of 'a gang of shopmen & City Temple young men at back of pit & gallery.'[11] During the evening, a crowd of medical students broke the windows of the Women's Press. When, the same evening, small groups of women broke windows at the Home Office and the Local Government Board, they were hustled and jeered by 'men seeking "sport"'.[12]

---

* According to Sylvia Pankhurst, Nurse Pitfield sustained a wound on Black Friday which never healed, and in which cancer subsequently developed (*The Suffragette Movement*, p. 379). It is not possible now to determine whether an injury sustained on Black Friday brought about or hastened Nurse Pitfield's death.

Shortly before 10 o'clock the following evening, 5 March, about twenty detectives entered Clement's Inn, armed with a warrant for the arrest of Christabel and the Pethick-Lawrences. (Mrs Pankhurst and Mrs Tuke were also named, but they were already in prison.) The police searched the WSPU's offices, and arrested the Pethick-Lawrences. Christabel, however, could not be found. The police did not know that, several months earlier, Christabel had ceased to reside at Clement's Inn, taking a flat of her own nearby. She was immediately informed by Evelyn Sharp of the Pethick-Lawrences' arrest, and spent the night in hiding with friends.[13] In the morning, Christabel crossed to Paris, virtually undisguised. Nevinson, who subsequently visited her in Paris, wrote that she[14]

> Said her escape was not really premeditated but the thought came instinctively when she awoke fr sleep the night of the arrest. 'We must not all be shut up at a time of confusion & shock. . . .'

While Christabel was *en route* to Paris, the Pethick-Lawrences, Mrs Pankhurst, and Mrs Tuke were being charged at Bow Street police court with having[15]

> wantonly conspired and combined together unlawfully and maliciously to commit damage and injury to an amount exceeding £5 to plate-glass windows. . . . Also with unlawfully aiding, abetting, counselling, and procuring the commission of offences against the Malicious Injury to Property Act.

Early on the morning of 7 March WSPU members again broke windows, this time in the vicinity of Oxford Circus. On the same day, *Votes for Women* appeared with a number of blank spaces, the printers having suppressed articles 'considered by them to be inflammatory matter.'[16]

As the WSPU had mounted its offensives against the plate glass of central London, both the press and the Cabinet had reacted with anger and dismay. On 2 March 1912, *The Times* referred to the WSPU as 'Mrs Pankhurst and her maenads. . . . None of its previous follies has been so thoroughly calculated to discredit the suffragist cause.' The *Manchester Guardian* spoke of 'the madness of the militants . . . the small body of misguided women who profess to represent the noble and serious cause of political enfranchisement of women, but who, in fact, do their utmost to degrade and hinder it.' The *Morning Post* stated: 'Nothing could indicate more plainly their lack of fitness to be entrusted with the exercise of political power.'[17] The *Daily Chronicle* stated: 'All sensible people are being forced to the conclusion that there can be no women's franchise legislation under the present conditions.'[18] And the *Pall Mall Gazette* claimed on 2 March: 'Somewhere deep in the councils of the suffrage movement there surely lurks a persuasive "Anti" in disguise, who is sworn to the prompting of just such self-defeating raids as yesterday's.'[19]

Within the Cabinet, the chances of the Conciliation Bill were increasingly regarded as dim. On 7 March, Lady Frances Balfour wrote to Mrs Fawcett:[20]

> Betty [Lady Betty Balfour] reports that at Grillion's on
> Monday [March 4], . . . Haldane, Grey, and Asquith
> all agreed nothing more could be done this session for
> suffrage. Asquith told them the police believed that there
> was a plot to assassinate Lloyd George. Betty says she
> knows L. George threatened resignation if a clause
> enabling women was not permitted in the Manhood
> Suffrage Bill. Asquith was so angry he would not speak to
> him for some days.

On the same day as the discussion at Grillion's, Harcourt wrote to Gladstone: 'I am quite hopeful of defeating their Conciliation Bill . . . largely owing to the folly of their proceedings.'[21] On the following day, Haldane, a suffragist, wrote to his sister: 'The Suffragettes are behaving like mad women. They are spoiling the chances of the Conciliation Bill.'[22]

The projectors of the Conciliation Bill themselves were also disheartened by the WSPU's tactics. Lord Robert Cecil, one of the leading Unionist sponsors of the Bill, said:[23]

> If the deplorable outrages committed by the so-called
> Suffragists were devised for the purpose of advancing the
> cause of Women's Suffrage, they can only be described as
> senseless. But if their object was to put all possible

difficulties in the way of the Constitutional Suffragists, and particularly in the way of the Conciliation Bill, then the proceedings, however unscrupulous, were exceedingly well designed.

Within the fortnight before the Bill's Second Reading, a number of MPs indicated that suffragette militancy had brought them to vote against the Bill. Sydney Buxton, the President of the Board of Trade, wrote to *The Times*, on 16 March, that he was in favour of women's enfranchisement, and under ordinary circumstances would have voted for the Conciliation Bill, hoping it would be widened in Committee, but that he now planned to vote against the Bill, because[24]

> I feel convinced that to pass the Bill just now might appear to be, and would undoubtedly be claimed by the militants and their admirers to be, a justification for and an endorsement by the House of Commons of their methods and actions.

E. Crawshay Williams, Lloyd George's secretary, expressed similar sentiments, as did G. Wilson, T. Bridgeman, W. Ashley, and E. Wason.[25] Churchill too declared against the Bill, though his reasons were somewhat murkier: he had consistently opposed the Bill on the grounds that it was too narrow. On 23 January, however, after lunching with him, C. P. Scott had written in his diary that Churchill 'practically admitted that his present wrecking tactics are the outcome of resentment at the treatment he has received from the WSPU.'[26] Scott's suspicions may well have had solid foundations, for after being denounced by H. N. Brailsford for voting against the first Conciliation Bill, Churchill had angrily replied:[27]

> Your accusation of 'treachery' is not well-grounded. Under what obligations had you or your friends ever placed me? For the last five years you have disturbed or tried to disturb almost every meeting I have addressed. During the last four elections that I have fought your organizations have opposed me with their utmost strength: & if I have been returned on three occasions it has been in spite of every effort on the part of the militant suffragists to prevent me.

Moreover, a week after giving this retort, Churchill had written, in a private memorandum:[28]

> Mr. Churchill's view has been that although in principle the obsolete sex barrier is illogical, yet there is no great practical grievance; and, further, that in any case the militant suffragists have less claim on him than on any other public man.

Thus, Churchill's opposition to the second Conciliation Bill very likely stemmed in part from his belief that women had 'no great practical grievance', and in part from his strong resentment at the treatment he had received from the WSPU.

On 28 March 1912, the second Conciliation Bill failed to pass its Second Reading, by a margin of fourteen. Two hundred and twenty-two MPs voted against the Bill, and 208 voted in its favour. The *Westminster Gazette* commented:[29]

> If there were no obvious explanation for it, the fact that the same Bill had in the same Parliament been passed by a majority of 167 and rejected, within a year, by a majority of 14 would be one of the strangest incidents of our time. In the case of the Conciliation Bill there is, of course, one very obvious explanation, and that is the window-breaking campaign . . . the atmosphere was unfavourable to any action which might have been construed by the unthinking public as yielding to pressure on the part of the House of Commons. . . .
>   The woman's movement, in fact, if it is to come to a successful issue, must have some regard to the psychology of the male . . . the electorate and its representatives have been put in a position in which they feel they would look weak and ridiculous if they yielded to this agitation.

A number of MPs certainly claimed to have voted against the Bill because of the WSPU's tactics. Reasons and rationalizations cannot, however, be easily separated: it is simply not possible to know how many of the Liberals who claimed to have been influenced by suffragette violence would have voted against the Bill anyway, being privy to the results of the secret poll taken during the previous autumn at the behest of the Master of

Elibank (see p. 151), or at least generally aware that the Bill would probably benefit the Tories. It would seem most unlikely that, for example, as Lloyd George's secretary, Crawshay Williams would have taken a position unlike that of Lloyd George, who for months had opposed the Bill as detrimental to Liberal interests.

In addition, at least three factors other than WSPU militancy influenced the fate of the Conciliation Bill. By pre-arrangement, 41 Irish Nationalist MPs had voted against the Bill, while 10 abstained – Redmond had urged his followers to oppose the Bill in order to avoid any possibility of Asquith's resigning and the Cabinet breaking up, such an occurrence being viewed as detrimental to the prospects of independence for Ireland.* (The previous year, 31 Irish Nationalists had voted in favour of the Conciliation Bill.) In addition, as a result of an outbreak of strikes in the north, only 25 out of 41 Labour MPs were present to support the Bill.

Given the extremely narrow margin by which the Conciliation Bill had been defeated, and the fact that at least six MPs – almost enough to have altered the outcome had all six voted in favour – professed to have voted against the Bill as a result of feminist militancy, it is at least possible that militancy brought about the failure of the Bill to pass its Second Reading. Yet, the Bill's subsequent fate in Committee – where, without doubt, Liberals like Lloyd George, Buxton, and Williams would have supported widening amendments which would have made the Bill far less palatable to its Unionist supporters – would have been another matter. Given the forces against the Bill, it is highly unlikely that success at the Second Reading would have been followed by the passing of the Bill into law.

After the arrest of the Pethick-Lawrences on 5 March 1912, and Christabel's subsequent flight to Paris, the WSPU momentarily

* Following the defeat of the Conciliation Bill, the WSPU issued a statement that the leaders of the Union had 'for many months past had private knowledge of the Nationalist leaders' intention to wreck the Conciliation Bill in the supposed interests of Home Rule. This knowledge was a prime cause of the refusal of the Women's Social and Political Union to trust any longer to the Conciliation Bill or any other private member's proposal' (*The Times*, 1 April 1912).

lacked firm leadership. About a week after Christabel arrived in Paris, Annie Kenney received a note from her that said:[30]

> I want you to take supreme charge of the whole Movement
> during my absence, and while Mother and Mr. and Mrs.
> Lawrence are in prison. . . . I give you complete control over
> the Whole Movement until the leaders are released and
> we are all once again united. Come quickly [to France]. . . .

Christabel had no intention of giving Annie Kenney control in the sense of giving her autonomous power to make major decisions; rather, Annie became Christabel's agent, the medium through which Christabel continued to set Union policy. Annie began to travel to Paris each weekend, in disguise, to confer with Christabel and receive instructions. Her virtually symbiotic relationship with Christabel was resented by some of the Union's members – Christabel later wrote that[31]

> the cry was raised that 'Annie is nothing but blotting paper
> for Christabel.' This was, in reality, a high compliment to
> Annie, proving that she perfectly knew and was faithful to
> her duty as my representative. . . . Annie . . . was in the
> habit of signing her letters to me: 'The Blotter'.

Christabel also maintained her control over the Union by writing, each week, both the leading article and political notes for *Votes for Women*.[32]

Disguised as 'Amy Richards', Christabel lived in some comfort in Paris, at first as the guest of the Princesse de Polignac, later in her own apartments at 11 Avenue de la Grande Armée.[33] When, in April 1912, Sylvia Pankhurst visited Paris, disguised as a nurse, she found Christabel relaxed, gay, and confident.[34] After so many years of nearly incessant political meetings, and the myriad pressures of Clement's Inn, life in Paris was serene. The London newspapers arrived but a few hours late, and a stream of friends and followers crossed the Channel to consult and be instructed. Annie Kenney later wrote of her weekends in Paris with Christabel:[35]

> We would walk along the river or go into the Bois, or visit
> the gardens. Whoever saw us would also see stacks of

newspapers, pockets stuffed with pencils, and always a
knife to sharpen them. To her aristocratic and literary
French friends we were a source of amusement, wandering
through Paris, I in travelling clothes – I could not be
troubled with luggage, – arm in arm, talking incessantly.

On 28 March 1912 Mrs Pankhurst, the Pethick-Lawrences, and
Mrs Tuke were committed for trial on the charges which had
been brought against them three weeks earlier. After prelimin-
ary hearings, the Pethick-Lawrences were released on bail, but
Mrs Pankhurst remained in prison to serve the sentence imposed
on her for breaking Asquith's windows on 1 March. On the
evening of 28 March, the WSPU raised £10,000 in the Albert
Hall. Eleven days later, Mrs Pankhurst was released from
prison, her sentence having been remitted until after the
conspiracy trial. She went to the country to recuperate, the
conspiracy trial being postponed until she could recover her
health sufficiently to conduct her own defence.

On 5 April, the twenty-eight WSPU members who were in
Aylesbury prison as a result of the window-breaking of 1 March
began a hunger strike. WSPU prisoners in Winson Green and
Holloway soon followed suit. The hunger-strikers were fed by
force. In protest, the WSPU held meetings in Hyde Park, where
Sylvia Pankhurst's appeals for 'the women who are dying of
tortures and are at this moment facing death' were greeted by
howls of derision.[36] (Resentment of the suffragettes was now
frequently in evidence – on 22 March, in Glasgow, a mob of 200
men had broken up the WSPU shop, throwing iron bolts and
weights through the windows.) Faced with increasingly hostile
audiences, the Union's more radical members were now asserting
that outdoor propaganda meetings were useless – only the
destruction of property could be effective.

The second week of April saw the introduction of an Irish
Home Rule Bill. The WSPU bitterly opposed the Bill:[37]

The Irish party has set itself to wreck the cause of women's
enfranchisement, but Mr. Redmond will find that two can
play at that game . . . now war is declared. The Nationalists
have come out into the open as opponents of the enfranchisement of women. They have thrown down their challenge.

That challenge has been taken up. It is a fight to a finish
between Suffragists and the Nationalist Party!

The immediate result of this rodomontade was a poster parade
('No Votes for Women – No Home Rule') outside the Houses of
Parliament.[38]

On 15 May 1912, the conspiracy trial of Mrs Pankhurst and the
Pethick-Lawrences opened at the Old Bailey. Mrs Pankhurst
argued, movingly, that militant deeds had been done for purely
political reasons, and should be treated accordingly. On 22 May,
the jury found all the defendants guilty, but recommended
leniency, in view of the 'undoubtedly pure motives' underlying
the suffrage agitation.[39] Justice Coleridge sentenced each de-
fendant to nine months in the Second Division, and ordered Mrs
Pankhurst and F. W. Pethick-Lawrence to pay the costs of prosecution. Mrs Pankhurst and the Pethick-Lawrences announced
that unless they were transferred to the First Division
within a week, they would hunger-strike. Among those who
signed appeals to Asquith in support of the WSPU leaders' claim
to be political prisoners were Jean Jaurès, Romain Rolland,
Madame Curie, Edward Bernstein, Victor Adler, Upton Sinclair,
and over 100 British MPs.[40] On 10 June, Mrs Pankhurst and the
Pethick-Lawrences were transferred to the First Division.

Five days later, the WSPU held its twentieth meeting in the
Albert Hall. Mrs Tuke announced at the meeting that if the
seventy-nine WSPU members in prison were not all placed in the
First Division, all WSPU prisoners, including the leaders, would
hunger-strike. It was also announced, with little fanfare, that in
the autumn the WSPU would move to larger offices in a different
building. £6,000 was collected in the Albert Hall.

The hunger-strike started on 19 June. Three days later, forced
feeding began. Approached by wardresses carrying a feeding tube,
Mrs Pankhurst threw an earthen bowl at her captors, who
retreated. Mrs Pankhurst was not forcibly fed; weakened by
fasting, she was released on 24 June. Mrs Pethick-Lawrence was
released on the same day, having been forcibly fed once. F. W.
Pethick-Lawrence was released three days later, having been
forcibly fed five times. By 6 July all of the hunger strikers had
been freed, forty-five women having been released before their

sentences had expired. During the hunger-strike, Emily Wilding Davison had sought martyrdom by throwing herself over the railings of a prison staircase. She escaped serious injury or death by being caught by a wire mesh screen below.

On release from prison, Mrs Pankhurst and the Pethick-Lawrences were all badly in need of rest. When Mrs Pankhurst was well enough to travel, she joined Christabel in Paris. In early July, the Pethick-Lawrences were about to embark for a fortnight in Switzerland, when they received a message from Mrs Pankhurst asking them to stop in Boulogne to confer with her and Christabel. No completely reliable account of the meeting that followed survives. The only available accounts by any of the four principals are in the Pethick-Lawrences' respective autobiographies, both of which were written more than twenty-five years after the event.* Of the two autobiographies, that of F. W. Pethick-Lawrence is somewhat more reliable.† F. W. Pethick-Lawrence's recollection of the Boulogne meeting was as follows:[41]

> We broke the journey [to Switzerland] in Boulogne to have a talk with Mrs. Pankhurst and Christabel, who came from Paris to join us. We walked together up from the town on to the cliffs that lie between it and Vimereux, and resting there we discussed the future.

* In her autobiography, *Unshackled*, Dame Christabel did not describe the Boulogne meeting, referring only to a 'consultation' (p. 226) with the Pethick-Lawrences in France, and placing the consultation far later in the summer – after the return of the Pethick-Lawrences from Canada – than had actually been the case.

Mrs Pankhurst never really wrote an autobiography, *My Own Story* being primarily the work of Rheta Childe Dorr, an American journalist, who, according to Sylvia Pankhurst, produced the book 'from talks with Mrs. Pankhurst and from Suffragette literature' (*The Suffragette Movement*, p. 268). Produced hurriedly, in 1914, when Mrs Pankhurst was at the height of her fame, *My Own Story* is so replete with errors and glossings-over as to be virtually useless to the historian. The Boulogne meeting was not mentioned in *My Own Story*.

† In writing *My Part in a Changing World*, Mrs Pethick-Lawrence was not as careful as she might have been to check her facts with easily available sources, such as *Votes for Women*. To cite but one example, she claimed that Christabel's being in Paris was made public before the Boulogne meeting (p. 277) whereas, in fact, Christabel's whereabouts were a well-kept secret until September 1912.

The talk developed unfortunately, for we found that during our separation we had been thinking along different lines. I had always had a very high opinion of Christabel's political genius. She had had in my view an almost uncanny instinct for diagnosing public opinion and for choosing a line of action that would make the greatest appeal to it. But I did not feel the same about her present attitude. It seemed to me that her impressions, obtained for the most part second-hand, did not fully accord with the facts, and that the policy, based on them, that she proposed to adopt would not therefore have the reactions she anticipated. . . .

Broadly, the difference between us was this. I took the view that the window-smashing raid had aroused a new popular opposition, because it was for the first time an attack on private property; and that therefore before it was repeated, still more before graver acts of violence were committed, there was need for a sustained educational campaign to make the public understand the reasons for such extreme courses. I took it for granted that she herself would return to London. . . .

Christabel took the view that such popular opposition as there might be was not essentially different from that which had over and over again manifested itself when other new forms of militancy had been inaugurated, and that the right method of overcoming it was to repeat and intensify the attack in the early autumn. . . . She considered that, just because her policy was a revolutionary one, it was necessary that she herself should remain outside the reach of the Government, so that whatever happened she might be in a position to direct it.

Our discussion became somewhat heated, and attracted the attention of Mrs. Pankhurst and Emmeline, who were seated a few paces away. They came and joined us and expressed their views. Mrs. Pankhurst, as a born rebel, was even more emphatic than Christabel that the time had come to take sterner measures. She appeared to resent the fact that I had even ventured to question the wisdom of her daughter's policy. Emmeline, on the other hand, thought it would be a grave mistake to throw away the present unique opportunity of expounding our views to the public,

and considered that it was essential to consolidate our
position before striking again. We did not pursue the matter
further. . . . Next morning, after a friendly talk with
Christabel, we departed for Switzerland.

Christabel's exact relationship to the serious acts of militancy
that almost immediately followed the Boulogne meeting is not
clear. On 13 July, in the early morning hours, a P.C. Godden, of
the Oxfordshire Constabulary, apprehended one of two women
who were standing near the wall of Nuneham House, the
country residence of Lewis Harcourt, one of the Cabinet's
leading 'Antis'. The constable impounded a basket and a satchel,
which together contained a bottle and two cans of inflammable
oil, two boxes of matches, four tapers, nine 'pick-locks', twelve
fire-lighters, a hammer, an electric torch, and 'a piece of American
cloth smeared over with some sticky substance.'[42] In the bag of
the apprehended woman, Helen Craggs, was a note, addressed
to 'Sir', which said:[43]

I myself have taken part in every peaceful method of
propaganda and petition . . . but I have been driven to
realise that it has all been of no avail, so now I have
accepted the challenge given by Mr. Hobhouse at Bristol,
and I have done something drastic. . . .
   Women . . . see around them the most appalling evils in
the social order; they see children born into conditions
which maim them, physically and mentally, for life; they see
their fellow-women working in the sweated industries at a
wage which makes their life a living death – or sacrificed
as white slaves to a life which is worse than death.

Helen Craggs subsequently received nine months' imprisonment. She was, however, released after a hunger strike of
eleven days. Whether Christabel and Mrs Pankhurst had requested that Harcourt's house be burned is not clear. In a speech
on 21 October, Mrs Pankhurst did refer to Helen Craggs as 'acting
solely on her own responsibility.'[44] The abortive effort to burn
down Nuneham House had been, at any rate, both the first
serious attempt at arson by members of the WSPU and the first
occasion on which an act of destruction was attempted without
the perpetrators' intending to offer themselves for arrest.

Whatever the relationship between Christabel and the would-be burners of Nuneham House may have been, Christabel's growing belief in the political efficacy of destroying property had certainly not yet permeated the WSPU as a whole. Sylvia Pankhurst remained interested in promoting large, legal public demonstrations, and, on 14 July, under her leadership, the local London WSPUs sponsored a large meeting in Hyde Park. At this meeting, held in brilliant sunshine, there were twenty platforms and 150 brass bands. Keir Hardie and George Lansbury both spoke at Sylvia's behest, and the Women's Freedom League and the Actresses' Franchise League were among the organizations taking part. The demonstration had not been sponsored by the national WSPU, and was certainly not along the lines of agitation now being contemplated by Christabel.

Five days after the attempt to burn Harcourt's house, a more serious incident occurred. Mary Leigh had already been arrested nine times, and had spent over fifteen months in jail. On 18 July, in Dublin, Mary Leigh threw a hatchet into a carriage in which Asquith and Redmond were riding. She escaped. That evening, she and Gladys Evans tried to set fire to the Theatre Royal, where Asquith had just seen a performance. The two women ignited the curtains behind a box, threw a flaming chair down into the orchestra, and set off small bombs made of tin cans. They did not try to evade arrest, and were subsequently sentenced to five years in prison. *

On 30 August 1912, *Votes for Women* published a photograph of Mary Leigh 'as Drum-Major'. She was wearing a military uniform and saluting, and had signed the photograph, 'No Surrender'. In an accompanying photograph, Gladys Evans appeared in a military uniform 'as Drummer in the W.S.P.U. band'.[45] Christabel later wrote that she had no prior knowledge of the specific acts the two women intended to perpetrate in Dublin.[46]

---

* After prolonged hunger strikes, Mary Leigh was released on 21 September and Gladys Evans on 3 October, on licences that restricted their movements and activities. Substantial and prolonged legal complications followed, and the cases were eventually allowed to drop, though the two women had between them served but sixteen weeks of their five-year sentences.

In mid-July the Pethick-Lawrences had returned to England
from Switzerland. They soon received a letter from Mrs Pankhurst saying that she would remain in Paris for some time, and
encouraging them to visit Mrs Pethick-Lawrence's brother, on
Vancouver Island. The Pethick-Lawrences left for Canada, *Votes
for Women* announcing that they and Mrs Pankhurst would be
welcomed back to active leadership at a mass meeting in the
Albert Hall on 17 October.[47]

The Pethick-Lawrences had not paid the costs levied on them in
connection with the conspiracy trial of the previous May, and
while they were in Canada, they learned that on 19 August
bailiffs had seized their country house. They soon received a
letter from Mrs Pankhurst in which she urged them to remain
in Canada and take up legal domicile there to protect their
extensive assets from confiscation by the British government.[48]
Surprised, the Pethick-Lawrences declined to accept the suggestion, and planned to return to England in early October.

Over the summer of 1912, various members of the WSPU had
created a variety of incidents, in one of which a suffragette
clutched Asquith by the lapels of his suit, and shook him. In turn,
the Union encountered opposition from a variety of quarters:
on 22 August, Mrs Fawcett claimed that the militants had a
'large share' in bringing about the defeat of the Conciliation Bill
the previous March, and were now 'the chief obstacles in the way
of the success of the Suffrage movement in the House of Commons, and far more formidable opponents of it than Mr. Asquith
or Mr. Harcourt.'[49]

Considerably less genteel opposition presented itself in Wales.
At the Eisteddfod, on 5 September, suffragettes who heckled
Lloyd George were attacked by the crowd and had their clothing
torn. Then, on 21 September at Llanystymdwy, when Lloyd
George, who had come to address his constituents, was heckled by
two WSPU members, the two women were assaulted by the
crowd: they were struck, their hair was pulled, and their clothing
was torn, one of the women being stripped to the waist before
being rescued by the local constabulary. Before the end of the
meeting, the two women's shirts were cut up and pieces were
distributed amongst the crowd as souvenirs of the occasion.[50]

The incident in Llanystymdwy resulted in some rather lurid

publicity: the *Daily Mirror* devoted its entire front page to a photograph of the women being mauled, and the *Illustrated London News* devoted a full page to similar photographs. Such publicity was of dubious benefit to the WSPU. Sylvia Pankhurst later wrote that[51]

> some of the sheltered habitués of Clement's Inn objected to the attitude of the girls who had faced the fray; it was too bold and defiant for their approval, and lacking in appropriate womanly distress. Quietly they were replaced by a more orthodox type of young woman.

On 13 September 1912, a week before Llanystymdwy, *Votes for Women* had finally announced that Christabel was in Paris, and published photographs of her at work in exile. Prior to deciding to make her whereabouts known, Christabel had privately sought legal advice, and had been assured by French officials that she would not be extradited. Her motives for revealing her whereabouts were not immediately apparent.

"The Suffragette," October 17, 1913.

Registered at the G.P.O. as a Newspaper

The Suffragette

The Official Organ of the Women's Social and Political Union.

Edited by Christabel Pankhurst.

No. 53—Vol. II.   FRIDAY, OCTOBER 17, 1913.   Price 1d. Weekly (Post Free)

THE FORCES OF EVIL DENOUNCING THE BEARERS OF LIGHT.

15   At the height of the Moral Crusade: *Suffragette*, 17 October 1913

16 St Catherine's Church, Hatcham, 6 May 1913

17 Unknown suffragette

14 The Pethick-Lawrences Depart

In early October 1912, the Pethick-Lawrences returned from Canada. On arrival at Clement's Inn, they were warned that the Pankhursts were moving to oust them from the Union. Inside Clement's Inn, the Pethick-Lawrences found that the WSPU's offices had been repossessed by the landlord – during the previous week, the WSPU had completed the move, announced in June, to palatial new offices in Lincoln's Inn House, Kingsway, a five-storey building constructed of Portland stone in Italian Renaissance style. The Pethick-Lawrences went to the new headquarters. There they found that no office space had been allotted to them, and that, in the corridors, conversations stopped as they passed by. The following day, the Pethick-Lawrences visited Mrs Pankhurst. She informed them that their connection with the Union was at an end.[1]

The Pethick-Lawrences were shattered. They had not expected such a sudden and complete ouster, and they could not believe that Christabel had agreed to the decision. Mrs Pankhurst invited them to a second meeting, which was held a few evenings later. When the Pethick-Lawrences arrived at the meeting place, Christabel was there, having crossed from Paris in disguise. Christabel was as adamant as her mother.[2] She would direct the Union's affairs herself, and from Paris. If the Pethick-Lawrences insisted on speaking in the Albert Hall on 17 October, no officers of the WSPU would attend the meeting.

As the Pethick-Lawrences themselves came to realize, their ouster had been carefully planned in advance.[3] The publicizing of Christabel's presence in Paris had served to make it clear to the Union's members that Christabel was in active control of *Votes for Women*, and through it the Union's policy. The move to Lincoln's Inn House had involved the Union's departure from offices at Clement's Inn which had been leased in Mrs Pethick-Lawrence's name, and which adjoined the Pethick-Lawrences' private

G

apartments.[4] In the new building, the Union could far more easily refuse to allot office space to the Pethick-Lawrences. Finally, plans for the split had obviously not been kept secret from the WSPU staff.

The Pethick-Lawrences discussed between themselves the course they would take. Emmeline Pethick-Lawrence wished to resist, but her husband counselled otherwise: if they opposed the Pankhursts publicly, they would split the membership of the WSPU, ruin the organization, and with it, perhaps, the cause to which they had devoted the last six years of their lives.[5] F. W. Pethick-Lawrence wrote privately to George Lansbury, on 26 October:[6]

> The whole situation has come upon us with startling suddenness and at the time nearly stunned us. To be asked to leave the W.S.P.U. to which we have contributed our life blood, was like a mother being asked to part from her little child. And yet as we faced the situation in all its aspects we saw that the only other alternative was to carry into the public arena our difference with the inevitable result that the Union would be smashed to bits. It was better we felt to leave it intact in the hands of those from whom we differ.

Leave it intact they did, in a remarkable act of self-abnegation. The Pethick-Lawrences never expressed to those not their intimates the bitterness they felt at the ouster which had been so carefully planned in their absence.

Once the Pethick-Lawrences had decided not to resist being thrown out of the Union, only the manner of their departure remained to be determined. Once again they crossed the Channel to Boulogne. There, in a small hotel facing the quay, terms were agreed upon. The Pankhursts would take over complete control of the WSPU, including the Women's Press. The Pethick-Lawrences would retain control of *Votes for Women*, which would cease to be the official organ of the WSPU. A joint statement was drawn up:[7]

> At the first re-union of the leaders after the enforced holiday, Mrs. Pankhurst and Miss Christabel Pankhurst outlined a new militant policy, which Mr. and Mrs. Pethick-Lawrence found themselves altogether unable to approve.

Mrs. Pankhurst and Miss Christabel Pankhurst indicated that they were not prepared to modify their intentions, and recommended that Mr. and Mrs. Pethick-Lawrence should resume control of the paper, *Votes for Women*, and should leave the Women's Social and Political Union.

Rather than make schism in the ranks of the Union, Mr. and Mrs. Pethick-Lawrence consented to take this course.

In these circumstances, Mr. and Mrs. Pethick-Lawrence will not be present at the Meeting at the Royal Albert Hall on October 17.

> Emmeline Pankhurst
> Christabel Pankhurst
> Emmeline Pethick Lawrence
> Frederick William Pethick Lawrence

As a sop to formality, the statement was read to a meeting of the Union's committee before being made known to the Union's membership. Mary Neal and Elizabeth Robins, the two committee members who had not been privy to what was taking place, were shocked at the breach. However, since neither woman had any power in the Union, and the committee itself had no authority, opposition was out of the question. During the meeting, Mrs Pankhurst announced that the committee would be disbanded. There was no real opposition to the crumpling of a body which had only existed on the letterheads of WSPU stationery anyway.

There remained now only the announcement of the split to the members of the WSPU. As in 1907, the members were presented with a carefully-planned *fait accompli*. On 17 October 1912, the day of the Albert Hall meeting, two journals appeared – *Votes for Women*, now edited by the Pethick-Lawrences alone, and a new weekly, the *Suffragette*, edited by Christabel.* Both publications announced the split. That evening, in the Albert Hall, Mrs Pankhurst handled the situation with mastery. Had she simply read the Boulogne statement and said little else, there might well have been a dangerous slack, a moment or longer of doubt and questioning from which serious divisions might have emerged.

---

* *Votes for Women*, and *Suffragette*, 18 October 1912. Both issues were post-dated, being placed in circulation on 17 October 1912.

But Mrs Pankhurst followed her reading of the Boulogne statement with an impassioned speech:[8]

> Why are we militant? The day after the outrages in Wales I
> met some of the women who had exposed themselves to the
> indecent violence of that mob . . . those women suffered
> from assaults of a kind which it was impossible to print in
> a decent newspaper . . . one woman . . . said, 'All the time
> I thought of the women who, day by day, and year by year,
> are suffering through the White Slave Traffic, and I said
> to myself, "I will bear this, and even worse than this, to
> help win power to put an end to that abominable slavery." '
> Until by law we can establish an equal moral code for men
> and women, women will be fair game for the vicious section
> of the population, inside Parliament as well as out of it. . . .
> When I began this militant campaign I was a Poor Law
> Guardian, and it was my duty to go through a workhouse
> infirmary, and never shall I forget seeing a little girl of
> thirteen lying in bed playing with a doll. . . . I was told she
> was on the eve of becoming a mother, and she was infected
> with a loathsome disease, and on the point of bringing, no
> doubt, a diseased child into the world. Was not that
> enough to make me a Militant Suffragette? . . .
> We women Suffragists have a great mission – the greatest
> mission the world has ever known. It is to free half the
> human race, and through that freedom to save the rest.

In a superb peroration, Mrs Pankhurst announced the new policy of destruction of property:

> Those of you who can express your militancy by facing
> Party mobs at Cabinet Ministers' meetings when you
> remind them of their falseness to principle – do so. Those of
> you who can express your militancy by joining us in our
> anti-Government bye-election policy – do so. Those of you
> who can break windows – break them. Those of you who
> can still further attack the secret idol of property so as to
> make the Government realise that property is as greatly
> endangered by Women Suffrage as it was by the Chartists
> of old – do so. And my last word to the Government: I
> incite this meeting to rebellion. I say to the Government:

You have not dared to take the leaders of Ulster for their incitement to rebellion, take me if you dare.

With such oratory, Mrs Pankhurst carried the meeting with her. The immorality of both ordinary men and privileged politicians would be ended: votes for women would save both women's souls and theirs. In the light of so glowing a future, what matter the departure of the Pethick-Lawrences? Immediately after Mrs Pankhurst's speech, Annie Kenney rose to announce that the Union would henceforward oppose Labour candidates as well as Liberals at by-elections. Labour MPs were supporting a Government responsible for forced feeding and mass imprisonment, so they were enemies of women as much as were the Liberals.[9]

In the days after the Albert Hall meeting, the ouster of the Pethick-Lawrences met with little real opposition from WSPU members. Many members were shocked, but there was no way in which the ordinary member could influence the policies decreed from Lincoln's Inn House. The lack of substantial opposition within the WSPU was due not only to the Pankhursts' deft strategems, but to the Pethick-Lawrences' determination to avoid schism in the Union's ranks. Mrs Pethick-Lawrence stated on 18 October, 'We do not call upon anybody to follow us, and leave the W.S.P.U.'[10] The Pethick-Lawrences kept completely secret the great disparity between their public statements and their private reactions. H. W. Nevinson wrote in his private journal:

Nov. 25 [1912][11]

called on poor Lawrence in his new office. . . . He was overcome in speaking of the breach: felt bitterly hurt especially at the long underground preparation & sudden explosion upon their innocence. Said the only tangible cause of quarrel was that they upheld militancy on large & open scale, and the Pankhursts upheld these sporadic separate attacks on post-offices &c.

Dec. 23 [1913][12]

Talked to Mrs. Lawrence. . . . She also spoke of the Pankhursts saying Mrs. Pankhurst was the extreme & violent person: They used to call her 'enfant terrible'. Christabel

was always moderate & reasonable. Mrs. P wd not let them
see Christabel alone before split, nor Mrs. Tuke nor Annie
Kenney.

July 19 [1914][13]
Sunday: at Holmewood. Walked with Lawrence through
woods. . . . He talked again of the shameful behaviour of
Mrs. Pankhurst at time of split, wh had been carefully
prepared long before. It seems the origin was my work for
the paper when they were all arrested. I was supposed to
be intimate friend of HNB. [H. N. Brailsford] Whom I
seldom saw at that time, and he of Ld. George. So the
silliness went on. His contempt of her meanness and hatred
of her 'playing acting' for sympathy are very violent:
almost an 'obsession'.

Whether or not the Pankhursts were actually suspicious of
Pethick-Lawrence's relationship with Nevinson and Brailsford
cannot now be ascertained. Christabel did remark to Nevinson,
when he visited her in Paris on 23 November 1912, that she
'rather disapproved of men's intimate concern in the movement'.[14]
Pethick-Lawrence had been, after all, the only man ever to take
a large part in directing the Union's affairs.

The immediate result of the Pethick-Lawrences' departure was
a substantial alteration in the organizational structure of the
WSPU. Prior to March 1912, WSPU policy had been determined
by Christabel and the Pethick-Lawrences acting in concert. Now
Christabel alone set policy from Paris, through Annie Kenney and
other go-betweens, and the London headquarters was obedient to
her command. The London offices were by now staffed by women
completely loyal to Christabel, women who lacked the experience
in movements other than the WSPU that the Pethick-Lawrences
and the organizers of earlier days had possessed. The process of
the previous six years whereby persons of some independence of
thought had been progressively eliminated from the inner
councils of the Union had now reached its logical climax, with the
achievement of a complete autocracy.

In the past, Mrs Pethick-Lawrence had been responsible for
the Union's financial affairs, and F. W. Pethick-Lawrence had
seen that the Union's offices were conducted efficiently. Now

Mrs Pankhurst became treasurer of the Union. She had always been the Union's most famous speaker, but in the years of the Pethick-Lawrence ascendancy she had not normally been involved in routine day-to-day planning. Annie Kenney herself later wrote that after October 1912 the Union lacked the efficiency and order that the Pethick-Lawrences had brought to it.[15]

Whereas the immediate effect of the Pethick-Lawrences' departure on the organizational structure of the Union is clear, the effect of their departure on WSPU policy is less easy to assess. To be sure, the policies the Pethick-Lawrences had previously advocated were increasingly pushed aside. But the militant campaign had never been static – militancy had always taken on progressively more extreme forms, and it is unlikely that the process of radicalization would have halted had the Pethick-Lawrences not been ousted. The nature of WSPU policy had they stayed cannot, of course, be known, but the Union's choice of tactics certainly would have continued to have been influenced by F. W. Pethick-Lawrence's concern with the relationship between the nature of militant tactics and the likely response of both the public and the Government to use of those tactics, for that concern had always distinguished his handling of the practical side of the militant campaign.

15 Bromley and Bow, and its Aftermath

In early October 1912, almost unnoticed by Lincoln's Inn House, Sylvia Pankhurst had begun a suffrage campaign of her own in the East End. She received financial assistance for her new endeavour primarily from local WSPUs of the London area, as the national WSPU had long since ceased to attempt to organize working-class districts. Under Sylvia's supervision, WSPU shops were opened in Bethnal Green, Poplar, Limehouse, and Bow, and street-corner meetings were held. The first such meetings were not without tumult; in Bow, a swarm of urchins threw stones, and in Bethnal Green WSPU speakers were pelted with fish heads and newspapers soaked at a nearby public urinal.

The East End would have continued to go unnoticed at Lincoln's Inn House, had it not been for George Lansbury, who was sitting as MP for the East End seat of Bromley and Bow. Lansbury had long been a friend to the Union. As early as June 1906, he and his wife had donated £2 to the then obscure WSPU.[1] In ensuing years, Lansbury had become a fervent apologist for women's suffrage, a gadfly on the issue to the Labour Party in the House of Commons. In October 1912, he took the position that his fellow Labour MPs should vote against the Government until women were granted the vote. The Labour Party did not wish to vote against the Government on issues unrelated to women's suffrage, and Lansbury was informed that as the party had paid part of his election expenses and his seat had been won under its sponsorship, he should support the party's policy or leave the party. In protest against this treatment, Lansbury resigned his seat in order to seek reelection as an independent Labour candidate, fighting primarily on the suffrage issue. In early November, he crossed to Boulogne to confer with Mrs Pankhurst and Christabel, who gave him the Union's full support.[2] It was the first time that a Parliamentary seat would be fought for primarily on the women's suffrage issue, and the first time that the Union had agreed to support a candidate.

Lansbury was certainly a most attractive candidate. Sylvia Pankhurst later wrote of him:[3]

> I think what most endeared George Lansbury to working class audiences was his phrase 'men like you and me'. You could hear it once or twice in every one of his speeches. It summed up the general brotherliness of his attitude. It was rather elder brotherly and toward women he was inclined to be fatherly.
> He was a big long-legged, loose-limbed man, unconventional in his way, with a ruddy face. . . . One might have taken him for a farmer.

The *Suffragette* was confident: there was little doubt that Lansbury would be elected. Christabel wrote that work and money would not be stinted to ensure Lansbury's victory, and that Bromley and Bow would mark a turning point in the movement for votes for women.[4] Privately she was perhaps somewhat less optimistic, for she wrote to Lansbury on 24 November that: 'Whatever the result the fight has been gloriously worthwhile'.[5]

The Union's effort for Lansbury was not merely verbal. Lincoln's Inn House dispatched Miss Grace Roe, a young Irishwoman, to the East End to take over the WSPU campaign there from Sylvia Pankhurst. Sylvia was not pleased to be displaced, and she believed that Grace Roe was a singularly inappropriate replacement, 'entirely unsuited to the work before her'.[6] Still in her twenties, Grace Roe was one of the younger organizers completely loyal to Christabel, who had risen in the wake of the disaffection of more experienced organizers and the ousting of the Pethick-Lawrences. Grace Roe had none of the experience in working-class movements that the earlier WSPU organizers had possessed. Indeed, she had scant sympathy for Labour. As a result – Sylvia later alleged – Grace Roe and Joe Banks, head of the Poplar Labour Representation Committee which had followed Lansbury into independence, were unable to co-operate. Labour and WSPU competed for halls and open-air meeting places, and acrimonious discussions occurred, friction

G*

being increased by some Labour officials' resentment of WSPU attacks on the Parliamentary Labour Party. Moreover, some Labour supporters decried the WSPU as a middle-class movement agitating for a 'ladies' vote'.[7] The accusation was not unjustified, given the limited franchise the WSPU advocated. Difficulties were increased by the plethora of voices raised on Lansbury's behalf; all manner of organizations appeared in the constituency to grind their own axes, and the result was an ideological babel.

On election day – 24 November – it rained. The constituency was a large one, and the downpour made it imperative that sufficient cars be available to transport Lansbury supporters to the polls. The *Daily Herald* had previously appealed for cars in terms that suggested its readers were not likely to own them ('Will any of our friends who have a few spare motors knocking about').[8] The WSPU did have cars, obtained from wealthy supporters, but for much of the morning these stood unused, as Grace Roe and Banks argued over whether the cars would operate under the aegis of the WSPU or be dispatched to Labour headquarters, where Banks had the list of sympathetic voters. According to Sylvia Pankhurst, Grace Roe insisted that Mrs Pankhurst did not want the WSPU to 'work under the men'.[9] Grace Roe's cast of mind was not atypical of the mentality by now frequently found in the WSPU's predominantly maiden ranks; WSPU members, jealous of sexual and political autonomy, were becoming increasingly adverse to co-operation with male politicians.* Eventually, the cars were dispatched, after Mrs Pankhurst intervened.

Reginald Blair, the Unionist, received 4,042 votes; Lansbury received 3,291.[10] There were, no doubt, a number of reasons for Lansbury's defeat, not all of them related to the WSPU. As the *Suffragette* pointed out, with some justice, the very people for whom Lansbury was fighting – women – could not vote for him.[11] There were, however, other factors. G. S. Jacobs, a solicitor who had worked in Lansbury's campaign, wrote to Lansbury on 27 November:[12]

Dear Lansbury,
   I am sorry. You, of course, must attribute the result to

* With regard to the incidence of single women in the WSPU, see p. 210.

(1) Removals, (2) Women's Suffrage, (3) The bewilderment
caused by your hostility to the Labour Party. . . .

You cannot rely on all the workers of the Women's
organizations. Their cause is righteous, but it does not help
when some of their canvassers go round saying that they do
not agree with your socialism, but are supporting you on the
suffrage question – in fact, frankly, they are using you as a
tool. My wife and I and my son found a lot of that when we
were canvassing for you.

The letter alluded to a failing which was fundamental:
social reforms for working-class women, let alone 'socialism', had
long since ceased to be the primary goal of the WSPU. The
Union sought to appeal to women of all social classes, and denied
the existence of any fundamental antagonisms between class
interests, at least where women were concerned. Reforms that
would benefit working-class women were but part of the multitude of reforms that would somehow be made law once women
could vote – or, rather, once one woman in seven could vote, as
such would have been the result of extending the existing franchise to women, the measure so doggedly advocated by the
WSPU. The Union itself had never undertaken a stringent
analysis of the probable electoral effects of granting women the
vote by extension of the existing franchise, being content to rely
upon the hopelessly inadequate survey taken by the ILP in
1904. 'Votes for ladies!', the derisory cry heard in Bromley and
Bow, was probably an apt enough epithet.

For the WSPU, however, Lansbury's defeat on 24 November
had come as a shock after the confidence with which the immi-
nence of victory had been proclaimed.[13] The defeat seemed to
demonstrate, once again, the futility of using legal means –
speeches, demonstrations, and canvassing – as levers with which
to obtain enfranchisement, and WSPU patience with such
methods was now at an end. Lansbury's defeat had been the
straw that broke the camel's back.

On the evening of 26 November 1912, the day after the announcement of Lansbury's defeat, WSPU members poured acid, ink,
lampblack and tar into postal pillar boxes in the City of London,
the West End, and a host of provincial cities. Thousands of

pieces of mail were destroyed. In Newcastle alone, 2,000 letters were damaged. The destruction was carried out secretly, and the perpetrators escaped arrest, but Mrs Pankhurst and Mrs Drummond made clear to the public the Union's advocacy of and responsibility for the deeds committed.[14]

Letter-destroying marked the completion of a fundamental change in the aim of militant tactics. In earlier years, the WSPU had sought to enlist public support by evoking sympathy for its cause. The effort to win public support had reached its zenith with the great demonstration of June 1908. Now the public was to be *coerced* into asking the Government to grant women the vote. The *Suffragette* stated the new policy succinctly:[15]

> The Suffragists who have been burning and otherwise
> destroying letters have been doing this for a very plain and
> simple reason. They want to make the electors and the
> Government so uncomfortable that, in order to put an end
> to the nuisance, they will give women the vote.

The new tactic also differed from previously employed tactics in that it was completely indiscriminate: persons of all political opinions, women as well as men, could be affected. The *Suffragette* was not unduly concerned: 'The public acquiesced far too widely and easily in the sufferings of women; its dishonour is on its own head.'[16] In any case, the very unpopularity of letter-destroying was to be the key to its effectiveness: 'These militant women are being warned that letter-burning is very unpopular. That is just what they want it to be, because they know that if the electors and the Government liked to have letters burnt, they would do nothing to stop it.'[17]

The WSPU was correct in its belief that neither the public nor Parliament would be overjoyed to have letters destroyed. On 3 December, Lloyd George observed that to a large extent public opinion had been antagonized, and added that the House of Commons was very responsive to public opinion. There was, he said, a great deal of evidence inside the House that the ardour of suffragist MPs had been chilled 'by the very remarkable proceedings of a small section of the supporters of the cause.'[18]

Within the WSPU, the rash of letter-burning of late 1912 was accompanied by an increasing emphasis on votes for women as an instrument for enforcing the Union's growing concern with sexual morality. On 29 November, Mrs Drummond appealed to women workers:[19]

> the enemies of votes for women are saying that the
> Suffrage movement is a movement of rich women, and that
> the women workers are taking no real part in it. . . .
>   There are three questions which, above all others, are
> firing our indignation, and making us determined that we
> will now get the vote once and for all. These questions
> are: –
> 1. The sweating of women workers. The starvation of
> women is undermining the health of the mothers of the
> race, and is driving thousands to a life of shame.
> 2. The White Slave Traffic. Even under the new Bill
> which is now being carried a man can get less punishment
> for trapping an innocent girl and forcing her to a life of
> shame than for stealing a loaf of bread.
> 3. The outrages committed upon little girls, some of them
> only babies. This is a growing evil, which working-class
> mothers are determined to stamp out, and to do this they
> must have the vote.

The specific legislation through which the alleged evils would be ended was, as usual, not described. It is clear, however, that winning the vote was increasingly seen as involving the triumph of moral righteousness over monstrous depredations. The WSPU drew no sharp distinctions between the sexual exploitation of women and the alleged political immorality of male politicians; there was a growing tendency simply to identify opponents of votes for women with the forces of darkness. This tendency could result in the more adventuresome WSPU followers advocating deeds well beyond the pale of existing WSPU policy: the Metropolitan Police transcript of a speech that a Miss Gilliatt, speaking for the WSPU, made on Wimbledon Common on 8 December 1912, was as follows:[20]

> they were told that they had never taken human life and
> that it was impossible for them to do so. As regards the
> impossibility of killing a Cabinet Minister she (Miss Gilliatt)
> and her followers knew different. 'Attend their (Cabinet
> Ministers') political meetings' Miss Gilliatt said, 'and you

will find out for yourselves what an easy matter is their destruction.'

Before any such urge could be put into effect, a momentary lull took place, in the first weeks of 1913.

By January 1913, the non-militant National Union of Women's Suffrage Societies had come to place its hopes upon proposed women's suffrage amendments to the long awaited Franchise Reform Bill, which was to be debated in the Commons during the week of 20 January. The moderate suffragists put strong pressure on the WSPU to call a temporary halt to militancy in order not to jeopardize the amendments' chances. At first the Union refused, on the grounds that the amendments had no chance of passage. Not until 13 January was Evelyn Sharp (formerly of the WSPU) able to persuade Mrs Pankhurst to suspend militancy until the amendments had been acted upon; Mrs Pankhurst had agreed to the suspension only so that the WSPU would not be blamed for what she saw as the amendments' inevitable defeat. In a statement made on 13 January, she claimed that the amendments were foredoomed because anti-suffrage Cabinet Ministers had 'given members to understand that [in the event of passage] there will be a split in the Cabinet which will involve their resignation.'[21]

The Cabinet met on 22 January. Asquith reported to George V:[22]

Some discussion took place on the Franchise Bill, and on the possible acceptance or rejection of the various woman suffrage amendments. It was agreed, that whatever might be the decision of the House of Commons, the members of the Government holding diverse views would not regard the result of such decision this year as calling for their resignation of office.

Mr. McKenna pointed out that, in the not improbable event of the rejection of the women amendments, [sic] we must be prepared for a serious recrudescence of what is called 'militancy', and after some discussion, it was agreed that it might be necessary early next Session to ask Parliament to give the Home Secretary 'in and out' powers in regard to this class of prisoner.

On 23 January 1913, the Speaker of the House, J. W. Lowther, was asked by Bonar Law if the women's suffrage amendments would so change the character of the Franchise Bill that it would have to be reintroduced as a new Bill. The Speaker did not make a ruling immediately, but on that day or the next, he privately conveyed to some Cabinet Ministers his intention to rule that insertion of the women's suffrage amendments would indeed so change the Bill as to necessitate its withdrawal. On 25 January, Asquith wrote to George V: 'This is a totally new view of the matter, which appears to have occurred for the first time to the Speaker himself only two or three days ago.' Asquith further informed the King that the Speaker's ruling had been 'wholly unexpected', and that the Government was 'in no way responsible' for it.[23]

The Speaker's ruling was made public on 27 January. Despite Asquith's denials of complicity, the WSPU alleged that the decision had been a 'joint action' of the Speaker and the Government.[24]

> The Government deny that they had previous knowledge that the Speaker intended to explode this bomb. Official lying is, however, so much the rule that denials of the Government's foreknowledge of and complicity in the Speaker's action, carried [sic] no weight with us. . . . The only inference that can be drawn . . . is that they are scoundrels, and that this particular mode of torpedoing the women's amendments was an expedient held in reserve for use in the event of a Woman Suffrage amendment being carried. What we are prepared to believe is that the Speaker's disclosure of the torpedoing scheme in question was premature from the Government's point of view, and that they intended it to remain a secret unless and until a Woman Suffrage amendment should be passed.

In view of Asquith's denials of complicity, and the lack of evidence to the contrary, it would seem that the WSPU's allegations were groundless. The WSPU was increasingly slipping into a rather Manichean outlook in which Cabinet Ministers were 'scoundrels', Labour MPs were guilty of 'betrayal', and Lloyd George was an 'enemy in disguise', hand in glove with anti-suffragists in 'the common object of cheating the women.'[25] In

short, any politician not prepared to forsake all other considerations, including that of his own political survival, for the sake of
promoting women's suffrage, was an enemy. Given the facts of
political life, that the Liberal Cabinet remained divided on
women's suffrage and the Liberal Government was dependent
upon Irish Nationalist and Labour support to remain in office, a
very large number of Liberal and Labour MPs who were
sympathetic to women's suffrage, but more concerned with
keeping the Cabinet intact and the Government in office, had
become 'enemies'.

With the Commons so filled with foes, desperate measures now
seemed called for. During the final week of January 1913, Mrs
Pankhurst said that the suffragettes were 'guerrillists', warranted
in employing all the methods of war; human life would be held
sacred, but 'if it was necessary to win the vote they were going to
do as much damage to property as they could.' The WSPU had a
'plan of campaign', the details of which could not be made
public.[26] The 'plan of campaign' was not immediately put into
operation, for, clinging to the methods it had so often employed,
the WSPU attempted to march to the House of Commons on
28 January. Some windows were broken in Whitehall and about
thirty women were arrested, but the demonstration was ham-
pered by small numbers, heavy rain, and hostile crowds. Nevinson
wrote that the event was 'not like the old deputations: indeed the
organising & inspiring spirit has gone, the implicit confidence &
faith, ever since the split.'[27] Large numbers of supporters, so
necessary for the mass demonstrations of the Pethick-Lawrence
era, were not to be necessary for the campaign which was about
to begin.

16 The Arson Campaign

On the last day of January 1913, the WSPU began a concerted campaign of destruction of public and private property. Within the next three weeks, slogans were burned on to putting greens, a jewel case was smashed at the Tower, telegraph and telephone wires linking London and Glasgow were cut, an orchid house was burned at Kew Gardens, windows were smashed at London clubs, the refreshment house at Regent's Park was destroyed by fire, and at Harrow a railway carriage was set ablaze.[1] Most of the perpetrators escaped arrest, but the WSPU leaders made no secret of the Union's responsibility for the deeds – on 10 February, Mrs Pankhurst reiterated the arguments used to justify the destruction of mail two months earlier, saying:[2]

> We are not destroying Orchid Houses, breaking windows, cutting telegraph wires, injuring golf greens, in order to win the approval of the people who were attacked. If the general public were pleased with what we are doing, that would be a proof that our warfare is ineffective. We don't intend that you should be pleased.

At 6 a.m. on 18 February, a bomb set by Emily Wilding Davison and accomplices wrecked five rooms of a partly-completed house that Lloyd George was having built near Walton Heath, Surrey. Mrs Pankhurst had not known beforehand that the explosion was planned, but on 19 February she again said that she accepted responsibility for all that had been done; she had advised, incited, and conspired, and the authorities need not look for the women who had done what they did the previous night because she herself accepted full responsibility for the deed.[3] Eight days earlier, the Cabinet had instructed the Attorney General to initiate proceedings against Mrs Pankhurst for inciting others to violence and pillage.[4] On 24 February, Mrs Pankhurst was arrested for procuring and inciting women to commit offences contrary to the Malicious Injuries to Property Act of 1861.[5]

The burgeoning arson campaign and the bombing of Lloyd George's house did not fail to evoke the reaction which was always brought on by new and more extreme forms of militancy. The press spoke out in a chorus of dismay: on 20 February, the *Morning Post* spoke of 'dangerous and wicked violence', the *Yorkshire Observer* of 'mad women', the *Sheffield Daily Telegraph* of 'criminals', and the *Morning Advertiser* of 'silly malice'.[6] The *Yorkshire Post* called Mrs Pankhurst a 'foolish and wicked old woman'.[7] On 23 February, the *Observer* declared that 'during the last week what is called the "Women's Cause" has made a further movement backwards, and has continued with increased celerity the crab-like progress which has for a long time been carrying it away from the vote.'[8] The *Observer* alleged that the outrages were driving large numbers of people into the anti-suffragist camp.

Condemnation by the press was accompanied by more violent forms of reaction. On 23 February, suffragettes who attempted to hold a meeting on Wimbledon Common were attacked by a mob. The next day, the large plate glass window of the Croydon WSPU was smashed, and on the following day a WSPU stall in Walsall market-place was wrecked by an angry crowd, and a suffragist meeting in Worthing had to be closed because of the hostility of the audience.*

Table 16.1

Date	Location	Object	Est. Value (£)
9 March	Newcastle	Heaton Park Pavilion	400
10 ″	Saunderton	railway station	1,000
16 ″	Cheam	house	2,000
19 ″	Englefield Green	Lady White's house	2,300
29 ″	Croxley	station waiting rooms	1,300
		Total	7,000

* *The Seventh Annual Report, National Women's Social and Political Union*, 1 March 1912–28 February 1913, is, for purposes of comparison, treated in fn. *, p. 227–8.

The increase in the scale of secretly-performed destruction, and the parallel growth of violent opposition, continued throughout March. The major acts of arson attributed to the suffragettes in March 1913 were as in table 16.1.[9]

On 1 March, Mrs Drummond opened the first of a projected series of WSPU meetings in Hyde Park. Turf and mud were thrown at the speakers, and Mrs Drummond was drowned out by cat-calls and singing. That same day, at Wimbledon Common, a band of men rushed the WSPU platform and dragged the speakers away. On the next Sunday in Hyde Park there was again a disturbance, and on 16 March there was pandemonium. Bells were rung, and toy trumpets and whistles were blown. Before Mrs Drummond could utter a word, a clump of turf hit her in the mouth. For half an hour she tried to speak while the crowd pelted her with oranges, mud and stones. Before the afternoon was out, many suffragettes had their coats and hats torn by the mob, and had to be escorted from the park by the police. Nevinson, who was present, wrote in his journal that when a crowd on Oxford Street recognized the suffragette Brackenbury sisters it 'rushed to tear them to pieces. The police got them into the Tube station: a horrible time.'[10]

The Government was slow to stir. On 6 March the Cabinet discussed the treatment of suffrage prisoners, and McKenna, the Home Secretary, submitted the draft of a Bill which would authorize the re-arrest of prisoners who had been released because of self-induced ill-health. John Burns, an anti-suffragist, protested, saying that no steps beyond the provision of food and drink should be taken to stop prisoners from starving themselves.[11] On 12 March, the Cabinet again considered McKenna's Bill, and Asquith reported to George V that 'despite the doubts of the Prime Minister & one or two other Ministers as to its efficacy, its introduction was authorized.'[12]

On the same day, inspectors from Scotland Yard raided the Notting Hill studio of Olive Hocken, an artist, and found wire-cutters, fire-lighters, hammers, bottles of corrosive fluid, and five false motor car licence plates. Also found were strips of ribbon bearing the legends, 'No votes – no telegraphic connection' and 'No security by post or wire until justice be done to women.'[13] (WSPU arsonists normally left a message or other sign behind so that destruction would be attributed to the proper quarters.)

At the Old Bailey on 2 April, Mrs Pankhurst was found guilty of the charges which had been placed against her in February, and was sentenced to three years of penal servitude. That evening Annie Kenney told a meeting of 250:[14]

> Militancy will be more furious than before. . . . You, who sympathize with militancy, surely will come forward tonight and join the militant ranks and give in your name to do one deed within the next 48 hours. . . .
>   There are many things you can do. You don't need me to tell you. You all know. When you have done it don't forget that you have got to get away to do it again.

Militancy indeed became more furious than before. The damage attributed to the suffragettes during April 1913 was double that of March:[15]

Table 16.2

Date	Location	Object	Est. Value (£)
2 April	Hampstead	Garden Suburb Free Church	100
2 ,,	Manchester	Art Gallery pictures	110
4 ,,	Chorley Wood	Roughwood	2,500
5 ,,	Ayr	racecourse stand	2,000
7 ,,	Norwich	The Chase	2,000
11 ,,	Tunbridge Wells	Nevill Cricket Pavilion	1,200
15 ,,	St Leonards	Loveleigh	5,000
27 ,,	Perth	cricket pavilion	1,200
		Total	14,110

On 8 April, Annie Kenney was arrested under an obscure statute of Edward III, but was released on bail after undertaking temporarily to cease her involvement with the militant campaign. (The charge was later dropped in favour of a more serious charge.) Mrs Pankhurst, who had undertaken a hunger strike in prison, was released on 12 April on a fifteen-day special licence to recuperate.

Meanwhile, the reaction against the arson campaign began to curtail some of the legal activities of the WSPU. On 10 April, the Union held what was to be its last meeting at the Albert Hall; the management of the hall subsequently refused to let it to the Union. Then, on 15 April, E. R. Henry, Commissioner of Police of the Metropolis of London, informed the Union that it would no longer be permitted to hold meetings in the parks of metropolitan London. Recent meetings had been the occasion of grave disorder, and, given the nature of WSPU speeches, the police could not prevent such disorder from continuing. In view of this circumstance and of the fact that it was the policy of the WSPU to advocate the commission of crimes, the Home Secretary had directed the Metropolitan Police to prevent meetings being held.[16] The police subsequently refused to allow the entry of suffragette speakers' platforms into Hyde Park, but women did try to speak from the ground. The *Daily News* said of a meeting held towards the end of April that 'it was not a question of the police stopping meetings but of a crowd discovering a Suffragette and chasing her out of the Park.'[17]

During April, McKenna's 'in and out' legislation, now entitled the Prisoners' Temporary Discharge for Ill-Health Act, had rapidly passed through its various readings, and on 25 April the Bill received the Royal Assent. Under the Act, prisoners who damaged their health through their own conduct could be temporarily released to recover, and then be re-imprisoned. The time spent outside prison would not be counted as part of the currency of the sentence. Lord Robert Cecil had referred to the Bill as 'what is commonly called a cat-and-mouse proposal, namely, catching the women, then letting them go again; then catching them again'.[18] The measure soon became popularly known as the 'Cat and Mouse Act'.

On 30 April 1913, the police raided the WSPU's offices at Lincoln's Inn House, and arrested Mrs Beatrice Sanders, the financial secretary of the Union, Harriet Kerr, the office manager, Rachel Barrett, an assistant editor of the *Suffragette*, Geraldine Lennox, a sub-editor, Agnes Lake, the business manager, and Mrs Drummond. The women were all charged with conspiring to damage property. That same morning, the police also raided Annie Kenney's flat at 19 Mecklenburgh Square, and the Victoria House Press, which was printing the *Suffragette* for the first time that week, the former printer having quite understandably lost his nerve. On the following day, Annie Kenney was arrested as she returned from France, and a chemist named Clayton who had been aiding the WSPU was also arrested. They too were charged with conspiring to damage property. On Friday, Sidney Drew, the manager of the Victoria House Press, was arrested. The raid on the printers of the *Suffragette* and the arrest of Drew probably stemmed from a letter which Herbert Samuel, then Postmaster General and a foe of women's suffrage, had written to McKenna on 3 March:[19]

> I would suggest for your consideration whether the time
> has not come for the publishers and printers of this paper,
> and for the Union, to be prosecuted for illegal conspiracy. . . .
> If printers were deterred from publishing incitements to
> violence, the movement itself would be hampered not a
> little.

The raids of 30 April yielded some rather substantial evidence. At 19 Mecklenburgh Square, the police found, in Clayton's handwriting, a plan for simultaneously smashing a large number of fire alarms in London, lists of timber yards which could be burned, and a plan to set the National Health Insurance Commission on fire:[20]

> At a quite slack time . . . one might find oneself alone in
> the waiting room, as I did . . . one might have time to
> leave some fire-lighters, pour out some inflammable liquid,
> such as benzoline, methylated spirits, or paraffin, apply a
> light and instantly walk out of the building.

In Annie Kenney's room at Lincoln's Inn, the police found a satchel containing eight bottles of benzine.[21] At Lincoln's Inn they also found a collection of hammers with 'W.S.P.U.' inscribed on the handles, and a 'crimes record book', listing payments made to WSPU members as reimbursement for expenses incurred in purchasing supplies.[22] Those arrested were all charged with conspiring maliciously to damage property, and their trial was set for 9 June.

The raids and arrests did not in themselves cripple the Union. Arrests had not been unexpected, and trained understudies were ready to take the places of those imprisoned. Annie

Kenney's position as Chief Organizer was filled by Grace Roe. WSPU headquarters remained closed for only two days, and through the efforts of Gerald Gould and the *Daily Herald*, the *Suffragette* appeared as usual. Drew the printer was released on 2 May, having given an undertaking to cease printing the *Suffragette*.

Whereas in immediate and practical terms the Union coped with the raids fairly easily, the reactions the arson campaign had aroused in the winter and spring of 1913 – the baiting and bullying of suffragettes, the closing of the Albert Hall, the prohibiting of meetings in London parks, the Cat and Mouse Act, the raids on Lincoln's Inn and the WSPU's printers, and continued arrests of the Union's leaders – had a marked effect on the WSPU's tactics and ideology. The effect of repression seems to have been the opposite of what was intended. Repression had been brought on primarily by the arson campaign, and was intended to bring that campaign to an end. But as the arsonists themselves could seldom be caught, the Government was forced to clamp down on the Union's legal above-ground activities, which could more easily be got at. Large public meetings had previously been one of the principal means of legal expression utilized by the WSPU. The unintended result of the Government's moves to curtail such meetings was that secretly carried out destruction became a relatively safer and less-impeded tactic. House-burners were not assaulted by mobs in public parks. The positive results of the Government's acts are debatable, to be sure, but the acts certainly did not put a crimp in the arson campaign, as the increasing number of structures burned each month quite clearly demonstrates.

The proliferation of measures against the WSPU also influenced the Union's ideology. As repression mounted, the WSPU more and more tended to see its opponents as tyrants and bullies who embodied the quintessence of moral evil. Apropos the rows in public parks, Mrs Pankhurst said that the newspapers were deliberately rousing 'that element from which the White Slaver is drawn; from which the brute who lives on the immoral earnings of his own child is drawn'.[23] Forced feeding too was seen as a manifestation of untrammelled brutishness: on 28 March 1913 the *Suffragette* devoted an entire page to 'They tortured me', by Sylvia Pankhurst. In that same issue Christabel was moved to write:[24]

> After many years the martyr-spirit that seemed dead in our country shines out again in a blaze of glory. . . .
> Hysterical! Fanatical! So were called the saints and martyrs of the past . . . the so-called fanatics and hysterics are the glory of the human race. It is through them that all good things come into being. . . .
> In fighting against evil, the few are stronger than the many, women stronger than men. . . .

Christabel's writing was not atypical of the growing tendency in the WSPU to envisage the struggle for the vote as the working out of a dichotomy between the forces of good and evil, a process increasingly described in WSPU speeches and writing in the rhetoric of millenarian eschatology. On 10 April, at the last meeting held in the Albert Hall, Georgina Brackenbury said:[25]

> The powers of darkness pluck away our leaders one by one, but they only incite all the rest of the rank and file to greater action.
> . . . I want to say these words to you: 'When ye hear rumours of war and tumults, be not terrified, for these things must needs come to pass first.'

The millenarian vision requires villains: in the classical millenarian formula the good are first confronted by an ever-increasing tyranny or evil, and that evil must be extirpated for the millennium to come. For reasons which are not entirely clear, Christabel was now moving toward the belief that sexual disease spread by prostitution was the evil responsible for society's worst ills. She wrote on 11 April:[26]

> The chief fruits [sic] of woman slavery is the Social Evil [prostitution]. As a result of the Social Evil, the nation is poisoned morally, mentally, and physically. Women are only just finding this out. As their knowledge grows they will look upon militancy as a surgical operation – a violence fraught with mercy and healing.

Militancy would bring about a truly radical social regeneration:[27]

The militancy of women is doing a work of purification.
Nowhere was purification more needed than in the relationship between men and women. . . . A great upheaval, a
great revolution, a great blasting away of ugly things – that
is militancy. . . . The bad and the old have to be destroyed
to make way for the good and the new. When militancy
has done its work, then will come sweetness and cleanness,
respect and trust, perfect equality and justice into the
partnership between men and women.

The Union continued its efforts to bring about the great upheaval Christabel envisaged; the destruction attributed to
suffragettes in May 1913 was more than double that of April,
reaching a total of £36,475 (see table 16.3).[28]

Table 16.3

Date	Location	Object	Est. Value (£)
3 May	Aberdeen	Ashley Road School	400
6 "	Hatcham	St Catherine's Church	15,000
7 "	Fulham	Bishop's Park stand	200
9 "	Barrow	Oak Lea	6,000
10 "	Dundee	Faringdon Hall	10,000
10 "	Nottingham	boot warehouse	1,600
12 "	Nottingham	boat club house	1,600
14 "	Folkestone	The Highlands	500
18 "	Cambridge	buildings in Storeys-way	850
21 "	Edinburgh	Scottish Observatory	75
28 "	North Sheen	stables and outhouses	250
		Total	36,475

In turn, the Government continued its efforts to thwart the
advocacy of secret arson. In the first week of May, the Union
transferred the printing of the *Suffragette* to the National
Labour Press in Manchester, but on 9 May, the day the first
issue appeared, the manager of the press was arrested. On the
previous day, the Home Secretary had asked that customs
officials be instructed to hold at port of entry any issues of the
Suffragette that might be printed abroad.[29] The measure turned
out to be unnecessary, for the Union transferred the printing

of the *Suffragette* to the Athenaeum Press, whose manager, J. E. Francis, made a rigorous attempt to delete actionable material.

On 12 April, Mrs Pankhurst had been released to recuperate on a fifteen-day licence. Three weeks later, she wrote to Ethel Smyth from 'mouse haven', the nursing home in Pembridge Gardens run for the Union by Nurse C. E. Pine:[30]

> Today I had a glass of champagne, and fish. . . . All the old Adam (or, Eve, which is better) is coming back, and I begin to realize the glorious fight ahead of me when the 15 days are up. O kind fate that cast me for this glorious role in the history of women!

Mrs Pankhurst was not rearrested until 26 May, when she tried to attend a meeting at the London Pavilion. Re-imprisoned, she again refused to eat or drink, and on 30 May she was released once more on a seven-day licence.

Neither frequent arson nor hunger strikes seem to have had any positive effect on the Parliamentary outlook. On 6 May, a private member's women's franchise Bill, which included the wives of householders, had been easily defeated on its Second Reading by a vote of 266 to 219.[31] Defeat of the measure had been generally expected, as a number of suffragist Conservative MPs had opposed it on the ground that it would confer too wide a franchise.

Emily Wilding Davison had always been one of the Union's more erratic members. She had been the first to set a letter box ablaze, in December 1911, though doing so was not at the time sanctioned by WSPU policy. Subsequently, while in prison, believing that a martyrdom would benefit the Union, she had tried to kill herself by jumping from a balcony. At Lincoln's Inn there had been some scepticism regarding the seriousness of her intentions; she was regarded by some of the WSPU staff as a self-dramatizing individualist insufficiently capable of acting within the confines of official instructions.

On 3 June 1913, Emily Wilding Davison and her flat-mate decided to attend the Derby the following day, and disrupt the race by suddenly waving the WSPU colours before the horses at Tattenham Corner. At the Derby, Emily Wilding Davison did not wave the colours from the rail as planned, but, instead, dashed on to the course and was run down by the King's horse, Anmer. Her skull was fractured, and she died five days later without having regained consciousness.

After the collision, the attending constable reported that on removing Emily Wilding Davison's jacket he had found two flags of purple, white, and green, $1\frac{1}{2}$ yards by $\frac{3}{4}$ yards each, folded up and pinned inside the back of the coat. He had also found a return railway ticket from Epsom to Victoria.[32] Given the existence of the return ticket and the large flags, it is not clear whether she decided on her dash in advance, or acted on impulse having brought the flags in order to wave them as originally planned. She had not told anyone that she intended to run on to the course, and that doing so would result in death could hardly have been a matter of certainty. It is, however, clear that Emily Wilding Davison was imbued with the belief that a martyrdom would aid the WSPU; not only had she attempted suicide, but she had also written, but not made public, an article, 'The price of liberty', which concluded:[33]

sacrifice involves terrible suffeirng to [sic] the militant – old friends, recently made friends, they all go one by one into the limbo of the burning fiery furnace, a grim holocaust to Liberty. . . .

But a more soul-rending sacrifice even than that of friendship and of good report is demanded of the militant, that of the blood tie. 'She that loveth mother or father, sister or brother, husband or child, dearer than me cannot be my disciple', saith the terrible voice of freedom in accents that rend the very heart in twain.

'Cannot this cup of anguish be spared me?' cries the militant aloud in agony, yet immediately, as if in repentance for having so nearly lost the Priceless Pearl [of Freedom], in the words of all strivers after progress, she ejaculates: 'Nevertheless I will pay, even unto this price'; and in her writhing asks what further demand can be extracted from her.

The glorious and inscrutable Spirit of Liberty has but one further penalty within its power, the surrender of Life itself. It is the supreme consummation of sacrifice, than which none can be higher or greater.

To lay down life for friends, that is glorious, selfless, inspiring! But to re-enact the tragedy of Calvary for generations yet unborn, that is the last consummate sacrifice of the Militant!

Nor will she shrink from this Nirvana.

She will be faithful 'unto this last.'

Emily Wilding Davison apparently found a kind of ecstasy in the prospect of martyrdom. That the true militant 'ejaculates' and goes through 'writhing' before the 'supreme consummation of sacrifice' brings 'Nirvana' suggests that she may have found a quasi-sexual fulfilment in the contemplation of self-destruction. Be that as it may, her figures of speech were obviously not those of practical politics, but of Ruskin, Carlyle, and the Bible. Her vision of the militant's progress was not unlike the classical millenarian fantasy in which achievement of the perfect age 'demands of the faithful some kind of ordeal that will magically make them worthy – a difficult journey, the building of a city in the hills, the carrying out of ritual and of ascetic purification, or the perpetration of violence'.[34] However, in her vision the period of trial was to end with a Christ-like sacrifice of self through which Liberty would be brought into being.

On 14 June 1913, the remains of Emily Wilding Davison were carried by train from Epsom to London. The train arrived at Victoria at about two o'clock. The coffin, covered in purple, white, and green, was then escorted by a guard of honour, composed of over 2,000 suffragettes, through miles of spectator-lined streets to St George's Church in Bloomsbury. The marchers carried purple banners on which were written, in white, legends such as 'Thoughts have gone forth whose power can speak no more. Victory! Victory!' and 'Give me Liberty or give me death'.[35] Near St George's the crowds were dense. As the coffin was carried into the church, members of the WSPU, dressed in white, lined the way on either side and gave a military salute. Mrs Pankhurst, who was arrested as she attempted to enter the church, had issued a statement pledging to 'carry on our Holy War for the emancipation of our sex'.[36] After the service, the coffin was borne to King's Cross and placed on the 5.30 train to Morpeth, Northumberland, Emily Wilding Davison's birthplace.

Perhaps in part as a result of the death of Emily Wilding Davison, in June 1913 the Holy War of the WSPU resulted in £54,000 worth of damage (see table 16.4).[37]

Table 16.4

Date	Place	Object	Est. Value (£)
3 June	Oxford	Rough's Boathouse	3,000
4 ,,	Bradford-on-Avon	Elmscross	7,000
5 ,,	Muswell Hill	cricket pavilion	1,000
8 ,,	Hurst Park	racecourse stand	6,000
10 ,,	East Lothian	residence	2,500
18 ,,	Rowley Regis	parish church	6,000
20 ,,	Olton	residence	1,000
21 ,,	St Andrews	Batty's Marine laboratory	500
30 ,,	Balfron	Ballikinrain Castle	25,000
30 ,,	Leuchers Junction	railway station	2,000
		Total	54,000

The trial of those who had been arrested in connection with the raids of 30 April was held in mid-June. The five-count indictment included charges of conspiracy to destroy the contents of letter boxes, conspiracy to give false fire alarms, and conspiracy to inflict damage on 'houses, goods, and chattels belonging to divers subjects of the King.'[38] The defendants were found guilty and given sentences ranging from six to twenty-one months. After their imprisonment, there ensued a continuing round of hunger strikes, releases on licence, evasion of arrest on expiration of licence, and eventual re-arrest. All the prisoners served far less than their original sentences. Annie Kenney served less than one month, and Miss Lake served forty-eight days. Despite the relatively short times spent in prison, hunger-striking greatly taxed the prisoners' health and vitality.

In July and August 1913 arson decreased. WSPU members often went on holiday during the summer months, and the

Union never attempted major efforts at this time of year
(table 16.5).[39]

Table 16.5

Date	Place	Object	Est. Value (£)
4 July	Sutton Coldfield	unoccupied residence	3,000
7 ,,	Rivington	Sir W. Lever's bungalow	20,000
7 ,,	Southport	pier	100
		Total	23,100
4 August	Lynton	Hollerday	9,000
14 ,,	Willesden	Park Tea Rooms	250
20 ,,	Bedford	timber yard	200
22 ,,	Edinburgh	residence	300
26 ,,	North Finchley	Friern Watch	500
		Total	10,250

In July, the WSPU's London activities centred on the weekly
meetings at the Pavilion Theatre in Piccadilly Circus.
Mrs Pankhurst and Annie Kenney, both of whom were free
under the Cat and Mouse Act and eluding re-arrest, attempted to
attend a meeting held on 14 July. Annie was re-arrested after a
fight between WSPU women and the police. Seven days later,
Mrs Pankhurst was re-arrested after a similar struggle, fifty
officers being used to secure her arrest. After yet another hunger
strike, she was released from prison on 24 July in a state so
weak that her doctors gave her a transfusion.[40] On 28 July,
Mrs Pankhurst was brought on to the stage of the Pavilion
Theatre seated in a wheelchair. At the end of the meeting,
plainclothes officers arrested Annie Kenney once again, after
yet another fight with Union members. In a report filed on the
following day, Superintendent Sutherland of the Metropolitan
Police outlined the history of the disturbances at the Pavilion,
and recommended that its directors be asked to cease leasing the
hall to the WSPU; in the event of the directors' refusing to do
so, the police might consider opposing a renewal of the various
licences granted to the hall by the London County Council.[41]

17 The Great Scourge

During the spring of 1913, the leaders of the WSPU had become increasingly alarmed by what they saw as the widespread social consequences of venereal disease. In the 25 July issue of the *Suffragette*, Christabel published the first of a series of articles on the effects of prostitution and venereal disease. These articles appeared weekly until 26 September, and were reprinted in December 1913 as a book – Christabel's first – entitled *The Great Scourge and How to End It*.

In her articles, Christabel combined essentially Victorian beliefs regarding sexuality, morality, and prostitution with a series of allegations of her own concerning the prevalence and pathological consequences of venereal disease. For purposes of explication and analysis, it is probably helpful to treat these two facets of her work – the received and the idiosyncratic – separately.

Christabel's central argument was that prostitution, and a resultant spread of venereal disease, were the direct consequences of men's failure to live up to the moral standards of women (i.e. women who were not prostitutes). According to man-made morality, wrote Christabel, an immoral man was simply obeying the dictates of masculine nature. Therefore, she wrote,[1]

> One is forced to the conclusion, if one accepts men's
> account of themselves, that women's human nature is
> something very much cleaner, stronger, and higher than
> the human nature of men. But Suffragists . . . believe that
> a man can live as pure and moral a life as a woman can.
> The woman's ideal is to keep herself untouched until she
> finds her real mate. Let that be the man's ideal, too!

This basic argument was not at marked variance with beliefs which had been commonly accepted during Christabel's youth.

Victorian theorists held sexual continence in high esteem, and equated continence with moral superiority. The respectable woman was thought to have a nature more noble than that of men, because she was held to have little or no inherent sexual desire, and was therefore continent by nature. 'As a general rule', wrote Dr William Acton, 'a modest woman seldom desires any sexual gratification for herself. She submits to her husband's, but only to please him; and, but for the desire of maternity, would far rather be relieved from his attentions.'[2] In contrast, Victorian theorists were ambivalent about and troubled by male sexuality. Continence was a virtue for both the sexes, but whereas continence in women was considered natural, continence in men involved feats of character and will. F. W. Newman had written:[3]

> at no time of life is any man — married or unmarried —
> exempt from the essential duty of curbing animal impulses.
> In the struggles of a young man against unchaste surround-
> ings and raw passions, nothing so paralyzes his force of
> Will as to be told that some men have from God the gift of
> continence, and others *have it not*, and that to the latter
> class marriage is the rightful *vent*.

Belief in inherently unequal sexuality formed part of the web of social practice that both sanctified and subjugated the Victorian middle-class wife, whose legal and economic position had its sexual analogue. Women's subjection, O. R. McGregor has written, was[4]

> sexual as well as social. It is significant that submissiveness
> is always the quality most stressed by the manuals of
> conduct. Men thought of women, and women thought of
> themselves, as passive, submissive instruments of male
> gratification who must dutifully and joylessly endure the
> lawful embraces of their husbands. Their only legitimate
> satisfactions from sexual intercourse were those of mother-
> hood, and these issued from pain and suffering.

Christabel's ideas reflected Victorian orthodoxy not only with regard to the moral value of continence, but with regard to prostitution as well. 'The Great Social Evil' was, after all, the common Victorian euphemism for prostitution. Estimates of the

number of prostitutes in Victorian London alone ranged at least
as high as 80,000.* The Victorians had produced a spate of books
and articles on prostitution, and Christabel's remedy – male
chastity – had certainly been proposed often enough before.†
The entire campaign against the Contagious Diseases Acts had,
after all, been based on the premise that the alternative to
licensing and inspecting female prostitutes was male self-
control.

While Christabel's concerns with continence and prostitution
were, then, by no means unusual, her factual assertions regarding
the prevalence and consequences of venereal disease were
grossly exaggerated. Christabel wrote in the *Suffragette* of
1 August 1913 that it was 'widely accepted by medical authorities' that '75 per cent to 80 per cent of men' had been infected
with venereal disease before marriage. Some men might seem
to be cured, but among them were men whose cure was only
apparent, and who later infected their wives. 'It is therefore
hardly too much to say', wrote Christabel, 'that out of every
four men there is only one who can marry without risk to his
bride.'‡

* H. Mayhew, *London Labour and the London Poor*, vol. 4, London,
1861, p. 211. No systematic investigation of the total number of
prostitutes in Victorian London was ever made. Contemporary estimates
varied widely because of the clandestine nature of the profession and
because the incidence of prostitution increased and decreased in
inverse relation to the availability of other forms of employment
(E. M. Sigsworth and T. J. Wyke, 'A study of Victorian prostitution and
venereal disease', in *Suffer and Be Still* (ed. M. Vicinus), pp. 78–9).
† For a bibliography of Victorian writing on prostitution, see O. R.
McGregor, 'The social position of women in England, 1850–1914, a
bibliography', *British Journal of Sociology*, vol. 6, no. 1, March 1955,
p. 55, fn. 47.
‡ *Suffragette*, 1 August 1913. Christabel gave no source for her statistics. That those statistics were by no means 'widely-accepted by medical
authorities' was made clear by the report of the Royal Commission on
Venereal Diseases, established in 1913 and reporting in 1915. After
extensive inquiries, the commission stated that adequate statistics for
the incidence of venereal disease among the population of Britain as a
whole were not available. The one general estimate of the incidence of
venereal disease given by the commission related to large cities only,
and was primarily based on research in the East End of London: 'While
we have been unable to arrive at any positive figures, the evidence we

H

In an article published on 8 August, Christabel dwelt on the many illnesses brought on or fostered by specific venereal diseases: syphilis was not only a 'powerful predisposing cause' of both tuberculosis and cancer, but 'the most potent single cause of physical degeneracy and of mortality.' Gonorrhoea was 'acquired before marriage by 75 per cent. or 85 per cent. of men', and the common result of gonorrhoea in women was sterility.[5] (Christabel later wrote, on 19 September: 'Perhaps more cases of blindness are due to gonorrhoea than are due to any other cause.')[6] The cure for venereal disease was 'Votes for Women, which will give to women more self-reliance and a stronger economic position, and chastity for men.'[7]

In 'Chastity and the health of men', published on 5 September, Christabel argued that sexual immorality caused bodily weakness, since the sexual act involved a great expenditure of male energy, which energy could 'if it is not expended in that way, be transformed and expended in other ways, either physical or mental.' She added: 'Chastity for men is not only morally imperative, but is also physiologically imperative. Incontinence on the part of men causes a waste of vital force which impoverishes their moral nature and weakens their body.'[8] The belief that frequent sexual intercourse could drain men of their capacity for 'higher' endeavours had been commonly held in the Victorian era, and within the WSPU itself the belief that intense sexuality could be pernicious was certainly not held by Christabel alone. The Suffragette's (anonymous) reviewer of H. G. Wells's The Passionate Friends found the protagonist 'terribly oversexed' and one of the heroines 'morbidly over-excited about sex', and went on to state that men were in need of sexual reformation, and that 'unless a new man develops in greater numbers than at

---

have received leads us to the conclusion that the number of persons who have been affected with syphilis, acquired or congenital, cannot fall below ten per cent. of the whole population in the large cities, and the percentage affected with gonorrhoea must greatly exceed this proportion' (Royal Commission on Venereal Diseases, Final Report of the Commissioners (Cd 8189–90), HMSO, London, 1916, p. 23). No specific estimate was given of the incidence of gonorrhoea in large cities, let alone in Britain as a whole, nor were statistics presented regarding the incidence of venereal disease in males before marriage – no figures remotely resembling the percentages mentioned by Christabel appeared in the Royal Commission's report.

present, the new woman will certainly not find sex a disturbing factor in her life.'[9]

In 'The dangers of marriage', published on 12 September, and in subsequent articles, Christabel moved to the obvious conclusion of the arguments she had been presenting: marriage was to be avoided. Marriage as a physical union involved 'appalling danger to women'. Noegerath, a 'great authority', had stated that three out of five married women were infected by gonorrhoea. Wrote Christabel:[10]

> Let every woman not yet married remember that the vast majority of men contract sexual disease in one of its forms before they are married. Let every woman learn that to cure a man of such disease is long and difficult and strictly speaking impossible, since no doctor can give a guarantee that his patient is cured and will not immediately or in years to come infect his wife. . . .
>
> Never again must young women enter into marriage blindfolded. From now onwards they must be warned of the fact that marriage is intensely dangerous, until such time as men's moral standards are completely changed and they become as chaste and clean-living as women.

To the present-day reader, the exaggerations of *The Great Scourge* may seem palpable. Yet Christabel's articles were not widely criticized within the WSPU – on the contrary, the Union launched a campaign called the Moral Crusade, to propagate her ideas. It is not easy to explain why the officials and the ordinary members of the WSPU neither took exception to Christabel's allegations nor questioned seriously her fitness to continue to set WSPU policy.

That Mrs Pankhurst herself supported Christabel is not particularly surprising, given her complete loyalty to her eldest daughter in all matters. Anyway, support of the Moral Crusade did not really involve a complete change in Mrs Pankhurst's attitudes; she had often spoken of the woes that were in marriage. In August 1907, in a letter to her old political ally Sam Robinson, the Secretary of the Manchester ILP, she had congratulated Robinson on his forthcoming wedding, and added: 'There is no doubt that Miss Wilkie will do her part to make your venture one

of the few happy marriages.'[11] Sylvia Pankhurst wrote that her
mother often told women: 'Don't get married unless you care
so much that you cannot help it.'* Mrs Pankhurst's support of a
campaign which warned innocent women against the dangers
of marriage was not, then, completely out of character. From
the start, her support of the Moral Crusade was most enthusiastic: in a speech delivered on 5 August 1913, Mrs Pankhurst
said that 'the problem of prostitution' was 'the greatest evil in
the civilized world' and was 'perhaps the main reason for
militancy.'[12]

As to the lack of criticism of Christabel's ideas by her closest
associates, by 1913 the more independently-minded WSPU
leaders had either left the Union or been thrown out; those who
remained were women for whom absolute loyalty to Christabel
and Mrs Pankhurst took precedence over other considerations.
Christabel's two closest subordinates, Annie Kenney and the
WSPU's Secretary, Mrs Mabel Tuke (a widow), were child-like
women who worshipped Christabel, and were totally dominated
by her.† Mrs Pethick-Lawrence later wrote of Annie Kenney:[15]

> Her strength lay in complete surrender of mind soul and
> body to a single idea and to the incarnation of that idea in a
> single person. She was Christabel's devotee in a sense that
> was mystical . . . her devotion took the form of unquestion-
> ing faith and absolute obedience.

Christabel always eschewed romantic involvement with men,
but she could on occasion give warm affection to loyal female

* E. S. Pankhurst Papers, Internationaal Instituut, Folder 35, cancelled
pages of a chapter of *The Suffragette Movement* not included in the
published version. Such sentiments would not seem congruent with the
idyllic marriage Mrs Pankhurst claimed to have had. But the autobiographies of Sylvia and Christabel make it clear that the mild-
mannered, ultra-idealistic Dr Pankhurst had been regarded by his wife
and daughters as an exceptional man, far superior to ordinary men.
† Mrs Mabel Tuke's husband, a Captain in the South African Constabulary, had died in 1905. Early in 1906 Mrs Tuke met the Pethick-
Lawrences, while *en route* from South Africa to England. She joined the
WSPU a few months later, and was the Union's Secretary from 1906 to
1914. She was a frail woman, with limited physical endurance, and was
affectionately called 'Pansy' by her friends. The nickname had been
coined by Mrs Pethick-Lawrence.

subordinates. In late 1912 or 1913, Christabel wrote a letter to Mrs Tuke, who had collapsed and been sent to the WSPU's nursing home. The letter began 'My dear & darling Pansy', and Christabel went on to say that Mrs Tuke had 'overdone' her 'dear and precious Self', that 'even we who are really strong have been a bit under the weather at times and you are not strong', and that Mrs Tuke should visit Paris, where 'a little time with your own S.A.L. [Christabel's pseudonym] wd not be injurious perhaps. We wd look at shops but talk none. My own brave and dear, take care of yourself because you are very precious to us.'*

Granted the unquestioning devotion of Christabel's immediate subordinates, it is still possible to ask why Christabel's exaggerations did not cause the ordinary members of the WSPU to query her judgment. At least part of the explanation would seem to lie in the changing characteristics of the WSPU's membership. As has been pointed out, British feminism had largely been founded by spinsters.† Within the WSPU, a large number of leaders and subscribers were spinsters and widows; Mrs Pankhurst was a widow, and her three daughters remained unmarried during their years as WSPU leaders. Moreover, between 1906

---

* Pankhurst Papers, in the author's possession, C. Pankhurst to M. Tuke. Unfortunately, neither the date nor the place of writing appear on the letter. It was certainly written from Paris.

The reader should not be misled into believing that the salutation in itself indicated that Christabel was a Lesbian. Effusive salutations were not uncommon in letters between women in Georgian England, and as has already been mentioned Mrs Tuke was commonly called 'Pansy' by her friends.

Christabel may well have been a Lesbian, but the evidence is circumstantial rather than explicit: she never married, and the copious documents relating to her life and career do not allude to any heterosexual involvements. All the available evidence indicates that she had stronger emotional attachments to women than to men, and the markedly dominant/submissive character of her relationships with Mrs Tuke and Annie Kenney certainly seems to resemble the psychology of many Lesbian relationships. There is, however, no reason to believe that Christabel's affection for Mrs Tuke and Annie Kenney ever involved conscious sensuality, and as far as the history of the WSPU is concerned the exact nature of Christabel's sex-life is less significant than the fact that by 1913 she had grown into a state of mind in which she was completely adverse to any form of co-operation with men.

† See p. 5.

and 1913, as militancy had grown more physically demanding and therefore more attractive to relatively youthful women, the percentage of unmarried subscribers of funds to the WSPU had risen markedly. Whereas in the 1906–7 fiscal year, 45 per cent of the WSPU subscribers were unmarried, by the 1913–14 fiscal year, 63 per cent of WSPU subscribers were listed as 'Miss'. Unfortunately, the number of widows is incalculable, being subsumed under 'Mrs'. The changes in marital status of WSPU subscribers had been as in table 17.1.*

Table 17.1   Marital status of subscribers listed in WSPU *Annual Reports*

	1906–7	1907–8	1908–9	1909–10
Miss	45% [184]	60% [872]	60% [1059]	66% [2605]
Mrs	55% [221]	40% [576]	40% [718]	34% [1313]
	1910–11	1911–12	1912–13	1913–14
Miss	67% [3023]	64% [2967]	61% [2356]	63% [2612]
Mrs	33% [1496]	36% [1666]	39% [1475]	37% [1522]

The predominance of unmarried women was not confined to subscribers. All of the twenty-three WSPU organizers listed in *The Suffrage Annual of 1913* were unmarried.†

Given the high percentage of WSPU subscribers who were spinsters, and the frequent lauding of the unmarried woman law-yer, doctor, mountain-climber, etc., in articles in the *Suffragette*, it is possible that ready acceptance of Christabel's ideas stemmed in part from many unmarried WSPU members' desires to legitimize the socially and economically precarious role of the unmarried woman. WSPU members had often alluded to

* *Annual Reports* of the WSPU, 1906–14. As many donations were made either anonymously or through local branches of the WSPU, the number of subscribers does not indicate the total membership of the WSPU. Nor should these figures be taken to represent the relative support of the Union in different years, as under the circumstances prevailing from late 1912 on, many women preferred to subscribe funds anonymously because of the increasing threat of Government moves against financial supporters of the WSPU.

† *The Suffrage Annual and Women's Who's Who*, 1913 (A.J.R., ed.), London, 1913.

heterosexual activity as a vehicle for the satisfaction of selfish male pleasure, and frequently associated active heterosexuality with either immorality or the male domination involved in marriage. If marriage was as intensely dangerous as Christabel claimed, then fortunate the woman who had not married!

It is also possible to inquire into the effects of Christabel's articles on the size of the membership of the WSPU. The Union never divulged total membership figures and claimed not to keep a membership list.* From 28 February 1909 to 28 October 1913, however, the WSPU did publish the membership fees it received from new members, who were required to pay one shilling to join. The number of new members who joined each year, as derived from new members' fees, was as shown in table 17.2.†

Table 17.2 Number of new members per fiscal year as calculated from new member fees

	1909–10	1910–11	1911–12	1912–13	28 Feb.–28 Oct. 1913 [First 8 months of fiscal year only]
New Member Fees	£222/19/0	£217/0/0	£180/0/0	£119/0/0	£46/3/0
New Members	4459	4340	3600	2380	923

There had clearly been a marked decline in the rate of new memberships between 1909 and 28 October 1913. If each fiscal

* 'They have confirmed at their office at Clement's Inn . . . that they do not know their numbers, they assured us that they do not keep any list, and do not even know their London membership!' Letter to the editor from E. L. Somervell, Hon. Sec. Women's National Anti-Suffrage League, in *The Times*, 13 October 1909.
† Based on membership fees published in *Annual Reports* of the WSPU, 1909–13. During 1913–14, the WSPU ceased giving new members' fees as a separate item in the *Annual Report*. For the first eight months of the fiscal year beginning 28 February 1913, summaries of new members' fees received were published in the *Suffragette*, which is the source of the figures given.

year is compared with the previous fiscal year, new memberships had declined by about 3 per cent in 1910–11, 17 per cent in 1911–12, 34 per cent in 1912–13, and at least 42 per cent in fiscal 1913–14, assuming that the rate of new memberships in the four months after 28 October 1913 was not greater than the rate of new memberships during the previous eight months. It is probable that the Union ceased to publish new members' fees after 28 October 1913 in order to avoid publicizing the WSPU's rapidly decreasing ability to attract converts.

By the time Christabel's articles on prostitution and venereal disease had begun to appear – the first article was published on 25 July 1913 – the marked decline in the rate of new memberships was already well established. The arson campaign itself was undoubtedly the most important single factor that fostered the decline, and given the highly unfavourable public reaction which the arson campaign aroused, the effect that Christabel's articles may have had in furthering the decline is incalculable. She was certainly propagating ideas to which only a small minority of British women could conceivably have given unreserved assent; in particular, her claim that the danger of contracting venereal disease through marriage was so great that marriage itself should be avoided was hardly calculated to foster the transformation of vast numbers of married women into ardent supporters of the WSPU.

The WSPU's espousal of Christabel's ideas affected not only the Union's ability to attract new members, but its attitudes toward individual male suffragists as well as toward all parties and organizations in which men took part. Prior to the summer of 1913, the WSPU had not been, in principle, anti-male. Between 1906 and 1912, F. W. Pethick-Lawrence had provided the Union with indispensible legal and financial expertise, and writers and journalists such as Brailsford, Nevinson, Zangwill, and Laurence Housman had contributed articles to *Votes for Women* and spoken from WSPU platforms.* In addition, the WSPU

* Moreover, an organization called the Men's Political Union had been founded in 1910 to support the WSPU. I have been unable to obtain any concrete information regarding the size and activities of the MPU, beyond the fact that it ceased to be closely tied to the WSPU after the Pethick-Lawrences were ousted in October 1912.

had given its full support to George Lansbury's ill-fated campaign in Bromley and Bow.

After the summer of 1913, however, the WSPU was unwilling to permit either the active involvement of individual men in its affairs, or to work in conjunction with any organization which had male members. An emphasis on the exclusively female character of the WSPU underlay Christabel's subsequent refusals to co-operate either with newly emergent suffrage organizations in which men took part (see pp. 217–26), with suffragist politicians such as Lloyd George and Grey, or – more broadly – to consider any form of alliance with the more rebellious sections of the Labour movement or the Ulster Unionists. In *The Strange Death of Liberal England*, George Dangerfield quite rightly pointed out that the suffragettes, militant trade unionists, and Ulster Protestants were all in revolt against the emphasis placed by 'Liberal England' on security, respectability, and the virtue of political compromise. Dangerfield delineated, with considerable literary ability, the psychological characteristics which the suffragettes, trade unionists, and Ulstermen had in common, but he did not suggest that their revolts were allied, save in terms of a similarity of unconscious motivation. After the summer of 1913 – if not well before – the WSPU would have been psychologically incapable of alliance with either the Labour movement or the Ulster Unionists, for following Christabel's dictum that Mr Punch's 'advice to those about to marry – Don't!' had a 'true and terrible application to the facts of the case', and that 'self-respecting women' would increasingly find men unfit companions, the WSPU was no longer interested in the possibility of aid from male allies.[14] The belief that women would become conscious of their own worth only through independence of men and men's movements was one of the most important determinants of Christabel's policies from the summer of 1913 until the outbreak of war, one year later.

H*

18 The Arson Campaign, Continued

By July 1913, the physical strength of Mrs Pankhurst and Annie Kenney had become sapped by repeated hunger strikes, and in August the two women departed for a much-needed holiday on the continent. While abroad, Mrs Pankhurst decided that in October she would go on a lecture-tour of America. She felt that the tour would give her the relaxation of two sea-voyages, that she would be able to speak in public without fear of re-arrest, and that she could raise funds for the Union.* Annie Kenney, on the other hand, decided to risk re-arrest on her expired licence by returning to England to speak at the Union's first major autumn meeting.

That meeting was held at the Pavilion Theatre on 6 October 1913. It was attended by about a thousand women. WSPU leaders were now being re-arrested repeatedly, and Mrs Drummond, the first speaker, exhorted her audience:[1]

> Stand together. You don't need to depend on leaders. You
> have got the spirit of leaders in each one of your bosoms,
> and whatever you do, keep the flag flying until the
> Government realize that the movement does not depend
> upon leaders. . . . Build up your Organizations, strengthen
> them, and keep the movement going.

As Mrs Drummond was sitting down, police rushed on stage to arrest Annie Kenney. The Chief Inspector was then, he later reported, 'seized by about half a dozen strong muscular women, who acted more like wild animals than like human beings. Miss Kenney was released from my custody'.[2] After a struggle, ten women were arrested and Annie Kenney was spirited back to prison in a hansom cab. In the wake of the fighting, the directors of the Pavilion Theatre refused to permit further

---

* The US tour netted £3,684 for the WSPU. See *Eighth Annual Report*, fn. *, p. 227.

meetings of the WSPU on the premises. In the ensuing months, Christabel was forced to devote much correspondence to the search for a large hall in London. *

Annie Kenney did not remain in prison long. She went on a hunger strike and was released on a five days' licence on 13 October. She was not re-arrested until 22 May 1914, and ultimately served only twenty-eight days of her original eighteen-month sentence, yet the very hunger-striking that procured her release had undermined her health, and ill health and the desire to avoid re-arrest led her to remain in hiding or abroad for most of the seven months that she was free. Between 13 October 1913 and 22 May 1914 she delivered only two speeches.

The Prisoners' Temporary Discharge for Ill-Health Act had been designed to make forced feeding unnecessary, and forced feeding had indeed been suspended after the final ratification of the Act on 25 April 1913. However, the licencees' unwillingness to permit re-arrest and their involvements in illegal activities while free on licences and after the expiration of licences were making a mockery of the Act. In early October, Mary Richardson, who was evading re-arrest on an expired licence, was captured in the vicinity of a flaming mansion. Convicted of arson, she proceeded to go on a hunger strike. Rather than simply release her to commit arson once again, the Government re-introduced forced feeding, which now once again became widely used against hunger-striking suffragettes.

Forced feeding or no, the Government's efforts to halt the arson campaign were rendered ineffectual by the inability of the police to apprehend more than a handful of arsonists. Between 25 April 1913, the day the Cat and Mouse Act took effect, and 15 November 1913, forty-two cases of major arson were reported, but arrests were made in connection with only eight cases.[3] Arsonists were particularly hard to catch because they did not confine their activities to any one locale or to any single class of building; the Union's sole criterion in choosing structures to be burned was that no human being or animal be inside. The files of the Metropolitan Police give some indication of just how fumbling efforts at apprehension could be. The following minutes were written on 1 October 1913:[4]

* See Pankhurst Papers, in the author's possession, correspondence of C. Pankhurst, October 1913–April 1914.

It would be a great convenience if two motor cycles were purchased for the use of the C.I. Department. . . . The want of them is much felt in the Special Branch. The W.S.P.U. have two cars which they use both for committing acts of incendiarism and for escaping arrest, and it has been useless to keep observation on the cars because as soon as they are out in the country they travel too fast for any conveyance that Police officers can obtain. A motor bicycle would make it possible to follow them.

As a start one motor bicycle would perhaps suffice.

The CID was not willing to purchase a new motorcycle, let alone a car as powerful as those utilized by the WSPU. Instead, Sir Edward Henry suggested the hiring of a motorcycle as an experiment. He was informed that it was difficult to hire motor-cycles 'except at an exorbitant price', and that 'it would be cheaper' to augment the salary of a policeman named Smith who already owned one and who would be paid extra to use it to follow the WSPU cars.[5] Smith's efforts did not meet with success, as his motorcycle could not match the speed of the WSPU cars, and tended to stall easily. The experiment was eventually discontinued, in January 1914.[6]

As the arson campaign continued without check, suffragist MPs continued to complain that arson was damaging the very cause it was supposed to promote. On 15 October 1913, Philip Snowden wrote to Mrs Arncliffe-Sennett:[7]

I am convinced that the doings of the Pankhurstians are inflicting such injury on the suffrage movement that it is the duty of all who want women to have the vote to protest against their conduct.

On 23 October, Lloyd George said:[8]

in a Parliamentary sense, the movement has gone back. . . . In the last two Sessions we have been beaten, and you may depend upon it that, in a movement like this, Parliament represents the temporary mood of the nation. . . . For the moment, the militants have created a situation which is the worst I have ever seen for woman suffrage in Parliament.

Protestations or no, the burning of buildings continued, the major destruction in the autumn of 1913 being as shown in table 18.1.[9]

Table 18.1

Date	Place	Object	Est. Value (£)
5 Sept.	Dulwich	college laboratory	300
12 ,,	Sutton	Stanstad	500
13 ,,	Kenton	railway station	1,000
23 ,,	Seaforth	asylum	20,000
26 ,,	Yarmouth	timber yard	30,000
		Total	51,800
6 Oct.	Hampton-on-Thames	The Elms	1,500
23 ,,	Bristol	Combe Dingle Pavilion	2,000
26 ,,	Slough	residence	1,000
27 ,,	Bramshott	Mill House	1,000
28 ,,	Bradford	Shirley Manor	5,000
		Total	10,500
11 Nov.	Manchester	Alexandra Park House	200
11 ,,	Bristol	Begbrook	4,000
21 ,,	Oxford	timber wharf	2,000
23 ,,	Bath	Bathford	3,000
		Total	9,200

Though the WSPU remained impervious to criticism levelled at it from outside, the Union was not immune from internal dissension, and in November 1913 a serious dispute developed between Christabel and Sylvia Pankhurst. After George Lansbury's defeat in November 1912, Sylvia had devoted her considerable energy to rebuilding the East End branches of the WSPU into a semi-autonomous organization, the East London Federation of the WSPU. The ELF differed from the national WSPU in some important respects: it advocated universal adult suffrage, its membership was working-class, it did not sponsor arson, and it did not espouse anti-male attitudes. In fact, the

ELF welcomed both men and women as members, and Sylvia worked closely with the male-led Labour movement. While the ELF rejected secret arson as such, it did not eschew violence: in August 1913 Sylvia advised her followers to learn ju-jitsu and to bring sticks to meetings.[10] By October, Sylvia's lieutenant, Zelie Emerson, was openly advocating violence against the police, saying:[11]

> If you do not care to break their heads you can knock off their helmets and present them to the East London Federation. . . . You want to be strong, and there is no better object to practice your strength upon than some of McKenna's pups who stand out in the entrance there. They are large and fat and you cannot miss them if you aim right.

The meeting ended in tumult. On 5 November, Sir Francis Vane was introduced to an ELF meeting. He proposed drilling under officers, and Sylvia Pankhurst told the meeting that as Sir Edward Carson was arming his men, the ELF was justified in doing likewise.[12]

Sylvia was also pursuing a path independent of the policies of the national WSPU in that she did not restrict her political activities to the campaign for women's enfranchisement. On 1 November 1913, the *Daily Herald* held a meeting at the Albert Hall to protest against the lockout of the Dublin workers and the imprisonment of James Larkin. Sylvia appeared on the platform along with Lansbury and Connolly. Five days later, the *Daily Herald* announced the ELF's formation of a 'People's Army', and stated that 'every day the industrial rebels and the Suffrage rebels march nearer together'.[13] Lansbury and his associates had sent emissaries to Christabel in early August, and she had rejected the overtures made at that time. Christabel now wrote to Sylvia:[14]

> I shall repudiate any connection between the Herald League & the WSPU & in this & every possible way shall make it clear that we are absolutely independent of this and of all men's parties & movements. . . .
>
>   Before you were approached to speak at the Herald League Albert Hall meeting, I had been asked whether

Annie Kenney or Miss Richardson wd speak. I said *no*.
Upon getting this refusal from me – which was also a
refusal to have the W.S.P.U. represented on the platform,
they approached you & got your consent to speak.

Christabel soon used the pages of the *Suffragette* to deny the
possibility of an alliance with the *Daily Herald* League.
Independence of all men's parties was the basis of the WSPU.
The League was a men's organization and a 'class' (i.e. working-
class) organization, whereas the Union welcomed women of all
social classes.[15]

In reply, Sylvia issued a circular in which she declared that
the ELF had not formed an alliance with the *Daily Herald*
League. She went on to say:[16]

I went to the Albert Hall meeting to put the question of
Votes for Women before a great audience of 10,000 people.

There was a time when the W.S.P.U. held far more meetings than any other society. That is not the case today . . .
we must surely recognize the fact that the holding of public
meetings is an important part of our work, if only for the
making of new militants.

In stressing the importance of mass public meetings (the weekly
meetings at the Pavilion were for Union members and sympathizers), and in remaining free of involvement with the secret
arson campaign, Sylvia had clearly been turning away from the
tactics decreed by Christabel. On 27 November, Christabel wrote
to her revisionist sister:[17]

I have seen a circular letter sent out by you. I disapprove
and condemn it very strongly.

In a recent letter to me you referred to the fact that we
do not ask you to speak out at meetings. The reason for
this is that it is essential for the public to understand that
you are working independently of us.

As you have a complete confidence in your own policy &
way of doing things, this should suit you perfectly.

There is room for everybody in the world, but conflicting
views and divided counsels inside the W.S.P.U. there cannot
be.

For the moment, however, the ELF remained at least nominally affiliated with the WSPU.

Fissiparous tendencies were not limited to those on the Union's left. At the end of November, a number of politically moderate members, former members, and sympathizers began meeting in secret. The group included H. W. Nevinson, who wrote in his journal:

30 November [1913][18]
We discussed . . . Christabel's wrecking of WSPU by absences & suspicions. I urged delay & attempt at terms, but all others agreed it would be useless, all were for founding a new mixed society under chosen com[ee]. The thought of ruin now threatening that wonderful old WSPU filled me with distress. What power it had 18 months ago. . . . And now all going to pieces through one young woman's simple mistake.

3 December [1913][19]
Gathering in Gillespie's to discuss idea of new men & women's union. All very mournful about condition of WSPU, espec. as Mrs. Pankhurst returns fr. America tonight, & is to be arrested on board.

Mrs Pankhurst was indeed arrested on landing at Plymouth. A meeting of welcome had been planned for her at the Empress Theatre in Earl's Court on 7 December. Now 4,500 women attended what became a meeting to protest against her re-arrest. At the meeting, Mrs Drummond asked for recruits for the bodyguard, a new female strong-arm group which would protect Mrs Pankhurst and other 'mice' from re-arrest. The forming of the bodyguard had come in part as a response to the deteriorating physical condition of Mrs Pankhurst and other WSPU leaders. Hunger-striking brought about release from prison, but it also undermined the hunger-striker's health. Annie Kenney had to be carried into the Empress Theatre on a stretcher. The possibility that a women's strong-arm group might give rise to spectacles which would discredit the WSPU in the public eye does not seem to have occurred to the Union's members. To doubt the wisdom of Union policy would have

been to doubt the judgment of Christabel, of whom Mrs Drummond said at the meeting on 7 December:[20]

> She knows everything, and she can see through everything
> (applause) . . . Miss Christabel Pankhurst has taken you
> step by step along the dangerous path, and every time she
> has told you when there was a pitfall, and you who are
> members of the W.S.P.U. are the only people who stepped
> over them.

Mrs Drummond was not alone in attributing virtually clairvoyant
powers to Christabel. Christabel herself had written to a
Mrs Bradley on 17 November:[21]

> . . . one sees a great work to be done by the Union in the
> future. The future & its tasks were never so clearly visible
> to me as now. It is like a journey – the higher one climbs –
> the further one sees.

Within two days after Mrs Pankhurst's arrest at Plymouth on
4 December, three major burnings occurred. In December 1913
the amount of damage attributed to suffragettes was higher than
in any previous month, as table 18.2 shows.[22]

Table 18.2

Date	Place	Object	Est. Value (£)
5 Dec.	Wemyss Bay	Kelly House	27,000
6 "	Liverpool	exhibition	2,000
6 "	Rusholme	exhibition	15,000
15 "	Aigburth	St Anne's	3,000
15 "	Devonport	Roundabouts	2,000
15 "	Devonport	timber yard	5,000
21 "	Cheltenham	Alstone Lawn	350
25 "	Eastchurch	hay sheds	140
		Total	54,490

There was a lull in January, but the value of those structures
destroyed in February 1914 was again the highest ever, though
only by dint of the burning of a building valued at £40,000
(see table 18.3).[23]

Table 18.3

Date	Place	Object	Source	Est. Value (£)
8 Jan.	Cheltenham	St Paul's College	*Daily Chron.*, 9 Jan.	6,000 to 10,000
24 ,,	Lanark	mansion	*The Times*, 26 Jan.	many thousands
24 ,,	Lee	pavilion	*Lewisham Journal*, 30 Jan.	200
			Total	8,200 to 12,200
3 Feb.	Perth	House of Ross	*The Times*, 5 Feb.	5,000
3 ,,	Perth	Abercuhill Castle	*The Times*, 5 Feb.	several hundred
3 ,,	Perth	St Fillian's Castle	*The Times*, 5 Feb.	several thousand
7 ,,	Perth	highland villa	*Scotsman*, 9 Feb.	2,000
12 ,,	Birmingham	Carnegie Library	*The Times*, 13 Feb.	2,000
22 ,,	Surbiton	pavilion	*Surrey Comet*, 25 Feb.	1,000
24 ,,	Somerset	Redlynch House	*Western Gazette*, 27 Feb.	40,000
26 ,,	East Lothian	Whitekirk	*The Times*, 27 Feb.	10,000
			Total	62,000 to 65,000

A drawing of Bristol in flames, captioned 'How Men Fought for Liberty' and 'The Burning of the City of Bristol, 1831', appeared on the front page of the *Suffragette* of 16 January 1914. In that issue, Christabel claimed once again that the vote would be won when the WSPU had created 'a difficulty so great as to be found intolerable by the politicians.'[24] The arson campaign did not, however, appear to be creating such a 'difficulty'. The inconvenience created was not insufferable, in part because the scope of the campaign was limited. It was not really a campaign of terror, in that the Union took care not to burn down buildings with people or animals inside. Yet neither were the buildings to be burned chosen with an eye to their commercial value – no effort was made to burn down factories owned by wealthy Liberals. The lack of any economic intent to the arson campaign was symptomatic of the WSPU leaders' inability to analyse political forces in terms of economic interests. Finally, the burnings were clearly the work of a relatively small group of women; the campaign obviously did not involve the threat of a mass uprising or an orgy of destruction. What the political reaction would in fact have been, had truly intolerable difficulties been created, must remain a matter for speculation.

Although the arson campaign actually involved a somewhat circumscribed attempt at coercion, Christabel was thoroughly convinced of the ultimate effectiveness of her policies, and it was because Sylvia Pankhurst and the East London Federation had failed to follow those policies that Christabel now repeatedly asked Sylvia to visit her. In mid-January 1914, Sylvia travelled to Paris, where she was told by Christabel that the ELF must become totally separate from the WSPU. When Sylvia asked for reasons, she was told that her speaking at the meeting for Larkin's release was against WSPU policy, that the national WSPU did not have men in the bodyguard whereas the People's Army included men, and that although she had faith in what might be accomplished by stirring up working-class women, the national leaders had most faith in what could be done by women of means and influence.[25] At the end of January, Sylvia agreed that the ELF would become a separate organization. For the first time, a Pankhurst had been cast out of the WSPU. Yet the ELF had already achieved such a degree of *de facto* independence that no real change took place, the ELF's affiliation with the WSPU having been merely nominal for almost a year.

The ELF was not the only suffrage group that established itself outside the WSPU early in 1914. The narrowness of WSPU ideology and policy had alienated not only Sylvia Pankhurst and her working-class followers, but also some of the WSPU's most influential upper middle-class supporters. On 6 February, the suffragists who had met on 30 November and 3 December (and surely at intervals thereafter) announced the establishment of a new organization, the United Suffragists, which would be open to both men and women, and to militants and nonmilitants.[26] Many of the officers of the new organization had been important supporters of the WSPU. The Committee of the United Suffragists included Gerald Gould, H. W. Nevinson and Evelyn Sharp. Among the vice-presidents were Mrs Hertha Ayrton, Dr Louisa Garrett Anderson, Mrs Evelina Haverfield, George Lansbury, Mrs Israel Zangwill and Laurence Housman. Nevinson, Evelyn Sharp, and Laurence Housman had all written regularly for *Votes for Women* when it was still the official organ of the WSPU. Gould, the publisher of the *Daily Herald*, had printed the *Suffragette* when its presses were raided, had sought the WSPU's alliance with the *Daily Herald* League, and had given the Union financial support. Dr Louisa Garrett Anderson, the daughter of Dr Elizabeth Garrett Anderson, Mrs Hertha Ayrton, a well-known scientist, and Mrs Evelina Haverfield were all women of distinction in their own right who had given active support to the WSPU. All three had marched on Black Friday. In addition, Mrs Ayrton, Dr Anderson and Mrs Zangwill had all made substantial yearly contributions to the Union's funds between 1907 and 1913. Mrs Ayrton was one of the Union's largest contributors; she had given over £1,000 a year to the WSPU in 1909–10, 1910–11 and 1912–13.[27]

One of the members of the Committee of the United Suffragists, Mrs H. D. Harben, was the wife of a wealthy barrister who had himself given financial support and legal advice to the WSPU. A political admirer of Christabel, H. D. Harben had visited her in Paris several times and carried on a regular correspondence with her in 1913 and 1914. In January or early February 1914, Harben wrote Christabel a long letter in which he severely criticized her policies. The letter, a substantial part of which follows, is one of the few surviving instances of a knowledgable and sympathetic insider's critical assessment of the problems of the WSPU in early 1914: *

* Pankhurst Papers, in the author's possession, H. D. Harben to C. Pankhurst, Newland Park, Chalfont St Giles, Bucks, n.d., typescript draft or copy. The letter was almost certainly written in January or early February 1914, for Christabel replied to it on 15 February 1914. She did not answer the criticisms in detail, but wrote, 'it is impossible

[I] should have tried to tell you frankly how the whole
situation strikes me as one outside the W.S.P.U. It is not
easy to say but I will put it baldly for what it is worth and
I hope you will take it quite impersonally. For two years at
least and especially during the last twelve months the whole
efforts of the Government have been concentrated on the
attempt to isolate you and make you appear to the public as
an extremely discredited section which no respectable or
sensible people will have anything to do with . . . those
efforts of the Govt. would have been foredoomed to failure
were it not that from inside your own organisation and as I
suppose from you yourself they have found their most
valuable assistance. One by one every approach towards you
has been cut off from the inside and your chief officials at
Lincoln's Inn House have been going round the Branches
turning people out neck and crop. Loyalty and concentra-
tion (magnificent things in themselves) have been interpreted so as to exclude to my knowledge some of your most
loyal and arduous workers – people whom you yourself if
you knew them personally would I feel sure love and
admire. People are now saying that from the leader of a
great movement you are developing into the ringleader of
a little rebel Rump; and though I personally do not feel and
never have felt that actual numbers counted for anything, I
am as convinced as ever I was of anything in my life from
what I have seen of your Meetings and the personnel of
your organisation during this last six months that the
quality of your following is not what it was either in ability,
originality, spontaneity, human sympathy or any of those
characteristics which have been so striking a feature of your
Movement until quite recently.

   . . . in any case you can rely on me to help you
financially. . . .

   I should not have written at all were it not that you are

---

that the occupants of certain positions in the W.S.P.U. shall be self
chosen. We who are responsible for the campaign must decide who is
most fitted for each particular piece of work. Also if we are not satisfied
that a person occupying a given position is suitable to *retain* it, she
cannot retain it' (Pankhurst Papers, in the author's possession. C.
Pankhurst to H. D. Harben, Paris, 15 February 1914).

not in England, you govern largely by hearsay, and it may
be that you do not always hear all.

Harben was not the only informed suffragist who believed that
Christabel had become out of touch with the movement she
commanded. H. W. Nevinson later wrote:[28]

> During her residence in Paris it seemed to me that Christabel
> lost touch with the remaining members of the W.S.P.U.
> and of the political situation in London . . . in her absence
> the Union proceeded from one phase of destructive violence
> to another, and its general tone appeared to me to degenerate.

The Moral Crusade, the increasingly exaggerated claims of
Christabel's infallibility, and the increasingly frequent use of a
rhetoric of violence together involved a marked change in the
tone of the WSPU. The change in tone was exacerbated by the
ever-present danger of re-arrest of the Union's leaders, a danger
which was increasingly imparting a frenetic quality to the
WSPU's public activities.

Still subject to the three-year sentence she had received on
3 April 1913, Mrs Pankhurst could no longer address a public
meeting without being re-arrested, so the newly-formed
bodyguard, which comprised about thirty women, was now used
to protect her from re-arrest. On 8 February 1914, she addressed
a crowd from one of the windows of 2 Campden Hill Square, and
she later escaped with the aid of the bodyguard, who managed to
divert the police. On 21 February, she spoke from a balcony in
Glebe Place, Chelsea, and the following evening she once more
escaped with the aid of the bodyguard, who used Indian clubs to
attack the police surrounding the house.[29] Mrs Pankhurst was
able to take a certain macabre relish in the battle. She wrote to
her friend the composer Ethel Smyth:[30]

> Sunday night, as you know, we pulled it off. . . . How I
> wish you could have seen the masterly way the attack was
> made simultaneously from outside and inside. The police
> were between two fires. While the battle raged, I, with two
> others, dashed up the area steps and into the car. The big
> detective stood at the area door and was trying to block the
> car, and a girl engaged him single-handed with an Indian

club; he had his umbrella, and she kept him off until I was
away. All I regret is that I saw so little of the fight,
being otherwise engaged myself. The sequel you will have
seen. – only two arrested and *three days*' imprisonment!!!
What an encouragement to fight! The whole affair hushed
up. . . . As for our fighting women they are in great form
and very proud of their exploits as you can imagine. The
girl who had her head cut open would not have it stitched
as she wanted to keep the scar as big as possible! The real
warrior spirit!

At Campden Hill Square and Glebe Place, Mrs Pankhurst had
managed to address crowds from the windows of private houses
without being re-arrested. She now made more ambitious plans
to address a public meeting at St Andrew's Hall in Glasgow on
9 March.* On the day before the meeting, Mrs Pankhurst wrote

* Meanwhile, the fiscal year of the WSPU had ended on 28 February
1914. The annual report for 1913–14 stated that the total cash receipts
were £46,876. A total of £35,710 in receipts had been claimed in
1912–13, so a substantial increase had been achieved (*Seventh and Eighth
Annual Reports, National Women's Social and Political Union*) (see
table).

Cash Statements

1 March 1912 to 28 February 1913		1 March 1913 to 28 February 1914	
Subscriptions	£23,156		£28,157
Sale of Tickets for Meetings and Collections	£5,002		£4,694
		[Incl. Fair & Fete Receipts & Membership Fees]	
Interest	£345		£361
Brought Forward	£7,208		£9,980
Mrs Pankhurst's American Tour	—		£3,684
Total	£35,711	Total	£46,876

The apparently large increase in total receipts represented not an upsurge of popular support, but an adept handling of WSPU finances
and bookkeeping. The total for 1913–14 included both the nonrecurring
income from Mrs Pankhurst's American tour, and the exceptionally
large amount of cash brought forward from the previous fiscal year,

to Ethel Smyth: 'There is now a Scotch bodyguard and they are eager for the fray.'[31] In St Andrew's Hall, hidden behind flowers and foliage and enclosed in a covering of green muslin, two strands of barbed wire were stretched from one side of the speaker's platform to the other.

Mrs Pankhurst entered the hall well before the meeting began, and the bodyguard gathered around her on the platform. She had already begun to address the audience of 4,000 when a large body of Glasgow police rushed into the hall and stormed the platform. The bodyguard hurled chairs and potted plants, and one woman fired a number of blanks from a revolver.[32] The police used their truncheons. After much violence, Mrs Pankhurst was seized by detectives and carried off in a cab in which, bruised and shocked, she was forced to sit on the floor at the feet of the police.

Imprisoned once more, Mrs Pankhurst again went on a hunger strike, and was released five days after her incarceration. She was exhausted by the ordeal she had gone through, and did not appear in public again until 21 May. In Glasgow, the bodyguard had been a liability in that it had been unable to prevent her re-arrest, and had caused the police to use violence in effecting it, whereas in earlier days she had been arrested with a modicum of civility which had on occasion approached the ceremonial.

The day after Mrs Pankhurst's arrest in Glasgow, Mary Richardson, in protest against the arrest, slashed Velazquez' *Rokeby Venus* at the National Gallery. In fact, four of the five

---

over £2,700 more than had been brought forward in 1912–13. The large sum obtained from subscriptions in 1913–14 would seem to show a substantial increase in the members' financial support of the Union, but in reality the increased receipts from subscriptions largely reflected the Union's ability to attract a few more major donors: whereas in 1912–13 two persons had given sums of £1,000 or more, the total of the two donations being £2,105, in 1913–14 five persons gave £1,000 or more and the total was £5,878. Thus, the total subscriptions in 1912–13, omitting major donations of £1,000 or more, had been £21,051. Such subscriptions had risen to £22,278 in 1913–14, an increase of about 6 per cent. The markedly higher total receipts of 1913–14 did not then represent a great upsurge of popular support for the WSPU – indeed, receipts from meetings and collections had decreased. Nevertheless, the WSPU had shown a phenomenal ability to garner funds from a variety of sources.

major acts of arson committed in March 1914 occurred within five days after Mrs Pankhurst's arrest (see table 18.4).[33]

Table 18.4

Date	Place	Object	Source	Est. Value (£)
10 Mar.	Nottingham	Bulcote Farm	*Nottingham Guardian*, 11 March	2,000–3,000
12 "	Ayrshire	Robertsland House	*The Times*, 13 March	6,000
13 "	Birmingham	pavilion	*Birmingham Daily Post*, 14 March	300–400
14 "	Bristol	timber yard	*Bath and Wilts Chronicle*, 15 March	3,000
27 "	Belfast	Abbeylands (residence)	*The Times*, 28 March	20,000
			Total	25,900 to 27,000

That the last act of arson in March 1914 had occurred in Belfast was not mere chance. In a letter dated 10 September 1913, the Secretary of the Ulster Unionist Council, R. L. Bates, had informed the Ulster Unionist Women's Council that draft articles for a Provisional Government included the enfranchisement of women. This policy was not, however, confirmed by the subsequent speeches of Unionist leaders, and on 9 March 1914 Sir Edward Carson informed a WSPU delegation that he could not commit the Unionists to women's suffrage, as his colleagues were not united on the question, and he did not propose to cause dissension by introducing the matter. Dorothy Evans, the WSPU's organizer for Ulster, immediately accused Carson of 'a breach of faith and a betrayal of Ulster women', and announced that the Ulster WSPU declared 'war upon you and the Ulster Unionist Parliamentary Committee.'[34] One week later, Abbeylands, a mansion on the grounds of which Ulster Unionists had been holding military drills, was destroyed by fire. The WSPU always viewed Irish politics strictly in terms of their relationship to the campaign for the vote, and from this time on the suffragettes regarded the Ulster Unionists as political enemies and competitors for public attention.

For over a year, the WSPU had been legally barred from holding meetings in the parks of metropolitan London. The Ulster Unionists were not so prohibited, and the Union Defence League planned to hold a large meeting with fourteen platforms in Hyde Park on 4 April. The WSPU decided to stage a competing demonstration of its own. On 4 April, Mrs Drummond and a few hundred women entered Hyde Park, where vast throngs had assembled to hear Balfour, Milner, Carson and Long. Mrs Drummond and her small band were soon surrounded by a jeering crowd and pushed away from the Unionist platforms. Mrs Drummond managed to speak for a time seated on a supporter's shoulders before being arrested by the police and escorted out of the park.

During the following months, the militant campaign of the WSPU was increasingly overshadowed by the Ulster crisis. Christabel wrote in the *Suffragette* on 1 May 1914:[35]

Arrest Carson! Arrest Bonar Law! Such is the demand made
not by the W.S.P.U. only, but by all right-thinking people
in the country. Either arrest these men and their associates,
or cancel the sentences already passed upon militant
Suffragists, and never again arrest and imprison women who
break the law, in order, as the Ulster militants express it in
their case, to vindicate their right to be British citizens and
to be governed, through their consent expressed as voters,
by the Imperial Parliament!

Of the seven cases of arson committed by WSPU members between 10 April and 3 May 1914, five were in Ulster (see table 18.5).[36]

The WSPU's anti-Unionist foray into Hyde Park had been a rather impromptu affair. In contrast, the major demonstration held on 21 May 1914 was carefully planned months in advance. The WSPU had announced in early January: 'Ministers having degraded themselves by their cruelty and treachery, the WSPU desires no further interviews with them and will therefore make a direct approach to the King as the head of the nation.'[37] On

Table 18.5

Date	Place	Object	Source	Est. Value (£)
10 April	Belfast	Orlands Mansion house	*The Times*, 4 June	several thousand
16 ”	Derry		*Northern Whig*, 17 April	500
17 ”	Yarmouth	pier	*The Times*, 18 April	10,000
18 ”	Belfast	tea house	*The Times*, 20 April	several thousand
22 ”	Belfast	Annadale House	*The Times*, 23 April	500
28 ”	Felixstowe	Bath Hotel	*The Times*, 29 April	40,000
			Total	53,000 to 57,000
3 May	Belfast	pavilion	*Northern Whig*, 4 May	500
15 ”	Birmingham	pavilion	*Birmingham Daily Post*, 16 May	600–700
17 ”	Birmingham	grandstand	*Birmingham Daily Post*, 18 May	several thousand
22 ”	Dundee	hospital	*People's Journal*, 23 May	2,000
			Total	4,100 to 6,300

29 January, the Union sent its members a duplicated letter signed by Mrs Pankhurst:[38]

> I earnestly hope that every member of our Union who is not already engaged in active service will enroll herself as a member of the deputation that will, on behalf of the W.S.P.U., approach the King early in the Session.

As Mrs Pankhurst's letter was addressed to the generality of WSPU members, and was sent weeks before any request was sent to George V, it is clear that, from the start, a large public demonstration rather than an actual deputation to the King was envisaged. Not until 25 February did Mrs Pankhurst write to George V asking for an audience:[39]

> we frequently hear of the influence exerted by Your Majesty in political crises. . . .
>
>   Our right as women to be heard and to be aided by Your Majesty is far stronger than any such right possessed by men, because it is based upon our lack of every other Constitutional means of securing the redress of our grievances. We have no power to vote for Members of Parliament. . . .

Mrs Pankhurst's letter was brought to the attention of the Home Secretary, McKenna, who advised against receiving a deputation. McKenna later stated that by constitutional practice he was required to advise His Majesty in such matters, that requests for audiences could but rarely be granted, and that 'If the request for an audience comes from a person under sentence of penal servitude openly defying the judgment of the Court, it is clearly the duty of the Home Secretary to advise His Majesty not to grant an audience.'[40] Its request refused, the Union completed plans for a demonstration in which women would attempt to gain entrance to Buckingham Palace, just as they had attempted to gain entrance to the House of Commons in previous years. In order to minimize the possibility of a repetition of Black Friday, the WSPU scheduled the demonstration during daylight hours and launched a publicity campaign to draw thousands of spectators, who might attest to any police misconduct.

On the afternoon of 21 May, large crowds lined the roads near Buckingham Palace. Fifteen hundred constables were drawn up in a cordon which stretched from the two sides of the palace all the way around the Victoria Memorial. The WSPU had mustered a relatively small deputation of about two hundred women, who walked together as far as the Wellington Arch, where their little procession was broken up by the police. There followed a series of efforts to breach police lines on Constitution Hill. As in so many earlier demonstrations, women rushed against a wall of policemen, only to be thrown back. In contrast with earlier demonstrations, however, some of the women carried clubs, and these were used freely against the police, one constable being rendered unconscious.[41] The police retaliated in kind, and several women were roughly treated by a crowd of young men who had come seeking sport.

In the course of the afternoon, sixty-six women and two men were arrested. Only one woman managed to slip through the police lines, and she slipped and fell twenty paces from the main gate of Buckingham Palace. Mrs Pankhurst, who looked very weak, had been arrested early on, being lifted into the arms of Chief Inspector Rolfe and carried to a cab which waited behind the lines of police in front of the palace. Some of the constables who manned the cordon ended the day covered with red and yellow paint which had been thrown in eggshells.

The deputation to the King produced no concrete results other than the appearance in the newspapers of large photographs, lurid for their day, of disarrayed women locked in combat with the police. Such publicity was by now of dubious aid to the WSPU's effort to create an 'insoluble political crisis', for as the American suffragist Anna Shaw later observed: 'Women never show up their real weakness so much as when they attempt force.'[42] Two hundred women, of whom a few were armed with clubs and paint, had little but revolt itself in common with the armed bands of hard-faced men drilling in Ulster. Predictably enough, politicians and the press reacted to the disorders in front of Buckingham Palace with rage and dismay, though pity might have been more appropriate.

On the same day as the deputation to the King, the police had raided a flat in Maida Vale and found there seventy-two black bags and half a hundredweight of stones intended for window-breaking after the deputation. Also found were a plan of a private house and the approaches to it, twenty-two coils of fuse, a hundred yards of inflammable cord, a typewritten description of an 'improved shrapnel grenade', and cards giving instructions on how to reach the flat in Maida Vale.[43] At the flat the police arrested five women, including the wife of Leonard Hall of the Manchester ILP and her two daughters, one of whom, Nellie, had become a WSPU organizer.

The trials of those arrested in the deputation to the King and at the flat in Maida Vale began on 22 May. After her arrest in Hyde Park on 4 April, Mrs Drummond had continually disrupted court proceedings. At the trial which began on 22 May, court-room disruption was adopted as WSPU policy; the accused women refused to acquiesce in a trial based on laws made by men alone. One woman refused to walk into court and had to be carried, another wrestled with officers, another threw a boot at the magistrate, and others shouted incessantly. Eggs and a bag of flour were thrown from the galleries. Despite the uproar, most of the defendants were dismissed, and the longest sentence given was four months. Hunger and thirst strikes followed, and all of the prisoners were released within a few days.

The courtroom disruptions of the last week of May were accompanied by a rash of attacks on museum collections. On 22 May, five paintings in the National Gallery and one painting at the Royal Academy were damaged. On 23 May, a glass case holding a mummy was smashed at the British Museum. To avoid further damage, the National Gallery, the Tate Gallery, and the Wallace Collection were all closed until further notice, and the British Museum announced that in future women would only be admitted with a ticket issued on receipt of a letter from a person 'willing to be responsible for their behaviour.'[44]

On 23 May, the police again raided the Union's offices at Lincoln's Inn. Grace Roe was arrested on a charge of conspiracy, and a list of subscribers to the Union's funds was impounded. The police kept possession of the offices at Lincoln's Inn, and the Union set up new offices at 17 Tothill Street, Westminster. On 8 June, the new offices were raided by a force of about eighty police, and all documents found on the premises were seized. The WSPU moved its offices once again, to 2 Campden Hill Square, and on 12 June the new offices were raided in turn, all papers again being seized.

The succession of raids involved what *The Times* described as a police policy of 'harrying' the suffragettes.[45] As before, the Government, unable to apprehend more than a handful of secret arsonists, struck at the aboveground, legal manifestations of the Union, and by doing so decreased the possibility of legal activity and thus forced the Union further underground. The Union's plans were now made secretly in private homes. (The directions for reaching the flat in Maida Vale had included the instruction: 'N.B. – It is exceedingly important that on no account you should ask to be directed.')[46] Many Union members now travelled by night and used pseudonyms in their correspondence. Christabel was 'Amy Richards' and 'S.A.L.'.[47] Jessie Kenney, the younger sister of Annie Kenney, became 'Constance Burrows' when carrying out liaison between Paris and London, and 'Mary Fordyce' when on WSPU business in Scotland.[48] Pseudonyms used by other women included 'Clorf Ears', 'Brer Rabbitt', and 'Auntie Maggie'.[49] To the extent possible, written communications were avoided altogether and messages were sent by word of mouth. Code messages were used on occasion, Cabinet members being referred to at one time by women's names.[50] Codes and false names or no, 'mice' were not always successful in avoiding re-arrest; on 18 June the police raided five houses where women with expired licences were supposed to be hiding and managed to make one arrest. Altogether, twenty-one women were re-arrested in the first seven months of 1914.[51]

As a result of the great pressures being brought to bear on the WSPU, a series of noisy and often violent incidents occurred in late May and June. On 22 May, George V was attending a matinée at His Majesty's Theatre when one woman shouted, 'You Russian Tsar!' while another climbed on stage and began a speech.[52] On 3 June, an irate feminist felled the editor of the *Belfast Evening Telegraph* with an unexpected blow. Expelled from his office, she proceeded to the office of the editor of the *Belfast Newsletter* and struck him too. (He had angered her by urging those who found suffragettes marring golf courses to take the law into their own hands.) In London, on the same day as the Belfast assaults, two women used a dog whip to assault Dr Forward, the medical officer of Holloway Prison, where forced feeding was being carried out. The following day a woman who had managed to gain entrance to a Court function suddenly fell on her knees before the King, and cried in a loud shrill voice, 'Your Majesty, won't you stop torturing the women?'*

Suffragettes were themselves physically assaulted on a number of occasions. On 3 June, a WSPU procession at Bournemouth was attacked by a crowd. The following Sunday, a suffragette who shouted during the services at the Brompton Oratory was assaulted by women of the congregation, and a suffragette ejected from Westminster Cathedral was seized, shaken violently, and slapped.

* *The Times*, 5 June 1914. The WSPU disavowed any official connection with the incident.

At Ilford, that same weekend, a suffragette was chased by a crowd and took refuge in a house, the windows of which the crowd smashed.

In early June, additional publicity of a doubtful benefit to the cause of militant feminism was generated by charges which were laid against Grace Roe, the Secretary of the WSPU, who had been arrested in the raid of 23 May and imprisoned after arraignment. It was alleged that on 26 May and 30 May one of the clerks employed by the WSPU's solicitors had smuggled to Grace Roe tablets of apomorphine hydrochloride, an emetic which would make forced feeding useless by causing her to vomit immediately, and which would thus secure her speedy release. On 26 May, the tablets had been wrapped in a note: 'Our friends were delighted with your protest in Court. Everything is going splendidly. This feeding is horrible and it shows that they are at their last gasp.'[53] WSPU officials did not deny that the emetic had been smuggled in, but claimed that it had been brought in as an antidote to sedative and narcotic drugs that prison authorities were giving to hunger strikers to reduce their ability to resist forced feeding.[54]

Grace Roe's friends might envisage the authorities as being 'at their last gasp', but the claim was unrealistic. On 11 June 1914, McKenna discussed possible antidotes to feminist militancy and dismissed that most obvious of remedies, letting women vote, with the words:[55]

> I certainly do not think, and I am sure the Committee will agree with me, that that could be seriously treated as a remedy for the existing state of lawlessness.

On 20 June, Asquith received a delegation from Sylvia Pankhurst's East London Federation and said:[56]

> On one point I am glad to say I am in complete agreement with you. I have always said . . . that if you are going to give the Franchise to women, you must give it to them upon the same terms that you do to men. That is, make it a Democratic measure. . . .
> If the change has to come, we must face it boldly, and make it thorough-going and democratic in its basis.[56]

Sylvia Pankhurst later claimed that Asquith's response marked

'an unmistakable softening in his long hostility.'* The Prime
Minister's tone was indeed more amenable than it had been on
previous occasions, but he had indicated no change in his
opposition to women's voting, only his willingness to make the
best of necessity if and when it should arise. Indeed, Asquith's
statement may very well have simply reflected his agreement
with the view held by Lloyd George and Churchill, and confirmed by the secret poll of the secretaries of the provincial
Liberal federations taken in the autumn of 1911, that to give
women the vote on the existing franchise or a similarly 'narrow'
franchise would probably enfranchise a preponderance of Tory
voters. Perhaps all Asquith had really said was that if women
were ever given the vote their enfranchisement was going to be
on terms favourable to the political prospects of the Liberal party.

At any rate, Asquith certainly in no way modified the Government's existing policy of bringing ever stronger measures to bear
against the militant feminists. On 11 June, the Home Secretary
had announced a tentative plan to begin proceedings against
WSPU subscribers, holding them personally liable for damage
done.[57] On 23 June he announced that[58]

> Crimes and outrages are believed to have followed the
> incitements to violence which have been made in speeches
> by members of the Women's Social and Political Union
> using public halls. It has been deemed advisable by the
> police to warn the owners or lessors of such halls of the
> possible consequences to themselves that may result from
> the facilities thus afforded by them.

* E. S. Pankhurst, *The Suffragette Movement*, p. 575. In *The Strange
Death of Liberal England*, George Dangerfield went so far as to claim
that 'when he [Asquith] answered them it was to say that, in his
opinion, women's suffrage could not be long delayed. . . Sylvia Pankhurst . . . had interviews with Mr. Lloyd George and other members of
the Cabinet. There could be no doubt about it. The Government was
now prepared to support a Woman's Suffrage Bill' (George Dangerfield,
The Strange Death of Liberal England, p. 384). Dangerfield's account
involves serious errors. There is no evidence in the transcripts of
Asquith's meeting with the ELF delegation that Asquith said that in his
opinion women's suffrage could not be long delayed, nor is this a
realistic paraphrase of his remarks. Moreover, there is no evidence that
the Government made any decision to support a women's suffrage
measure at any time prior to the Great War.

I

McKenna's announcements did not deter the WSPU's arsonists – indeed, most of the arson committed in June 1914 occurred in the last week of that month (see table 18.6).[59]

Table 18.6

Date	Place	Object	Source	Est. Value (£)
1 June Windsor		Willows	*Daily Citizen*, 2 June	200–300
6 "	High Wycombe	mansion	*Daily Telegraph*, 8 June	1,500
20 "	Bideford	pavilion	*Western Morning News*, 22 June	160
25 "	Barnes	pavilion	*Daily Telegraph*, 26 June	several hundred
26 "	Nottingham	Alderson's	*Nottingham Guardian*, 27 June	1,000–2,000
29 "	London	Liveridge & Co.	*Daily Mail*, 30 June	many thousand
29 "	London	Sharp's	*Daily Mail*, 30 June	many thousand
			Total	5,000 to 12,000

The police finally vacated Lincoln's Inn, and Mrs Pankhurst attempted to resume work there on 9 July. She was arrested at the door. Re-imprisoned, she hunger-struck and was released on 11 July, exhausted and suffering from gastric disturbance and a high fever. Five days later, on 16 July, she tried to attend a WSPU meeting at Holland Park Skating Rink. An attempt was made to carry her into the hall on a stretcher, but before she could enter she was re-arrested and taken away in a police ambulance. Immediately after the arrest, Mrs Mansel, a cousin of the Chief Liberal Whip, made a singularly frenzied and defensive speech to the distraught audience:[60]

Mrs. Pankhurst has been re-arrested (Shame!). This

monstrous outrage is the latest infamy of this abominable, cowardly Government. . . . this horrible outrage of rearresting the person of the great leader of this Movement twice within eight days. . . .

Now, can you imagine anything more absolutely wicked and farcical and abominable, and in every way . . . appropriate to this miserable Government and miserable Home Secretary, than this treatment of a great woman like Mrs. Pankhurst. . . .

Something has been said about our being underground. Are we underground? (No!) Does this meeting look as though we were underground? No, friends, we are underground, we are over ground, and we are everywhere!

The meeting at the Holland Park Skating Rink on 16 July 1914 was the last major meeting held by the WSPU before the outbreak of the Great War. Yet to describe WSPU activities in mid-July 1914 as overshadowed by the approaching war would be to miscast seriously the problems which most beset the militants. Continental affairs did not concern the WSPU. Indeed, on 10 July the *Suffragette* announced, under the heading 'Good News for Suffragettes', that in February 1915 two operas by Dr Ethel Smyth would be performed in Germany – 'The Wreckers' at the Munich Hof Oper and 'The Boatswain's Mate' at the Frankfurt Civic Opera House.[61] In June and July 1914, WSPU concern with foreign affairs was reserved for Ulster. On 2 June the anti-suffragist *The Times* had stated:[62]

Among public affairs of the moment the question of woman suffrage is, comparatively, unimportant. It says little for the political discernment of its adherents if they are unable to see that there is one paramount issue, of far greater importance than any other occupying the time and taxing the wit of all parties in Parliament, which must be settled both now and finally. To this issue all minor ones must give place.

Far from failing to discern that Ulster had pre-empted the centre of the political stage, Christabel and Mrs Pankhurst were desperately trying to promote the idea that the militant campaign had created a crisis grave enough for the WSPU to merit the treatment accorded to the Ulster Unionists. In June, George

Lansbury and Sylvia Pankhurst had entered into private negotiations with Lloyd George, who, according to Sylvia's account, believed that there would be a General Election before the next Parliament, and offered to refuse to join a new Liberal Cabinet unless a reform Bill containing a clause giving votes to women on a broad franchise was introduced, the clause to be considered by a free vote of the Commons.[63] In return, it seems, feminist militancy would have to cease. According to both Lansbury and Sylvia Pankhurst, Lloyd George's offer came to naught, for the negotiations were, in Lansbury's words, 'smashed up' by Christabel's refusing to pledge an end to militancy before votes for women was made law.[64] Christabel was absorbed by the Irish question and could only envisage women's enfranchisement being brought about by a similar crisis. She wrote in the *Suffragette* of 3 July:[65]

> Votes for Women *now*!
> Why not! . . .
> It is an amazing thing that some men – and some women even – who claim to be Suffragists, should be talking, not of Votes for Women *now*, but of Votes for Women in the 'next Parliament'. We know by experience what Votes for Women in the next Parliament means. We know that the next Parliament, like to-morrow, never comes!
> . . . the Prime Minister and the Government have changed their mind – or at any rate, their policy, where the Irish question is concerned.
> . . . why should they not, at the same time that they are carrying a Bill for the pacification of militant Ulster, carry a Bill for the pacification of militant women!

On 18 July, Mrs Pankhurst was released from prison and taken to a nursing home in a state of complete exhaustion. In the next few days she did manage to write a letter to George V, in which she said that while he had refused to receive a deputation from the WSPU, he had received 'militant men' – Sir Edward Carson, Captain Craig, Mr John Redmond, and Mr John Dillon. Militant women were 'equally responsible, sober-minded, and public-spirited', and the Irish Conference at Buckingham Palace had been taken on 'your Majesty's own personal initiative.' She concluded, rather lamely: 'Our right to be received by your

Majesty in person will be actively asserted at a time which seems to us appropriate.'[66]

Mrs Pankhurst's letter had no effect. During the last two weeks of July, the Government, far from showing any interest in conciliation, attempted to halt the public distribution of the *Suffragette*. The Home Office sent a letter to wholesale news-agents, citing the trial of the publisher Drew, and stating that[67]

in the event of future issues containing incitements to crime, proceedings may be instituted not only against the printers, but also against all persons publishing or distribu-ting these issues.

In an attempt to continue public circulation of the *Suffragette*, the WSPU announced that its members would distribute the paper themselves. Members were urged to sell the *Suffragette* from their homes by putting a poster outside. They were also asked to lend their homes as distributing centres, to canvass newsagents and deliver papers to them, and to lend their motor cars for newspaper distribution. London would be divided into districts, each with a distributing centre (in some cases members' homes, in other cases local WSPU offices) and these centres would take the place of wholesalers. Members would pick up papers at the distributing centres and deliver them to news-agents who had agreed to receive them.[68] In as much as the Government was threatening to prosecute 'all persons publishing or distributing' issues inciting crime, it does not seem likely that many newsagents would have deemed it worthwhile to co-operate in the system of distribution proposed by the WSPU. At any rate, the *Suffragette* was by now a ghost of its former self, carrying perhaps one-third of the advertising linage it had carried a year earlier.

In keeping with the usual slackening-off of WSPU activities during summer months, there were relatively few cases of serious arson in July 1914, and the only case in which damage was greater than £1,000 occurred when Ballymenoch House, Ulster, was gutted by fire on 3 July (see table 18.7)[69]

In the last days of July, several WSPU members staged impromptu interviews with Cabinet members. On the morning of 28 July, Herbert Samuel was accosted at breakfast at the Kensington Palace Hotel. Asked about the forced feeding of

Table 18.7

Date	Place	Object	Source	Est. Value (£)
3 July	Ulster	Ballymenoch House	*Belfast Newsletter*, 4 July	20,000
12 ,,	Leicester	Blaby Station	*Daily News*, 13 July	500
29 ,,	Newtownards	race stand	*Belfast Newsletter*, 30 July	750
			Total	21,250

Grace Roe and Nellie Hall, he replied: 'I can do nothing.' That evening Haldane was asked how long the Cabinet intended to torture women. He answered: 'What do you mean by torturing? They ought to take their food.' The following day Birrell told interlocutors from the WSPU: 'You should drop militancy, and get enough electors to push the matter through. How do you expect to get it otherwise?' That same day, John Burns, on being told that all suffrage prisoners should be unconditionally released or else Carson and the other male rebels imprisoned, became angry and said: 'Now stop this nagging! I'll do nothing at all. You have killed your case.'[70] On 30 July, Mrs Dacre Fox and another member of the WSPU were arrested at Buckingham Palace while attempting to deliver yet another letter from Mrs Pankhurst to George V.[71]

Christabel Pankhurst later claimed that on the eve of the Great War the militant campaign had reached its 'greatest height'. Arson had indeed continued without check, but by the end of July 1914 the WSPU had in other respects become a harried rump of the large and superbly organized movement it had once been. The policies adopted after the ouster of the Pethick-Lawrences had not only failed to win the vote, but had failed to alter significantly the considerably vexed political conditions that still made women's enfranchisement unlikely in the foreseeable future.

The tactics employed by the WSPU from January 1913 until

the outbreak of war had failed to force the Liberals to grant
women the vote, not necessarily because the tactics were too
extreme, but because they lacked broad appeal and yet were not
sufficiently coercive to compel concessions. The emergence of the
unalloyed Pankhurst autocracy, the secret arson campaign, and
the gross exaggerations of *The Great Scourge* had succeeded in
alienating most of those WSPU members and sympathizers who
possessed some intellectual independence and critical facility of
their own. The policies carried out in 1913 and 1914 had not
only deprived the WSPU of many of its most gifted and influential
supporters, but had also alienated a number of politicians who
earlier had been at least moderately sympathetic to the WSPU.
Extreme militancy had also alienated substantial segments of the
general public; the decline in popular support had been increased
by the fact that the new tactics had resulted in important parks
and large halls being closed to the WSPU, thus making it
impossible to stage the large rallies of earlier years. By July 1914,
the WSPU's last direct avenue to the public, the *Suffragette*, was
in grave danger of ceasing to be available through newsagents.

In theory, the arson campaign was supposed to make Britons
so angry that they would be eager to give women the vote in
order to end the outrages being perpetrated. Fortunately or
unfortunately, however, Christabel's considerable political experience did not extend to training in terrorist techniques, and
the tactics she chose were not bothersome enough to create a
crisis of magnitude sufficient to bring about the passing of a
women's suffrage measure. The WSPU leaders, who were,
after all, middle-class English women of their day, were jealous
of the Ulster Unionists, but do not appear to have ever seriously
considered either the use of armed force or the instigation of
uncontrolled rioting. They misled themselves by continually
comparing the Union's tactics with the violence of 1830–32 and
1866. Not even the spectre of uncontrolled uprising was generated by the arson campaign of 1912–14, for the campaign was too
carefully disciplined and too divorced from working-class movements and the lives of working-class women ever to have
aroused the fears which might have been evoked by a less
controlled movement with a broader social base. Moreover, in its
belief that mob violence had extended the franchise in 1832 and
1867, the WSPU exaggerated the importance of the breaking of

the park railings in 1866, and the burning of ricks, castles, and
part of the city of Bristol between 1830 and 1832. The reform
Bills of 1832 and 1867 had been passed in part because they had
been portrayed as 'safe' measures of consolidation which would
widen the basis of support for existing social arrangements by
enfranchising groups that had 'shown themselves ready'.[72]
Contrary to what was suggested by WSPU rhetoric, the rick and
castle burners had not been enfranchised in 1832. That the
WSPU had a somewhat simplistic view of the genesis of earlier
franchise reforms does not, of course, prove that effective
coercion would have been impossible in 1913–14. As has been
pointed out, arson might have been more effective if commercial
and industrial targets had been chosen more frequently. The
burning of large and expensive private houses seriously incon-
venienced only a very few people, who were usually compensated
by insurance anyway.

Repeated hunger-striking, the other tactic central to the
later phase of the militant campaign, was also somewhat limited
in its effectiveness. Hunger strikes opened prison doors, but
repeated hunger-striking was apt to so weaken the hunger-
striker that while free on licence she was physically incapacitated.
By July 1914, there were no leaders of any real stature and
political experience left in the Union who were in good health,
out of prison, and in England. Most of the speeches made at
WSPU meetings in later 1913 and 1914 were at an intellectual
level far below that of the speeches of earlier years. In adopting
hunger-striking, and then bitterly protesting against the painful
ordeals of forced feeding that followed, the WSPU also seriously
overestimated the political persuasiveness of martyrdom, particularly when that martyrdom could be seen as self-imposed.
The comfortable and secure are not always deeply moved by the
suffering of the oppressed, particularly if the oppressed can be
portrayed as in some sense having brought their fate upon
themselves through their own disagreeableness. Anyway,
within the confines of its blinkered ways, the Asquith Government was trying to save lives, not destroy them, and Birrell's
expostulation, 'What do you mean by torturing? They ought to
take their food',[73] rather resembled Dr Johnson's kicking the
stone to refute Berkeley, in that it evaded the central issues but
had a certain commonsense merit.

In the final analysis, the tactical shortcomings of the 1913–14 phase of the militant campaign stemmed from the WSPU's too-ready devotion to the politics of apocalypse. If the vote was indeed to be won by the virtuous (most women, and militant feminists in particular) fighting valiantly but being ever-increasingly tyrannized by the wicked (most men, and Asquithian Liberals in particular) until, somehow, the virtuous triumphed and the paradise of enfranchisement was at hand, then tactics that clearly invited ever-increasing repression were well chosen. However, as E. J. Hobsbawm has pointed out, one characteristic of millenarian movements is that they 'share a fundamental vagueness about the actual way in which the new society will be brought about.'[74] The WSPU, while obviously not a 'pure' (to use Hobsbawm's terminology) example of a millenarian movement, was incapable of a more or less objective analysis of the *likely* response of Georgian England to an arson campaign waged by a relatively small group of middle-class women.

I*

19 The End of the Militant Campaign

Prior to August 1914, Christabel Pankhurst had envisaged war only in terms of the developing Ulster crisis. In 'How men fight', which appeared on 19 June 1914, she had written:[1]

> Sir Edward Carson and his followers are providing themselves with Mausers and machine guns. These are deadly weapons and their use means the agony, the wounding, the death of thousands of human creatures.
>
> The fact is that warfare as developed by men has become a horror unspeakable – a horror upon which the mind's eye dare hardly look.
>
> The old days when personal valour counted have gone. War is now a mechanical and souless massacre of multitudes of soldiers. . . .
>
> The soldier, like the civilian, is a human being and a citizen. Why should we be so willing for him to suffer, merely because he enlisted it may be, very young, and not really knowing what the terrors of modern warfare are!

On 1 August, Christabel left Paris to join her mother at St Malo, where Mrs Pankhurst had gone to recuperate. Christabel was on the coast of Britanny with her mother and Ethel Smyth when the order for French mobilization came, and she sent the *Suffragette* an article in which she said:[2]

> As I write a dreadful war-cloud seems about to burst and deluge the peoples of Europe with fire, slaughter, ruin – this then is the World as men have made it, life as men have ordered it.
>
> A man-made civilization, hideous and cruel enough in time of peace, is to be destroyed. . . .
>
> This great war, whether it comes now, or by some miracle is deferred till later, is Nature's vengeance – is

God's vengeance upon the people who held women in
subjection. . . .

That which has made men for generations past sacrifice
women and the race to their lusts, is now making them fly
at each other's throats, and bring ruin upon the world. . . .

Women of the W.S.P.U. we must protect our Union
through everything. It has great tasks to perform it has
much to do for the saving of humanity.

Christabel's remarks appeared in the 7 August *Suffragette*,
which like all issues was postdated. The following week, the
Suffragette failed to appear.

Due to the lack of sufficient extant documentation, it is not
possible fully to account for the course taken by the WSPU
during the first week of August 1914. Kitty Marion, one of the
WSPU's arsonists, later wrote that[3]

the first Sunday in August [2 August] . . . I was on
'danger-duty' in Leicester, ready to send another reminder
to the Government that women still wanted to vote, when a
telegram arrived from headquarters, to stop all activity.

Kitty Marion's recollection may or may not have been completely
accurate, but it is certainly clear that on the outbreak of war the
arson campaign abruptly ceased.

Private efforts were at once made to secure the release of
imprisoned suffragettes. On 7 August, Reginald McKenna said
that he would free only those prisoners who would 'undertake
not to commit further crimes or outrages.'[4] Three days later,
McKenna reversed that policy, announcing that[5]

I have advised His Majesty to remit the remainder of the
sentences of all persons now undergoing terms of imprisonment for crimes committed in connection with the suffrage
agitation. This course has been taken without solicitation on
their part, and without requiring any undertaking from them.
I have also advised His Majesty to remit the sentences of all
persons convicted of assaults, and other offences, in connection with recent strikes. His Majesty is confident that the
prisoners of both classes will respond to the feelings of their
countrymen and countrywomen in this time of emergency,

and that they may be trusted not to stain the causes they have at heart by any further crime or disorder.

WSPU policy was finally clarified by Mrs Pankhurst on 13 August, in a circular sent to the Union's members:[6]

Even the outbreak of war could not affect the action of the W.S.P.U. as long as our comrades were in prison and under torture.

Since their release it has been possible to consider what should be the course adopted by the W.S.P.U. in view of the war crisis.

It is obvious that even the most vigorous militancy of the W.S.P.U. is for the time being rendered less effective by contrast with the infinitely greater violence done in the present war not to mere property and economic prosperity alone, but to human life. . . .

Under all the circumstances it has been decided to economise the Union's energies and financial resources by a temporary suspension of activities. The resumption of active work and the reappearance of the *Suffragette*, whose next publication will be also temporarily suspended will be announced when the right time comes.

As a result of the decision announced in this letter, not only shall we save much energy and a very large sum of money but an opportunity will be given to the Union as a whole and above all to those individual members who have been in the fighting line to recuperate after the tremendous strain and suffering of the past two years.

. . . matters having come to the present pass it was inevitable that Great Britain should take part in the war and with that patriotism which has nerved women to endure endless torture in prison cells for the national good, we ardently desire that our country shall be victorious – this because we hold that the existence of all small nationalities is at stake and that the status of France and of Great Britain is involved.

The militant campaign was over.

The rank and file of the WSPU did not publicly oppose the

Pankhursts' decision to suspend militancy; the decision was received as a *fait accompli* dictated by circumstances. Given the severely straitened situation into which the WSPU had manoeuvered itself by the eve of war, and the even more unfavourable setting for continued domestic militancy attendant upon Britain's entering the war, it is hard to see how the members of the WSPU could have done otherwise. As Mrs Pankhurst was well aware, many of her most militant followers were exhausted by the events of the previous two years. Janie Allen, one of the most important financial supporters of the WSPU, wrote to Mrs Arncliffe-Sennett on 15 August:[7]

> I am completely unsettled as to my future action about
> Suffrage work. . . . I am at the moment completely tired
> out, & have orders to rest. Also all suffrage work is ended
> for a time & we must all work to relieve distress arising
> from the war.

Patriotic feelings also affected many WSPU members. As of late August 1914, the legal position of 'mice' who had been free on licences at the outbreak of war had not yet been fully clarified by the Government, and members of the WSPU discussed going to McKenna's house to 'insist on seeing him and demanding our freedom as well as that of Mrs. P. and A.K.'; however, the majority of WSPU members who discussed the move were against it, 'everybody thinking it an act of disloyalty on the part of the Union at times like these.'[8] Kitty Marion wrote of her own feelings: 'I am most anxious not to do anything that could be misconstrued into "hostility and disloyalty" just now.'[9]

Although the militant campaign had been suspended, the WSPU still had substantial funds which had been collected prior to 1 August, and a large paid staff. Christabel returned to England in the first week of September, and the course the Union would take soon became apparent. A day or two after her arrival, Christabel told the *Daily Telegraph* that [10]

> the success of the Germans would be disastrous for the
> civilization of the world, let alone for the British Empire.
> All – everything – that we women have been fighting for
> and treasure would disappear in the event of a German

victory. The Germans are playing the part of savages, overriding every principle of humanity and morality, and
taking us back to the manners and methods of the dark
ages. . . .

Among certain people there is a sort of idea that present
events form part of evolution – that it is ordained that
Germany shall supplant England. We suffragists . . . do
not feel that Great Britain is in any sense decadent. On the
contrary, we are tremendously conscious of strength and
freshness.

Surely this was not that land in which venereal disease was so
rife that women ought not to marry! Christabel's ideas were
changing.

Christabel made her first public address after returning to
England at the London Opera House on 8 September 1914.
The purpose of the meeting was not entirely clear to all concerned.
Christabel's followers expected a gala homecoming meeting,
and placed bouquets of flowers in a semi-circle at Christabel's
feet. But flyers circulated in advance of the meeting by the
national headquarters of the WSPU stated that 'Miss Christabel
Pankhurst will speak on the great need of vigorous National
defence against the German Peril',[11] and though bouquets
welcomed home the leader of the militant suffragettes, the
Opera House was decked with the flags of the allies, and a
women's band played national airs. That evening, a radiant
Christabel informed her audience that[12]

In the English–speaking countries under the British flag
and the Stars and Stripes woman's influence is higher,
she has a greater political radius, her political rights are
far more extended than in any other part of the world. . . .
I agree with the Prime Minister that we cannot stand by
and see brutality triumph over freedom.

'This last remark startled her followers into laughter', reported
the *Manchester Guardian*.[13] Christabel ended her speech by
urging men to join the army.

Laughter or no, Christabel and Mrs Pankhurst were rapidly
becoming chauvinists. Mrs Drummond, Annie Kenney, Grace
Roe, and Mrs Dacre Fox soon followed the Pankhursts into

apostasy. The meeting at the Opera House was but the first of a series of meetings at which WSPU leaders spoke on 'The War Crisis', 'The German Peril', and similar themes.[14] At Brighton, on 21 September, Mrs Dacre Fox urged 'the young men of the nation to answer Lord Kitchener's call for fresh reinforcements', and Mrs Pankhurst said that it was 'absolutely clear to everyone who had studied what had been going on in Germany for years past that the German plan was first to crush France and then to invade England.'*

The political transformation of Christabel and Mrs Pankhurst was remarkable, yet within the transformation a familiar pattern of thought remained. The allies now became the good who faced the ever-increasing tyranny of Germany, which was evil. Germany, said Christabel, was 'a male nation, a country in which the counsels of women emphatically do not prevail', whereas Belgium was 'the Suffragette country . . . Belgium has said, "a Colossus is determined to ride over and destroy us, but we will stand up in defiance."'[15] Mrs Pankhurst wrote, 'we owe all the ideals of real democracy to France, the "feminine" State that was held to be weak'.[16] Germany was militaristic, tyrannical, and male; Belgium and France were innocent, threatened, invaded, and female. The good would triumph in the end, but great sacrifice and suffering would be necessary first, so Christabel and her mother made recruiting speeches urging men to go to war. The suffragist Mrs H. M. Swanwick later wrote of Mrs Pankhurst:[17]

  I heard her often, and I never found her dull, until a
  melancholy night in 1915, when the ghost of the woman
  she had been talked unbelievable nonsense about Germans
  at a Queen's Hall meeting. There was a man there, I
  remember, who maintained that the stewards at Liberal
  meetings between 1906 and 1914 had been 'Huns'. 'You
  will remember', he roared, 'with what brutality these
  stewards treated the women?' Then, after a dramatic pause,
  he leant forward and snarled, 'It was not for nothing that
  they spoke with a foreign accent and in a guttural tongue.'
  Mrs Pankhurst nodded approval. I was so startled by this

* *Sussex Herald*, 22 September 1914. During the 1930s, Mrs Dacre Fox became one of Sir Oswald Mosley's Fascist candidates.

absurdity that I let out a shout of laughter. But the
audience turned on me with a shocked 'Hush!' I had
brawled in church. Nothing was, at that time, too fantastic
to be believed against Germans.

The great majority of WSPU members had not followed the
Pankhursts and their lieutenants into the anti-German
campaign. As Kitty Marion wrote: 'There was much dissatis-
faction and withdrawal from the W.S.P.U. on the part of many
members at militancy and suffrage propaganda being suspended
in favour of war propaganda'.[18] After the cessation of militancy,
donations to the WSPU had fallen sharply and the staff at
Lincoln's Inn House had been greatly reduced, the spacious
offices themselves eventually being given up for smaller offices
in Great Portland Street. Publication of the *Suffragette* was
resumed on 16 April 1915, but the weekly was now devoted to
anti-German propaganda. On 28 June, Lloyd George, as
Minister of Munitions, was privately informed that 'His
Majesty feels strongly that we ought to do more to enlist women-
workers. . . . The King was wondering whether it would be
possible or advisable for you to make use of Mrs Pankhurst.'[19]
Through Lloyd George, the WSPU subsequently received a
£2,000 grant from the Ministry of Munitions to finance a parade
asserting women's 'right to serve'. On 17 July 1915, Lloyd
George and Churchill reviewed a two mile procession of 30,000
women, some of whom carried banners with inscriptions such as
'Shells made by a wife may save a husband's life'.[20] In the
following months, the Pankhursts, assisted by Grace Roe and
Annie Kenney, led a national drive to recruit women for the
munitions industry, and on 15 October 1915 the *Suffragette* was
rechristened *Britannia*.

The last annual report of the WSPU had contained a financial
statement for the fiscal year 1 March 1913 to 28 February 1914.
No annual report was issued for the fiscal year that would have
ended on 28 February 1915, so an accounting had been given
neither of the amount given to the WSPU between 28 February
1914 and the outbreak of war, nor of the deposition of funds
subscribed for suffrage work which had remained on hand after
the war had begun. It was unclear to many WSPU members
whether or not funds given to the Union to support the feminist

campaign were now being used to sponsor meetings devoted to exciting hatred of the Germans, an object upon which neither the Union's members nor the by now very large body of ex-members were by any means agreed that their donations be spent.

On 22 October 1915, a number of WSPU members and ex-members met at the Caxton Hall, with Mrs Rose Lamartine Yates in the chair. A resolution was passed that[21]

> This meeting protests against the action of the W.S.P.U. officials whereby the Union's name and its platform are no longer used for woman suffrage and to remedy the innumerable disabilities of unenfranchised womanhood, but for other purposes outside the scope of the Union; and this meeting calls for a properly audited statement of account and balance-sheet of the Union's funds, no financial statement having been issued since the Spring of 1914.

Copies of the resolution were sent to Mrs Pankhurst and Christabel by registered mail.

On 25 November 1915, another meeting of members and ex-members of the WSPU was held at the Brondesbury Hall under the chairmanship of Mrs Elinor Penn Gaskell. A manifesto, adopted unanimously, pointed out that in the WSPU constitution, to which all members were required to give written assent, the object of the Union was stated to be 'to secure the parliamentary vote for women on the same terms as it is or may be granted to men.' The Manifesto went on to object to the name of the WSPU being used for purposes outside the scope of its stated object and to the failure to issue a financial statement regarding the deposition of funds since the beginning of the war.[22]

On 3 December 1915, Mrs Pankhurst answered her critics, writing that[23]

> Since the war began our work has been diverted into entirely new channels, and the funds contributed for suffrage work have been set aside and not touched for the purposes of our war campaigns . . . .
> If we issue a report and balance sheet for the year 1914–15 it will mean introducing a record of the suffrage work

before the war, and that is most undesirable during the
present truce. All our accounts are periodically audited by a
firm of accountants.

Both the question of the deposition of the funds and the use of
the name 'Women's Social and Political Union' were finally
settled in 1917. It is not clear whether a financial statement was
ever made available to members and ex-members, but while
Mrs Pankhurst was in Russia during the summer of 1917, funds
identified as left over from the militant feminist campaign were
used to purchase and furnish Tower Cressy, on Campden Hill,
as an adoption home for female children.[24] The dispute over the
use of the name 'Women's Social and Political Union' was also
laid to rest, when the 2 November 1917 issue of *Britannia*
announced that the WSPU would henceforward be known as
'The Women's Party'.[25]

During 1916, at least two efforts had been made by former
WSPU members and organizers to form new organizations
named after the original WSPU. 'The Suffragettes of the
W.S.P.U.' was composed of former WSPU members who wished
to 'entirely disassociate themselves from the line Mrs. Pankhurst
has taken up since the outbreak of war',* and who agreed to
act together under a completely democratic constitution. The
'Independent Women's Social and Political Union', formed on
21 March 1916, was devoted to 'work in the spirit of the old
W.S.P.U.'[26] The newly formed groups attracted few adherents,
and scant record of their activities remains.

* *Suffragette News Sheet*, No. 8, September 1916. Publication of
Suffragette News Sheet continued at least until November 1918.

20 Epilogue: The Vote, and After

Prior to 1906, votes for women had been regarded by many supposedly suffragist MPs as a hardy perennial to which support in principle might safely be given without further commitment being implied. Between 1906 and 1910, the suffragettes had succeeded in bringing the Commons to cease regarding votes for women as a provider of more or less yearly occasions for jocular remarks and desultory debate – by 1910, women's claim to the vote was no longer of marginal interest to male politicians. The forming of the Conciliation Committee in that year particularly attested to the efficacy of militancy – in 1905, the forming of a committee with such a name and purpose would have been as inconceivable as it was unnecessary.

An equally direct connection cannot be drawn between the arson campaign of 1912–14 and the granting of the vote to women over thirty on 6 February 1918. War carried in its train such rapid social and political change that by 1917 the issue of women's enfranchisement appeared in a context fundamentally dissimilar to that of pre-war days. An exhaustive consideration of the many factors which led to the surprisingly easy passage of women's suffrage legislation through the Commons in 1917 must remain beyond the purview of this work. Yet to examine feminist militancy in the pre-war years without making at least a brief inquiry into the relationship between that militancy and the granting of the vote in 1918 would be to fail to evaluate fully the ultimate effectiveness of the suffragettes' efforts.

A substantial array of war-wrought factors would have helped to further the cause of women's enfranchisement whether castles, railway stations, piers, and cricket pavilions had gone up in smoke or not. As men left jobs to fight overseas, they were replaced by women. Women also filled many jobs brought into existence by war-time needs, and the net result was that the number of women employed rose from 3,224,600 in July 1914 to 4,814,600 by January 1918.[1] The rise in employment was to prove temporary – by 1921, the number of women employed had dropped to pre-war levels – but this fall was not foreseen during the war, when it was clear only that some 'adjustment' would be necessary when hostilities ended. Anyway, during the war years by far the most extensive publicity was given not to the sheer number of women employed, but to the fact that women were doing *kinds* of work they had not done before. In July 1914 only 1,500 women were employed by banks, but by April 1918 banks employed 37,600 women.[2] During the same period, the number of women employed by tramway and omnibus companies increased from 1,700 to 28,900.[3] There had been few women bank clerks and no women bus conductors before the war, and the women who now flocked to these highly visible occupations received much praise. Also well-publicized was women's taking up of jobs requiring heavy labour, such as barrowing coke into railway vans, rolling barrels at breweries, stoking furnaces, unloading coal wagons, and building ships. In September 1916, the War Office claimed that women had 'shown themselves capable of replacing the stronger sex in practically every calling'.[4] The greatest adulation was reserved, however, for women who took part in the extremely hazardous munitions industry, in which one explosion alone caused the death of twenty-four women. By April 1918, 701,000 women were employed in munitions (including ship-building), and over 60 per cent of the workers in shell-making were women.[5]

The glowing praise given to women's work on the home front, to women nurses and doctors on the continent, and to heroic individual women such as the martyred Nurse Edith Cavell fostered a marked change in male attitudes towards women's enfranchisement. On 4 May 1916, Mrs Fawcett wrote to Asquith:[6]

A very general rumour has prevailed since last autumn . . . that the Government will, before the end of the war, find it necessary to deal with the franchise question in order to prevent the hardship and injustice which would arise if men who have been serving their country abroad, or in munitions areas in parts of this country other than those where they usually reside, should in consequence of their patriotic service be penalised by losing their votes.

When the Government deals with the Franchise . . . we trust that you may include in your Bill clauses which would remove the disabilities under which women labour. An Agreed Bill on these lines would . . . receive a very wide measure of support throughout the country. Our movement has received very great accessions of strength during recent months, former opponents now declaring themselves on our side, or, at any rate, withdrawing their opposition. The change of tone in the Press is most marked.

These changes are mainly consequent on the changed industrial and professional status of women.

On 7 May, Asquith replied:[7]

I need not assure you how deeply my colleagues and I recognize and appreciate the magnificent contribution which the women of the United Kingdom have made to the maintenance of our country's cause.

No such legislation as you refer to is at present in contemplation; but if, and when it should become necessary to undertake it, you may be certain that the considerations set out in your letter will be fully and impartially weighed, without any prejudgement from the controversies of the past.

It is his letter of 7 May 1916, rather than the interview of 20 June 1914, the importance of which was later so overestimated by Sylvia Pankhurst and George Dangerfield, that marked the first step on Asquith's road to Damascus.

Although Asquith had stated in his letter of 7 May to Mrs Fawcett that new legislation was not being contemplated, by July 1916 the Cabinet had become much concerned with the case for revision of the franchise. Existing law required men qualified as householders to have occupied a dwelling for at least one year prior to the 15 July preceding an election, so an enormous number of men who were either serving abroad in the armed forces or had changed their residences to take up war work in new locales had been inadvertently disenfranchised. In the early summer there was considerable indecisiveness on the part of the Government as to what to do about the situation. On

16 July, Asquith announced that the Government would set up
a Select Committee to consider registration and franchise, but
on 19 July the motion was withdrawn for lack of support. The
Government still intended to introduce legislation of some kind,
and on 4 August, representatives of fourteen constitutional
suffrage societies, including the NUWSS and the United
Suffragists, sent Asquith a letter stating that if the Government
limited its intentions to ensuring that men previously on the
register were not disqualified because of absence on war service,
then suffragists would not oppose the legislation; if, however,
new qualifications or changes in the period of residence were to
add new names to the register, then suffragists would not stand
aside – if qualifications based on war service were to be introduced, then women's claims could not be ignored. After the war,
the problem of the 'readjustment' of men's and women's labour
would have to be faced, and the large number of women who
had entered skilled occupations during the war had a right to
some say in the matter.[8]

With the advent of the Coalition, the balance between
suffragists and 'antis' in the Cabinet had changed significantly,
as Balfour, Bonar Law, Lord Robert Cecil, and Lord Selborne,
all suffragists, became Cabinet Ministers, and Lord Lytton
became a Junior Minister. Arthur Henderson, also a suffragist,
entered the Cabinet on 18 August 1916. In early August,
Henderson, Lord Robert Cecil, and Lloyd George gave their
support to the position adopted by the fourteen women's
organizations on 4 August. Then on 13 August, J. L. Garvin of
the *Observer*, long an 'anti', announced his conversion to adult
suffrage.[9] On the following day, in the Commons, Asquith gave
an awkwardly constructed speech in which, in the course of
speaking *against* any attempt at large scale revision of the
franchise while the war was still on (as opposed to simply
reregistering those previously qualified), he said:[10]

> the moment you begin a general enfranchisement on these
> lines of State service, you are brought face to face with
> another most formidable proposition: What are you to do
> with the women? . . . I have no special desire or
> predisposition to bring women within the pale of the
> franchise, but I have received a great many representations

from those who are authorized to speak for them, and I am bound to say that they presented to me not only a reasonable, but, I think, from their point of view, an unanswerable case. They say they are perfectly content, if we do not change the qualification of the franchise, to abide by the existing state of things, but that if we are going to bring in a new class of electors, on whatever ground of State service, they point out – and we cannot possibly deny their claim – that during this War the women of this country have rendered as effective service in the prosecution of the War as any other class of the community . . . they fill our munition factories, they are doing the work which the men who are fighting had to perform before . . . they are the servants of the State, and they have aided, in the most effective way, in the prosecution of the War. What is more, and this is a point which makes a special appeal to me, they say when the War comes to an end, and when . . . the process of industrial reconstruction has to be set on foot, have not the women a special claim to be heard on the many questions which will arise directly affecting their interests, and possibly meaning for them large displacements of labour? I cannot think that the House will deny that, and I say quite frankly that I cannot deny that claim. It seems to me . . . that nothing could be more injurious to the best interests of the country . . . than that the floodgates should be opened on all those vast complicated questions of the franchise . . . at this stage of the War. . . .

In a strangely convoluted argument, Asquith had declared *both* his support for women's enfranchisement after the war and his opposition to its consideration for the duration of the war. In taking this position, he had cast aside his most basic objections to women's suffrage. By referring to the various suffrage societies as 'those who are authorized to speak for them', he had conveniently forgotten the argument to which he had clung for so many years, that women's suffrage societies did not necessarily represent the wishes of the majority of women. And his equally long-held tenet, that voting would injure women's character by leading to a change in their social role, was obviously irrelevant

to the war-wrought employment of almost two million previously unemployed women; whether Asquith liked it or not,
women's role appeared to be changing rapidly, and doing so in
the full glare of super-heated war-time publicity. Asquith was
willing to acknowledge the facts of a situation which he could
hardly ignore.

Curiously enough, what was left of the WSPU (it did not
become the Women's Party until 2 November 1917) at first
rejected Asquith's conversion, not on the grounds that Asquith
had failed to go far enough, but on the grounds that soldiers and
sailors should be given the vote without the issue of women's
suffrage being allowed to interfere. On 15 August 1916,
Mrs Pankhurst accused Asquith of using votes for women as[11]

> an excuse for disenfranchising the Sailors and Soldiers, who
> he appears to think would vote against him and put some
> other man at the head of the Nation's affairs. . . .
>   Mr. Asquith insults as well as injures women when he
> tries to use them as catspaws to prevent the best men of the
> country from recording a vote, while any and every crank,
> coward or traitor, is to be free to vote as usual.

Thus, the WSPU at first opposed the very justification for
women's enfranchisement which was to prove to be the key
factor in that enfranchisement being obtained. History is not
without its ironies! Fortunately for the women's cause, by the
summer of 1916 the WSPU carried little weight in suffrage
circles, and its opposition proved to be short-lived anyway.

On 16 August, the same day that the WSPU's indignant
rejection of Asquith's conversion was announced in the Commons
by Commander C. W. Bellairs, Walter Long, the president of
the Local Government Board, suggested that a 'representative
Conference' be set up to consider all aspects of electoral reform.[12]
Long's proposal appeared to provide a way out of a Parliamentary
impasse, and was subsequently accepted. On 18 August, Long
suggested to Asquith that, in addition to members of all parties
from both houses of Parliament, the proposed conference
should include 'Representatives of Women's Societies – for and
against Suffrage',[13] but this suggestion was not taken up. On
26 September, Asquith wrote to the Speaker of the Commons,
J. W. Lowther, asking him to chair the conference. Lowther

accepted, albeit with no great enthusiasm, being in 'fear that the number and complexity of the issues, which will be raised as we proceed, will overwhelm us'.[14] In selecting the thirty-two members of the Conference on Electoral Reform, Lowther attempted to make the membership 'as nearly as possible proportionate to the strength of pre-war parties in the House of Commons.'[15] There were thirteen Conservatives, twelve Liberals, four Irish Nationalists, and three Labourites in the conference as it was originally constituted. Lowther also stated that on the question of women's suffrage he 'endeavoured to obtain an equal division of opinion, so far as it could be ascertained'.[16]

The conference held its first meeting on 12 October 1916, and its last on 26 January 1917. Its proceedings were secret. Women's suffrage was made the last item on the agenda, and was not decided on until after 10 January; Lowther later wrote:[17]

> I endeavoured to push off the burning question of women's suffrage as long as I could, and succeeded, for I felt that if we could agree upon other matters . . . there might be a greater disposition to come to some satisfactory solution on the women's question.

The postponement of consideration of women's suffrage until mid-January turned out to be propitious, for during December two events occurred which strengthened the women's chances: first, on 9 December, Asquith resigned and Lloyd George became Prime Minister. The fortunes of war and politics had finally removed the suffragists' erstwhile foe, who, while recently converted to women's suffrage in principle, had not as yet declared his support for women being granted the vote in wartime. Second, the women's cause was also aided when, on 14 December, Sir Frederick Banbury and Lord Salisbury, both 'antis', resigned as members of the conference, and were replaced by G. A. Touche and Lord Wortley, both of whom were suffragists.

The Conference on Electoral Reform issued its report on 27 January 1917. The conference recommended unanimously that the qualifying period be reduced to six months, that the franchise be extended to anyone resident in any premises during the qualifying period, and that soldiers and sailors who

normally resided in an area be permitted to vote. The conference
also recommended, by a majority of unstated proportions, that
some measure of woman suffrage be conferred.[18] Mrs Fawcett
wrote that, 'The majority for W.S. [Women's Suffrage] was
said to be large although the Conference as originally constituted
was equally divided. The majority reflects recent conversions.'[19]

The conference's specific recommendation regarding women's
suffrage was that unmarried women on the Local Government
Register and the wives of men on the Register should be
entitled to vote, but only at a specified age. Various ages had been
discussed, with thirty and thirty-five receiving the most favour.
The age qualification had been proposed to avoid the sudden
establishment of an absolute female majority in the electorate,
it being unclear what electoral effects, if any, women's voting
would have.

After the conference's report was published, Asquith abandoned
any lingering reservations – he was no longer in a position to
block legislation anyway – and agreed to move, on 28 March, a
resolution calling for a Bill along the lines of the report. On
26 March, the War Cabinet recommended that the Commons
adopt the report, but that any amendments regarding women's
suffrage be left to a decision by the members of Parliament,
without the imposition of Whips.[20] Two days later, the speech
with which Asquith opened the Commons debate on the Report
marked the final collapse of any serious opposition to women's
suffrage:[21]

I think that some years ago I ventured to use the expression,
'Let the women work out their own salvation.' Well, Sir,
they have worked it out during this War. How could we
have carried on the War without them? Short of actually
bearing arms in the field, there is hardly a service which
has contributed, or is contributing, to the maintenance of
our cause in which women have not been at least as active
and as efficient as men, and wherever we turn we see them
doing . . . work which three years ago would have been
regarded as falling exclusively within the province of
men. . . . But what I confess moves me still more in this
matter is the problem of reconstruction when the War is
over. The questions which will then necessarily arise in

regard to women's labour and women's functions and
activities in the new ordering of things – for, do not doubt
it, the old order will be changed – are questions in regard to
which I, for my part, feel it impossible, consistently either
with justice or with expediency, to withhold from women
the power and right of making their voice directly heard.
And let me add that, since the War began, now nearly
three years ago, we have had no recurrence of that
detestable campaign which disfigured the annals of political
agitation in this country, and no one can now contend that
we are yielding to violence what we refused to concede to
argument. I, therefore, believe, and I believe many others
who have hitherto thought with me in this matter, are
prepared to acquiesce in the general decision of the
majority of the Conference, that some measure of women's
suffrage should be conferred.

Asquith's arguments were by no means atypical of the
apologies now tendered in both Houses, where steadfast suffragists and recent converts alike repeated, again and again, that
women had earned the vote by their work for the war. Lloyd
George said: 'There is no doubt that the War has had an
enormous effect upon public opinion as far as this question is
concerned. . . . Women's work in the War has been a vital
contribution to our success.'[22] A. C. Morton stated that 'opinion
outside, if not inside, this House is largely changing in favour of
giving women a vote as soon as possible, and no doubt that is
largely owing to the excellent work which they have done for us
and for the country during the War'.[23] There is no need for
further examples, though many more could be given.

Asquith's speech was also something of a paradigm in that in
the arguments of several other men fulsome praise of women's
war work was also discreetly buttressed by words which seemed
to suggest that before the war there had been a 'detestable
campaign', that it would be desirable to avoid the recrudescence
of pre-war quarrels after the war, and that at this time, when
there could be no appearance of giving in to a horde of maenads,
it would be expedient to give women the vote. J. R. Clynes
said,[24]

a period of compromise is, after all, possible to us in this country, that while War is being waged in other lands we here, in . . . a state of peace, can use that condition . . . to settle on lines of compromise those highly controversial questions . . . whether you admit the right or not, women will persist actively to clamour for their rights until those claims are met.

Walter Long, an erstwhile 'anti', warned against 'a renewal of those bitter controversies over which we have wasted so much time in the past'.[25] And Bonar Law said:[26]

since the War began they have refrained from the kind of agitation which alienated people from their cause. . . . They have said, 'So long as there is no extension of the franchise to men for new qualifications we will say nothing, but the moment there is an extension of the kind we will fight for ours.' . . . There really is the problem, as I see it, in a nutshell. You cannot avoid this controversy. I wish you could. You have got to have it anyway.

Such arguments were later to be amplified in stronger terms in the House of Lords, by the Marquess of Crewe:[27]

The atmosphere after the conclusion of the war . . . cannot be in the political sense calm. It may be very much the contrary. A great number of questions exciting controversial feelings among all Parties will emerge suddenly, will rise to the surface . . . without any of the patriotic checks which all men, however keen their desires, wish to apply to political discussion at this moment. I therefore venture to ask those who believe that the consideration of this question could properly be postponed, what advantages can be expected from its postponement?

I recall the political position on this subject as it existed just before the war. We all know how high feelings ran . . . it would have been no surprise to us, the members of the Government of that day, if any one of our colleagues in the House of Commons who had taken a prominent line either for or against the grant of the vote to women had been assassinated in the street. . . . It is quite true that the various leaders of the women's party had drawn the line at murder, although they did not draw it at any other kind of

outrage. . . . But we all know that every period of political
agitation is liable to have its Invincible wing, and nobody
was certain that some enthusiastic supporters of the movement might not take the life, either of one of the Ministers
who declared himself in strong opposition to the Bill, or
of one of those who was known to be strongly in favour of
it, on the ground that he was acting as a traitor in
remaining a member of the Government which refused
the vote. That is an atmosphere, if the grant of the vote
is refused, which will undoubtedly be recreated, one of these
days.

On the evening of 28 March 1917, after a debate remarkably
lacking in acrimony, the Commons approved the introduction of
legislation based on the report of the Electoral Conference, by an
overwhelming majority of 341 to 62.* This division marked the
real turning point in the Parliamentary progress of women's
suffrage – thereafter, the outcome was never seriously in doubt.
Just as before the war the passage of women's suffrage legislation
had been blocked by a combination of factors – the Liberals'
fear of too 'narrow' a franchise, the Tories' fear of too 'broad' a
franchise, Asquith's Premiership, and the desire of the Irish
Nationalists to keep him in office – so, now, a number of war-
wrought factors – the decreased importance of party divisions
under the Coalition, the remarkably lessened fear of adult
suffrage, the entry into the Government of several conspicuously
fervid suffragists, the replacement of Asquith by Lloyd George,
the strongly-felt need for a revision of electoral qualifications
affecting soldiers and sailors, admiration for women's war work
and war heroism, *and* a general desire to avoid the renewal of
pre-war conflicts after the war – *combined* to create a political
climate highly favourable to the enfranchisement of women.
Before the war, feminist militancy had succeeded in making
women's enfranchisement a political issue of considerable
importance. During the war, given that the importance of the
issue was *already* well-established, the suspension of militancy
enabled male politicians to sponsor women's enfranchisement

* *H.C. Deb.* 5s. vol. 92, 28 March 1917, cc. 566–70. Commander
C. W. Bellairs, who had acted as the WSPU's spokesman the previous
August, voted against the Resolution.

without seeming to look 'weak and ridiculous if they yielded to this agitation.'*

By 19 June 1917, when the Commons considered the Committee stage of Clause Four of the Representation of the People Bill, Ramsay MacDonald could remark that the matter had 'already been fought and won.'[28] The clause passed by a vote of 385 to 55. In the Lords, Lord Curzon, President of the Anti-Suffrage League, admitted defeat on 10 January 1918, and that evening the clause passed the Lords by a vote of 134 to 71. The Representation of the People Act received the Royal Assent on 6 February 1918. Under the terms of the Act, enfranchisement was conferred on women over thirty who were householders, the wives of householders, occupiers of property of £5 or more annual value, or university graduates. Limiting the franchise to women over thirty proved effective in achieving the end of avoiding the immediate establishment of a female majority in the electorate, for in the first register of Parliamentary electors under the 1918 Act, 12,913,166 men and 8,479,156 women were listed.[29]

As has been mentioned, on 2 November 1917, by which time it was clear that women would soon receive the vote, the WSPU had been renamed 'The Women's Party'. Mrs Pankhurst became the new party's treasurer, Annie Kenney was Secretary, Mrs Drummond was Chief Organizer, and Christabel continued to edit *Britannia*, which became the party's official organ. On its founding, the Women's Party published a programme, 'For the war and after', largely written by Christabel.[30] The programme combined a foreign policy based on acute xenophobia with a domestic policy which included proposals for widespread reforms affecting women and children. In foreign affairs, the Women's Party advocated 'war till victory', followed by 'reduction of Germany's mineral and other war-like resources' to the point that Germany would find it impossible to wage war again, 'ridding all Government Departments of officials having enemy blood or connections, and of all officials who have pacifist and pro-German leanings', opposition to surrender of the authority of Parliament in international politics to 'any so-

* *Westminster Gazette*, 29 March 1912 (see p. 162).

called League or Council of Nations', keeping the natural resources and transport systems of Britain and the Empire 'under strictly British ownership and control', and the exclusive manning of the British public service 'by officials of long British descent and wholly British connection'. Under the rubric 'Special women's questions', the Women's Party advocated equal opportunity of employment, equal pay for equal work, equal marriage laws including equal conditions of divorce, and a raising of the age of consent. The 'community' was to 'guarantee to the expectant and nursing mother the food and other conditions required to enable the bearing and rearing of healthy children', and every child was to be 'guaranteed by the community from birth until it becomes a fully grown and self-supporting member of society the material conditions of life, the medical supervision and treatment, and the general education followed by specialized education, necessary to make the child a worthy citizen.' In addition, 'over-work and undefined hours of labour, which constitute the special burdens of the married woman', were to be 'reduced to a minimum by adopting the principles of Co-operative Housekeeping',* which would involve

(a) Central heating and hot water supply. (b) Large scale and therefore economical purchasing of food, and its expert preparation by a trained staff in large and scientifically equipped central kitchens, whence it would be conveyed to the private apartments of each family. (c) Central laundry worked by a special staff at a minimum price, which would supersede the present wasteful and uncomfortable method of the individual family wash. (d) The provision of an infirmary and isolation hospital for the use of families in each co-operative dwelling. (e) The similar provision for use, if desired, of a crèche, nursery school, gymnasium, reading room, and so forth.

---

* *Britannia*, 2 November 1917. Christabel had broached the idea of co-operative housekeeping at least as early as December 1913 (see 'Married women's health', *Suffragette*, 5 December 1913). Co-operative housekeeping was not, however, a major concern of the pre-war WSPU which, unlike the Women's Party, always avoided committing itself to any specific programme to be fought for after the vote had been won.

Christabel had clearly advanced from her earlier emphasis on the symbolic importance of votes for women to a more concrete vision of radically reformed conditions for working-class women. She had no real conception, however, of how the reforms she proposed were to be financed – far from advocating redistributive taxation, the Women's Party simply claimed that greater industrial efficiency and productivity would bring to the working class the standard of comfort of the middle class, without, it seems, the middle class being forced to make economic concessions. Greater productivity could only be achieved, the Women's Party insisted, by 'captaincy in Industry. . . . In Industry, as on board ship, there must be captain, officers, and crew. In Industry, as in an orchestra, there must be a conductor and those who play to his beat.'[31] Christabel claimed that captaincy in industry would result not only in greater efficiency and higher productivity, but in shorter hours and higher pay. Christabel did not, however, describe the way in which shorter hours and higher pay would, in practice, be obtained from the captains of industry; she merely said that the hours of labour should be determined by 'engineering and organising experts' rather than by the workers themselves.[32] Christabel's programme begged many questions, as neither she nor her colleagues were much concerned with the economic basis of social reform, or with the ways in which her curiously varied proposals could possibly be implemented without clashing directly with each other.

Though the programme of the Women's Party was a strange amalgam of apparently conflicting ideas, the immediate aims of the party's leaders were by no means obscure; in late 1917 and 1918, Christabel, her mother, and Mrs Drummond spent much time in South Wales, the Midlands, and on Clydeside, where they harangued workers against striking in war time on the grounds that strikes and shop stewards' committees betrayed British soldiers and furthered Bolshevik aims. Many of their listeners agreed with them, and the campaign against Bolshevik pacifists and 'shirkers' met with considerable success.

Soon after its founding, the Women's Party stated that women could 'best serve the nation by keeping clear of men's party political machinery',[33] but following Lloyd George's decision to issue letters of approval to parliamentary candidates, the Women's Party decided not to follow its own advice – in

November 1918, shortly after the armistice, Christabel contacted
Lloyd George with regard to her possible candidacy in the
Westbury Division of Wiltshire. Lloyd George was pleased to
give her his support, writing to Bonar Law:[34]

> I am not sure that we have any women candidates, and I
> think it is highly desirable that we should. The Women's
> Party, of which Miss Pankhurst is the Leader, has been
> extraordinarily useful, as you know, to the Government –
> especially in the industrial districts where there has been
> trouble during the last two very trying years. They have
> fought the Bolshevist and Pacifist element with great skill,
> tenacity, and courage.

At the end of November, Christabel switched her candidacy to
the newly created constituency of Smethwick, an industrial
suburb of Birmingham, and a few days later Lloyd George and
Bonar Law prevailed upon a Major S. N. Thompson, already
approved as the Unionist and Coalition candidate for the seat, to
stand down.[35] Thompson duly abandoned his candidacy, thereby
giving Christabel a free run against a Labour candidate, J. E.
Davison, the national organizer of the Ironfounders' Society.
Christabel, in turn, pledged her support to Lloyd George,
Bonar Law, and the Coalition.

Christabel made anti-Bolshevism the central theme of her
campaign. The main issue of the election was, she stated, 'between the Red Flag and the Union Jack', and the Labour Party
was 'entirely dominated by Bolshevism and Pacifism.'[36] Both
Philip Snowden and Mary MacArthur were, she alleged,
Bolshevists, and Ramsay MacDonald was among the numerous
Labour leaders possessing 'Bolshevist and pro-German sympathies'.[37] In reply to the charges against the Labour Party,
J. E. Davison called Christabel a 'political flibbertigibbet' who
had been 'all things by turn and nothing long.'[38]

In the Coupon Election, which was held on 14 December
1918, J. E. Davison defeated Christabel by a small margin. He
received 9,389 votes whereas Christabel received 8,614, a
difference of only 775. With the issue of 20 December, *Britannia*
abruptly ceased publication. In 1919 the Women's Party itself
ceased to exist, and Mrs Pankhurst and Christabel withdrew
from electoral politics.

K

During the course of the next two years, Christabel became an ardent believer in the Second Coming of Christ. From 1921 to 1940 she spent most of her time as a travelling evangelist, preaching the gospel of the Second Advent in Britain, Canada, and the United States. She wrote five books on her new beliefs: *The Lord Cometh!* (1923), *Pressing Problems of the Closing Age* (1924), *The World's Unrest: Visions of the Dawn* (1926), *Seeing the Future* (1929), and *The Uncurtained Future* (1940). In *Pressing Problems*, Christabel professed disillusion with the results of women's enfranchisement, writing:[39]

> Some of us hoped more from woman suffrage than is ever going to be accomplished. My own large anticipations were based partly upon ignorance (which the late war dispelled) of the magnitude of the task which we women reformers so confidently wished to undertake when the vote should be ours.

Though Christabel was disillusioned, her new beliefs were not entirely unrelated to the ideas she had professed during the final phase of the militant campaign, in that she still believed that the world would in time be utterly transformed. Women, she now thought, were 'wholly unable, just as men are unable, even to form, much less to put into effect, a policy that will regenerate the world', but it was 'unmistakably certain' that Christ would 'come to initiate the Millennium.'[40] A 'season of tribulation and world-purification' would, however, be necessary before the 'new thousand year age' could begin.[41] Within this schema, some familiar elements remained. Evil, once primarily the province of males, and later associated with Germany, was now attributed to human nature as a whole; Christ was the 'only hope of the world, for by no human instrumentality can the world be cleansed and healed of its terrible ills.'[42] Christabel now believed that all human systems of government involved 'muddles, miscalculations, failures, tragic surprises, [and] tyrannies' and that the alternative was 'theocracy', which was 'the divine reality of the future – the rule of God! That is the remedy for the failure of human rule of every form and in every age.'[43]

During the 1920s and 1930s, Christabel's life was largely peripatetic. In 1925 she lived for about six months at Juan-les-Pins, on the French Riviera, where she, her mother, and

Mrs Tuke ran a tea-shop called the English Tea Shop of Good Hope. In 1936, while in England, Christabel was made a Dame Commander of the British Empire (DBE), in honour of her work for women's enfranchisement. Christabel had lived with Grace Roe in Santa Barbara and Hollywood, California, for about six months in 1921, and in 1940 she returned to Los Angeles where she lived until her death on 13 February 1958.

Mrs Pankhurst spent the early 1920s in Canada, lecturing on behalf of Moral Hygiene. After nearly a year spent in Bermuda and on the Riviera with Christabel, she returned to England at the end of 1925. She was subsequently adopted as a Conservative candidate for the strongly Labour East End constituency of Whitechapel and St George's, Stepney, but her health failed well before any election could be held, and she died on 14 June 1928, at the age of sixty-nine.

On 6 March 1930, Stanley Baldwin unveiled a statue of Mrs Pankhurst in the Victoria Tower Gardens, under the shadow of the Houses of Parliament. On the base of the statue was carved an inscription which praised Mrs Pankhurst's courageous leadership of the movement for women's suffrage. A plaque honouring Christabel was added later, as was a plaque dedicated to over 1,000 women who endured imprisonment for the sake of the enfranchisement of their sex.

Notes

1 Antecedents

1 See W. E. Houghton, *The Victorian Frame of Mind*, pp. 341–4.
2 J. A. Banks, *Prosperity and Parenthood*, pp. 70–85.
3 O. R. McGregor, *Divorce in England*, p. 65.
4 'What is woman's work?', *Saturday Review*, vol. 25, no. 642, 15 February 1868, p. 197.
5 G. Best, *Mid-Victorian Britain 1851–1875*, p. 224.
6 *Parl. Pap.* 1948–9, vol. 19 (Cmd 7695), *Royal Commission on Population Report*, HMSO, London, 1949, pp.24–5.
7 *Ibid.*, p. 26.
8 *Ibid.*, p. 38.
9 W. J. Reader, *Professional Men*, p. 172.
10 See M. J. Peterson, 'The Victorian governess: status incongruence in family and society', *Victorian Studies*, vol. 14, no. 1, September, 1970, pp. 7–26.
11 E. M. Sewell, *Principles of Education*, p. 411.
12 H. Blackburn, *Record of Women's Suffrage*, pp. 51–2.
13 *Ibid.*, p. 54.
14 *Ibid.*, p. 55.
15 See Manchester National Society for Women's Suffrage, *First Annual Report*, Manchester, 1868.
16 See Blackburn, *op. cit.*, p. 72.
17 *Ibid.*
18 Archives, Manchester Public Library, box M/50, H. Cook to L. Becker, London, 8 and 12 April 1867.
19 B. L. S. Bodichon, *Reasons for the Enfranchisement of Women* [pamphlet], a paper read at the meeting of the National Association for the Promotion of Social Science, Manchester, 6 October 1866, p. 10.
20 Blackburn, *op. cit.*, p. 28.
21 *Ibid.*, p. 48.
22 N. McCord, *The Anti-Corn Law League, 1838–1846*, p. 69.
23 *Ibid.*, p. 49.
24 From 'Policy of the M.N.S.W.S.', as printed in Manchester National Society for Women's Suffrage, *First Annual Report* [and subsequent annual reports], Manchester, 1868, p. 20.
25 Archives, Manchester Public Library, box 17/1, L. Becker, *Women's*

Suffrage, Directions for Preparing a Petition to the House of Commons [MNSWS leaflet], 1869, p. 3.

26 Manchester National Society for Women's Suffrage, *Second Annual Report*, Manchester, 1869, p. 8.
27 C. Rover, *Women's Suffrage*, p. 60.
28 *H.C. Deb.* 3s. vol. 288, 10 June 1884, c. 1962.

2 Enter the Pankhursts

1 See Archives, Manchester Public Library, box 17/1, MNSWS leaflet, January 1869.
2 *H.C. Parl. Pap.*, 1870 (31), 4, 799.
3 Dame C. Pankhurst, *Unshackled*, p. 21.
4 Fabian Society, *Special Report of the Proceedings of the Three Days Conference* [minutes], 9–11 June 1886, London School of Economics.
5 R. M. Pankhurst, *The House of Lords and the Constitution*, [pamphlet], n.d.
6 E. S. Pankhurst, *The Suffragette Movement*, p. 96.
7 *Is Marriage a Failure?* [pamphlet], n.d.
8 E. S. Pankhurst, *op. cit.*, pp. 112–13. See also Dame C. Pankhurst, *op. cit.*, pp. 25–8.
9 *Labour Leader*, 23 May 1896.
10 *Manchester Guardian*, 4 June 1896.
11 *Ibid.*, 13 June 1896.
12 *Labour Leader*, 27 June 1896.
13 *Manchester Guardian*, 30 June 1896.
14 *Ibid.*, 4 July 1896.
15 *Ibid.*

3 The Founding of the WSPU

1 See E. S. Pankhurst, *The Suffragette Movement*, pp. 148–52.
2 As quoted in E. Coxhead, *Daughters of Erin*, p. 82.
3 A. Marreco, *The Rebel Countess, The Life and Times of Constance Markievicz*, p. 62.
4 *Women's Suffrage Record*, October 1903, p. 1.
5 E. Roper, biographical introduction to E. Gore-Booth, *Poems of Eva Gore-Booth*, p. 10.
6 *Report of the Executive Committee of the North of England Society for Women's Suffrage*, Manchester, 1901, pp. 11–23.
7 See C. Rover, *Women's Suffrage*, p. 25.
8 North of England Society for Women's Suffrage, *Report of the Executive Committee*, Manchester, 1901, p. 4.
9 *Ibid.*, p. 7.
10 *Women's Suffrage Record*, October 1903, p. 1.
11 *Ibid.* See also *Labour Leader*, 21 March 1903, and H. A. Clegg, A.

Fox, and A. F. Thompson, *A History of British Trade Unions Since 1889*, vol. 1, p. 275.

12 *Women's Suffrage Record*, October 1903, p. 1.

13 E. Roper, 'The cotton trade unions and the enfranchisement of women', in North of England Society for Women's Suffrage, *Report of the Executive Committee*, Manchester, 1902, pp. 13–14.

14 E. S. Pankhurst, *op. cit.*, p. 164.

15 North of England Society for Women's Suffrage, *Report of the Executive Committee*, Manchester, 1903, pp. 9–11.

16 *Labour Leader*, 14 March 1903, letter to the editor from C. Pankhurst.

17 *Ibid.*, 30 May 1903, letter to the editor from C. Pankhurst.

18 E. S. Pankhurst, *op. cit.*, p. 167.

19 *I.L.P. News*, August 1903, p. 1.

20 Clegg, Fox, and Thompson, *op. cit.*, p. 482; see also B. Drake, *Women in Trade Unions*, pp. 44, 51.

21 *Labour Gazette, Journal of the Labour Department of the Board of Trade*, October 1903, p. 267.

22 Billington-Greig Papers, box: In Hand, 1903–1907, undated holograph notes.

23 *Ibid.*

24 Dame C. Pankhurst, *Unshackled*, p. 44.

25 Billington-Greig Papers, box: A.K./W.S.P.U./P., undated holograph notes. See also Dame C. Pankhurst, *op. cit.*, p. 44.

26 Billington-Greig Papers, box: The Despard Papers, undated holograph notes.

27 *Manchester City News*, 31 October 1903.

28 *Clarion*, 1 January 1904.

29 *Ibid.*, 4 December 1903.

30 *Manchester Guardian*, 20 February 1904.

31 *Ibid.*; see also *Manchester Evening News*, 20 February 1904.

32 Dame C. Pankhurst, *op. cit.*, p. 46.

33 *Labour Leader*, 16 April 1904.

34 *Ibid.*, 23 April 1904, letter to the editor from C. Pankhurst.

35 *Clarion*, 6 May 1904.

36 As reprinted in J. K. Hardie, *The Citizenship of Women* [pamphlet], p. 7.

37 *Ibid.*

38 *Ibid.*

39 'Report of a national convention of the National Union of Women's Suffrage Societies', London, 25 and 26 November 1904, *Women's Suffrage Record*, 31 December 1904, p. 12.

40 *Ibid.*, p. 9.

41 *Labour Leader*, 3 February 1905.

42 *Ibid.*

43 E. Pankhurst to D. B. Montefiore, Manchester, 19 February 1905, as quoted in D. B. Montefiore, *From a Victorian to a Modern*, pp. 117–18.

44 E. S. Pankhurst, *op. cit.*, p. 182.
45 *H.C. Deb.* 4s. vol. 146, 12 May 1905, cc. 228–9.
46 *Labour Leader*, 19 May 1905.
47 H. Mitchell, typescript autobiography, London Museum 61.139/2, p. 5.
48 *Ibid.*, p. 4.
49 *Ibid.*, p. 3.
50 H. Mitchell, typescript statement, London Museum 60.15/8–24, in folder: Suffragette Biographical Notes.
51 H. Mitchell, typescript autobiography, pp. 49–50.
52 *Ibid.*, pp. 54–5.
53 *Ibid.*, pp. 55–9.
54 *Ibid.*, p. 61.
55 *Ibid.*, p. 48.
56 See *Labour Leader*, 12 May 1905.
57 A. Kenney, *Memories*, p. 3.
58 *Ibid.*, p. 2.
59 *Ibid.*, p. 9.
60 *Ibid.*, p. 14; see also *Labour Record*, April 1906.
61 *Ibid.*, p. 4.
62 *Ibid.*, p. 60.
63 *Ibid.*, p. 26.
64 *Ibid.*, p. 30.
65 Blackman Papers, undated holograph notes.
66 *Ibid.*
67 *Ibid.*
68 Billington-Greig Papers, box: A.K./W.S.P.U./P., undated holograph notes.
69 Blackman Papers, undated holograph notes.
70 *Labour Leader*, 26 May 1905, 11 August 1905.
71 For example, see *Labour Leader*, 7 July 1905.
72 H. Mitchell, typescript autobiography, p. 88.
73 *Labour Leader*, 7 July 1905.
74 *H.C. Deb.* 4s. vol. 150, 26 July 1905, cc. 356–7.
75 *Labour Leader*, 4 August 1905.
76 *H.C. Deb.* 4s. vol. 150, 1 August 1905, c. 1184.
77 *Labour Leader*, 4 August 1905.
78 *Ibid.*, 18 August 1905.

4 Militancy Begins

1 *Labour Leader*, 29 September 1905.
2 C. Pankhurst, interviewed by the *Sunday Times*, 8 March 1908.
3 See *Manchester Guardian*, 25 October 1905, letter to the editor from C. Pankhurst.
4 See *Manchester Guardian*, 16 October 1905, *Sunday Times*,

8 March 1908, Dame C. Pankhurst, *Unshackled*, pp. 48–52, and T. Billington-Greig, *The Militant Suffrage Movement*, pp. 33–4.
5 Billington-Greig Papers, folder: Student Teacher, undated holograph notes.
6 C. Pankhurst, 'Politicians I have met: tussles and flattery', *Weekly Dispatch*, 17 April 1921; *Manchester Guardian*, 16 October 1905.
7 *Manchester Evening News*, 14 October 1905.
8 *Manchester Guardian*, 16 October 1905.
9 *Ibid.*
10 *Manchester Evening News*, 16 October 1905.
11 *Labour Leader*, 20 October 1905.
12 *Manchester Evening News*, 16 October 1905.
13 *Labour Leader*, 27 October 1905.
14 *Ibid.*
15 H. Mitchell, typescript autobiography, pp. 90–1.
16 Billington-Greig Papers, box: Social and Feminist Awakening, undated holograph notes.
17 *Labour Leader*, 29 December 1905.
18 *Ibid.*, 12 January 1906.
19 W. S. Churchill to Manchester Suffrage Society, n.d., as quoted in R. Strachey, *The Cause*, p. 296.
20 Billington-Greig Papers, box: A.K./W.S.P.U./P., undated holograph notes.

5   To London

1 E. S. Pankhurst Papers, holograph notes, 31c, p. 12.
2 *South Wales Daily News*, 7 November 1905.
3 See 'First meeting of unemployed women of South West Ham', Minute Book of the Canning Town Branch, W.S.P.U., 1906–7, London Museum 50.82/1133.
4 A. Kenney, *Memories*, p. 69.
5 *Daily News*, 20 February 1906.
6 For examples, see *Manchester Guardian*, *Daily News*, *Evening News*, and *Daily Mirror*, 20 February 1906.
7 Minute Book of the Canning Town Branch, W.S.P.U., 1906–7, London Museum 50.82/1133.
8 *Labour Leader*, 9 March 1906.
9 E. Pethick-Lawrence, *My Part in a Changing World*, p. 24.
10 *Ibid.*, p. 38.
11 *Ibid.*, pp. 34–5.
12 *Ibid.*, p. 57.
13 *Ibid.*, p. 58.
14 *Ibid.*, p. 67.
15 See F. W. Pethick-Lawrence, *Fate Has Been Kind*, pp. 51–2.
16 E. Pethick-Lawrence, *op. cit.*, p. 131.

17 Billington-Greig Papers, box: A.K./W.S.P.U./P., undated holograph notes.
18 Women's Suffrage Collection, London Museum, 57.116/69, folder: Demonstrations & Political Action, A. Kenney to Mrs Rowe, London, 4 March 1906.
19 PRO, Mepol 2/1016, Metropolitan Police Report, 9 March 1906.
20 *Daily Mirror*, 10 March 1906.
21 *H.C. Deb.* 4s. vol. 155, 25 April 1906, cc. 1571–2.
22 *Ibid.*, c. 1584.
23 *Ibid.*, cc. 1584–5.
24 *Labour Leader*, 4 May 1906.
25 *Labour Record*, May 1906.
26 Minute Book of the Canning Town Branch, W.S.P.U., 10 April 1906, London Museum 50.82/1133.
27 *Manchester Guardian*, 21 May 1906.
28 Women's Suffrage Collection, London Museum, folder: Violence and Imprisonment, undated holograph statement by M. Baldock, clearly written shortly after the incident of 21 June 1906.
29 PRO, Mepol 2/1061, Metropolitan Police Report, 21 June 1906.
30 *Ibid.*
31 Gladstone Papers, Brit. Mus. Add. MSS. 45989, H. H. Asquith to H. Gladstone, Treasury Chambers, Whitehall, 22 June 1906.
32 *Labour Leader*, 29 June 1906.
33 Lansbury Papers, vol. 2, letter 260, E. Pethick-Lawrence to G. Lansbury, London, 25 June 1906.
34 E. S. Pankhurst, *The Suffragette Movement*, p. 216.
35 See Dame C. Pankhurst, *Unshackled*, p. 66.
36 *Labour Leader*, 17 August 1906, letter to the editor from C. Pankhurst and T. Billington.
37 *Ibid.*, 24 August 1906, letter to the editor from M. Gawthorpe.
38 *Ibid.*, letter to the editor from R. Smillie.
39 *Ibid.*, 10 August 1906.
40 *Ibid.*, 7 September 1906.
41 See statement by E. How Martyn in WSPU [Women's Freedom League] *Report of the Second Annual Conference, 12 October 1907.*
42 Billington-Greig Papers, box: A.K./W.S.P.U./P., undated holograph notes.
43 See duplicated statement, NWSPU, autumn 1907, headed 'Letter sent to inquirers from 4 Clement's Inn', London Museum.
44 See A. P. Budgett, *Facts Behind the Press* [pamphlet], pp. 4–5; see also D. B. Montefiore, *From a Victorian to a Modern*, p. 92.
45 *The Times*, 25 October 1906.
46 *Ibid.*
47 *Daily News*, 25 October 1906.
48 *Daily Mirror*, 23 October 1906.
49 *The Times*, 27 October 1906, letter to the editor from M. G. Fawcett.
50 Diary of Alice Milne, Secretary, Manchester WSPU, 22 October

1906, as copied by T. Billington, in Billington-Greig Papers, box: A.K./W.S.P.U./P.
51 T. Billington-Greig, *The Militant Suffrage Movement*, pp. 73–4.

6   Rapid Growth

1 M. G. Fawcett, *What I Remember*, p. 184.
2 *Daily Chronicle*, 14 February 1907.
3 *Ibid.*
4 *Daily Mirror*, 15 February 1907.
5 Women's Suffrage Collection, Archives, Manchester Public Library, E. Pankhurst to S. Robinson, London, 2 March 1907.
6 P. Snowden, *An Autobiography*, vol. 1, p. 286.
7 *Daily Mail*, 21 March 1907.
8 *Ibid.*, 22 March 1907.
9 *The Times*, 22 March 1907.
10 *Ibid.*
11 As quoted in WSPU [Women's Freedom League], *Programme for Second Annual Conference, October 1907*.
12 Independent Labour Party, *Report of the Fifteenth Annual Conference*, p. 48; see also *Daily Express*, 2 April 1907.

7   The Split

1 E. Pethick-Lawrence, *The New Crusade* [pamphlet], a speech given at the Exeter Hall, 30 May 1907, p. 7.
2 Arncliffe-Sennett Collection, vol. 1, E. Pethick-Lawrence to M. Arncliffe-Sennett, 11 July 1907.
3 *Daily Mirror*, 20 July 1907.
4 *Women's Franchise*, 12 September 1907.
5 *Ibid.*
6 E. Pethick-Lawrence, *My Part in a Changing World*, pp. 175–6.
7 See four-page NWSPU statement, undated but clearly written in September or October 1907, London Museum.
8 See form letter, C. Pankhurst to Miss Thompson [a branch secretary], Clement's Inn, 31 August 1907, in folder: Demonstrations & Political Action, London Museum. See also Arncliffe-Sennett Collection, form letter, C. Pankhurst to Dear Madam, 3 September 1907.
9 Statement, Women's Freedom League, in folder: Constitution-Organization, London Museum.
10 *Daily Chronicle*, 12 September 1907.
11 *Ibid.*, 16 September 1907.
12 London Museum, Provisional Committee (E. How Martyn, C. Despard, T. Billington-Greig, *et al.*) to Miss Thompson, 17 September 1907.

13 See WSPU [subsequently Women's Freedom League], *Report of the Second Annual Conference*, 12 October 1907.
14 See S. Newsome, *Women's Freedom League, 1907–1957*, p. 2.
15 *Votes for Women*, October 1907.
16 *Ibid.*, 11 February 1909.

8   To Hyde Park!

1 Balfour Papers, Brit. Mus. Add. MSS. 49793, C. Pankhurst to A. J. Balfour, London, 6 October 1907.
2 *Ibid.*, A. J. Balfour to C. Pankhurst, Whittingehame, Prestonkirk, Scotland, 23 October 1907.
3 *Ibid.*, C. Pankhurst to A. J. Balfour, London, 28 October 1907.
4 *H.C. Deb.* 4s. vol. 3, 27 April 1892, c. 1510.
5 *Ibid.*, cc. 1512–13.
6 R. Jenkins, *Asquith*, p. 247.
7 *Votes for Women*, January 1908.
8 *Ibid.*
9 See *Daily Graphic*, 18 January 1908.
10 *Daily Chronicle* and *The Times*, 20 January 1908.
11 National Women's Social and Political Union, *Second Annual Report*, 1 March 1907–29 February 1908, London, 1908, p. 3.
12 *Ibid.*
13 Gladstone Papers, Brit. Mus. Add. MSS. 45985, H. Gladstone to Edward VII, Whitehall, 21 March 1908.
14 *Votes for Women*, April 1908.
15 *Manchester Guardian*, 25 April 1908.
16 *Daily News*, 25 April 1908.
17 W. S. Churchill to C. Hozier, Taplow, 27 April 1908, as quoted in R. S. Churchill, *Winston S. Churchill*, vol. 2, p. 260.
18 *Votes for Women*, 30 April 1908.
19 *Ibid.*, April 1908.
20 *Ibid.*
21 *Ibid.*, 30 April 1908.
22 *Ibid.*, 4 June 1908.
23 E. Pethick-Lawrence, 'The purple, white & green', in NWSPU, *The Women's Exhibition 1909, Programme*.
24 *Daily Chronicle* and *The Times*, 22 June 1908, and *Votes for Women*, 25 June 1908.
25 Women's Suffrage Collection, London Museum, folder: Constitution-Organization, H. Fraser to I. Seymour, Glasgow, 6 July 1908.
26 *Daily Chronicle*, 22 June 1908.
27 *The Times*, 22 June 1908.
28 *Votes for Women*, 25 June 1908.
29 *Ibid.*, 4 June 1908.
30 Nevinson Journals, Bodleian Library, Dep. e 71/1, 23 June 1908.
31 *Votes for Women*, 25 June 1908.

32 *Ibid.*, 2 July 1908, leader by E. Pethick-Lawrence dated 29 June 1908.
33 *The Times*, 1 July 1908.
34 *Daily Chronicle* and *The Times*, 2 July 1908.
35 *The Times*, 15 October 1908. Court testimony regarding interview of Mrs Pankhurst by Superintendent Wells on 2 October 1908.
36 *Votes for Women*, 16 July 1908.

9 Frustration Mounts

1 *Votes for Women*, 16 July 1908, *The Times*, 20 July 1908.
2 *Daily News*, 2 July 1908.
3 *Votes for Women*, 10 September 1908.
4 *Ibid.*, 8 October 1908.
5 See two handbills, one printed on pale green paper and one printed on purple paper, in Flatman Collection, vol. 3.
6 *Daily Mirror*, 13 October 1908.
7 *Votes for Women*, 15 October 1908.
8 See court testimony in *The Times*, 15 October 1908.
9 *Daily Mirror*, 13 October 1908.
10 See *The Times, Manchester Guardian, Daily Mirror, Daily Graphic*, and other dailies, 22–6 October 1908.
11 *Daily Telegraph*, 26 October 1908.
12 E. Pethick-Lawrence, *My Part in a Changing World*, p. 205.
13 *Votes for Women*, 5 November 1908.
14 See E. Pethick-Lawrence, *op. cit.*, p. 209.
15 Gladstone Papers, Brit. Mus. Add. MSS. 45986, D. Lloyd George to H. Gladstone, Treasury Chambers, Whitehall, 9 November 1908.
16 *The Times*, 23 December 1908.
17 National Women's Social and Political Union, *Third Annual Report*, 1 March 1908–28 February 1909, London, 1909.
18 *Votes for Women*, 21 May 1909.
19 *Ibid.*, 4 June 1909.
20 Arncliffe-Sennett Collection, vol. 7, M. G. Fawcett to M. Arncliffe-Sennett, London, 10 June 1909.

10 Violence Begins

1 *Daily News*, 30 June 1909.
2 *Daily Telegraph*, 30 June 1909.
3 *Votes for Women*, 16 July 1909.
4 Women's Suffrage Collection, London Museum, F. W. Pethick-Lawrence to M. W. Dunlop, Clement's Inn, 9 July 1909.
5 *The Times* and *Manchester Guardian*, 14 July 1909.
6 Balfour Papers, Brit. Mus. Add. MSS. 49793, C. Pankhurst to A. J. Balfour, London, 22 July 1909.
7 As printed in *Votes for Women*, 20 August 1909.

8 *The Times*, 8 September 1909.
9 *Daily Mirror*, 18 September 1909.
10 *The Times*, 23 September 1909.
11 *Ibid.*, 20 September 1909.
12 *Ibid.*, 23 September 1909.
13 Gladstone Papers, Brit. Mus. Add. MSS. 45985 (Royal Correspondence), Ponsonby to H. Gladstone, Marienbad, 13 August 1909.
14 M. Leigh, *Fed by Force, a Statement by Mrs. Mary Leigh, Who Is Still in Birmingham Gaol* [leaflet], 1909.
15 See, for example, the testimony of Laura Ainsworth in *The Times*, 7 October 1909.
16 *Ibid.*, 29 September 1909, letter to the editor from E. Pankhurst, E. Pethick-Lawrence, C. Pankhurst and M. Tuke.
17 *Ibid.*, 5 October 1909, letter to the editor from H. N. Brailsford and H. W. Nevinson.
18 *H.C. Deb.* 5s. vol. 12, 1 November 1909, c. 1433.
19 *The Times*, 15 and 16 November 1909.
20 Asquith Papers, vol. 22, Misc. Letters, Report (copy), Metropolitan Police, New Scotland Yard, 27 September 1909.
21 Asquith Papers, vol. 22, Misc. Letters, Report, E. T. Troup to H. Gladstone, 27 September 1909.
22 Gladstone Papers, Brit. Mus. Add. MSS. 45992, H. Gladstone to Lord Grey, 10 October 1909.
23 *Ibid.*, 46067, H. Gladstone to E. Hobhouse, London, 9 November 1909.
24 Marion Correspondence, 50.82/1120, J. Gonne to K. Marion, London, 2 December 1909.
25 *The Times*, 11 December 1909.
26 *Votes for Women*, 31 December 1909.
27 Lady C. Lytton, typescript statement regarding prison experiences as 'Jane Warton', signed 31 January 1910, London Museum, 50.82/1119/11.
28 D. Butler and J. Freeman, *British Political Facts 1900–1960*, p. 126.
29 *Ibid.*, p. 122.
30 *Votes for Women*, 21 January 1910.
31 Nevinson Journals, Bodleian Library, Dep. e 71/4, 18 January 1910.
32 Archives, Manchester Public Library, M/50, H. N. Brailsford to M. G. Fawcett, 18 January 1910.
33 *Ibid.*, H. N. Brailsford to M. G. Fawcett, 25 January 1910.
34 Dame C. Pankhurst, *Unshackled*, pp. 153–4.

11   The Truce

1 National Women's Social and Political Union, *Fourth Annual Report*, 1 March 1909–28 February 1910, London, 1910.
2 *H.C. Deb.* 5s. vol. 15, 15 March 1910, c. 178.
3 *Votes for Women*, 18 March 1910.

L

4 *H.C. Parl. Pap.*, 1910 (180) 4, 325.
5 Nevison Journals, Bodleian Library, Dep. e 72/1, 14 April 1910.
6 *The Times*, 7 June 1910, letter to the editor from Lord Lytton.
7 *Votes for Women*, 3 June 1910.
8 Balfour Papers, Brit. Mus. Add. MSS. 49793, C. Pankhurst to A. J. Balfour, Clement's Inn, 12 June 1910.
9 Asquith Papers, vol. 5, Cabinet Letters, H. H. Asquith to George V, 23 June 1910.
10 Balfour Papers, Brit. Mus. Add. MSS. 49793, C. Pankhurst to A. J. Balfour, 23 June 1910.
11 *Ibid.*, A. J. Balfour to C. Pankhurst, London, 27 June 1910.
12 *H.C. Deb.* 5s. vol. 19, 11 July 1910, cc. 51–2.
13 *Ibid.*, 12 July 1910, cc. 223–6.
14 *Ibid.*, cc. 323–34.
15 Nevinson Journals, Bodleian Library, Dep. e 72/1, 12 July 1910.
16 H. H. Asquith to Lord Lytton, 10 Downing Street, 23 July 1910, as quoted in *Votes for Women*, 5 August 1910.
17 Women's Suffrage Collection, London Museum, folder: Demonstrations and Political Action, form letter, Mrs Pankhurst to Dear Friend, Clement's Inn, 27 October 1910.
18 Nevinson Journals, Bodleian Library, Dep. e 72/2, 9 November 1910.
19 *Votes for Women*, 25 November 1910.
20 H. N. Brailsford and Dr J. Murray, *The Treatment of the Women's Deputations by the Metropolitan Police*, A Copy of Evidence Collected by Dr Jessie Murray and Mr H. N. Brailsford, and forwarded to the Home Office by the Conciliation Committee for Woman Suffrage, in support of its Demand for a Public Inquiry, London, 1911.
21 *Ibid.*, p. 9.
22 *Ibid.*, pp. 8–9.
23 *Ibid.*, p. 33.
24 *Ibid.*, pp. 28–9.
25 *Ibid.*, p. 32.
26 *Ibid.*, pp. 19–20.
27 *Ibid.*, pp. 4 and 8.
28 W. S. Churchill to Sir E. Henry, Home Office, 22 November 1910, as quoted in R. S. Churchill, *Winston S. Churchill*, vol. 2, Companion, part 3, 1911–1914, p. 1457.
29 *H.C. Deb.* 5s. vol. 22, 10 March 1911, cc. 1834–5.
30 *Votes for Women*, 25 November 1910.
31 H. N. Brailsford and Dr J. Murray, *op cit.*, p. 76.
32 *Ibid.*, p. 77.
33 *H.C. Deb.* 5s. vol. 20, 22 November 1910, c. 273.
34 C. P. Scott, *Political Diaries*, 2 February 1911, p. 35.
35 Nevinson Journals, Bodleian Library, Dep. e 72/2, 29 November 1910.
36 *Ibid.*, 2 January 1911.
37 D. Butler and J. Freeman, *British Political Facts*, p. 122.
38 *Votes for Women*, 30 December 1910.

12   The Truce Renewed

1 *H.C. Parl. Pap.*, 1911 (6) 5, 917.
2 *Votes for Women*, 17 February 1911.
3 National Women's Social and Political Union, *Fifth Annual Report*, 1 March 1910–28 February 1911, London, 1911.
4 A. E. Metcalfe, *Woman's Effort*, p. 171.
5 *Votes for Women*, 19 May 1911.
6 *H.C. Deb.* 5s. vol. 26, 29 May 1911, cc. 703–4.
7 Nevinson Journals, Bodleian Library, Dep. e 72/3, 30 May 1911.
8 Arncliffe-Sennett Collection, vol. 14, form letter, C. Pankhurst to Dear Friend, Clement's Inn, 1 June 1911.
9 *The Times*, 2 June 1911.
10 Nevinson Journals, Bodleian Library, Dep. e 72/3, 2 June 1911.
11 H. H. Asquith to Lord Lytton, 10 Downing Street, 16 June 1911, as printed in *The Times*, 17 June 1911.
12 *Votes for Women*, 23 June 1911.
13 Nevinson Journals, Bodleian Library, Dep. e 72/3, 18 June 1911.
14 *Votes for Women*, 23 June 1911.
15 *Ibid.*, 7 July 1911; see also Women's Suffrage Collection, London Museum, folder: Demonstrations and Political Action, C. Pankhurst to A. Flatman, Clement's Inn, 4 July 1911.
16 Elibank Papers, MS. 8802, f. 308, D. Lloyd George to Elibank, 5 September 1911.
17 PRO, CAB 37/108/148, Report, J. Renwick Seager, 21 Abingdon Street, 8 November 1911.
18 *Ibid.*
19 *Votes for Women*, 6 October 1911.
20 *Ibid.*
21 *The Times*, 8 November 1911.
22 Nevinson Journals, Bodleian Library, Dep. e 73/1, 8 November 1911.
23 Women's Suffrage Collection, London Museum, folder: Demonstrations and Political Action, form letter, F. Drummond to Dear Secretary, Clement's Inn, 8 November 1911.
24 *Votes for Women*, 10 November 1911.
25 C. P. Scott, *Political Diaries*, p. 57.
26 Arncliffe-Sennett Collection, vol. 15, form letter, E. Pethick-Lawrence to My Dear Colleague, Clement's Inn, 13 November 1911.
27 *The Times*, 18 November 1911.
28 Arncliffe-Sennett Collection, vol. 15, typescript circular, WSPU, Clement's Inn, n.d., with facsimile signature A. B. Hambling.
29 *Ibid.*, form letter, A. B. Hambling to Dear Friend, Clement's Inn, 18 November 1911.
30 See court testimony of Lilian Ball, as reported in *The Times* 27 March 1912.
31 *Daily Express*, 22 November 1911.
32 *Votes for Women*, 1 December 1911.

33 *Ibid.*
34 Archives, Manchester Public Library, box M/50, H. N. Brailsford to M. G. Fawcett, Hampstead, 26 November 1911.
35 Lloyd George Papers, C/8/1/1, D. Lloyd George to C. P. Scott, 11 Downing Street, 30 November 1911.
36 C. P. Scott, *op. cit.*, 2 December 1911, p. 58.

13 Violence, Flight, and Divided Counsels

1 Nevinson Journals, Bodleian Library, Dep. e 73/1, 6 December 1911.
2 *Ibid.*, 7 December 1911.
3 *Votes for Women*, 22 December 1911.
4 *Ibid.*
5 Archives, Manchester Public Library, box M/50, H. N. Brailsford to M. G. Fawcett, London, 22 January 1912.
6 *Votes for Women*, 23 February 1912.
7 E. Smyth to Lady B. Balfour, Holloway Prison, 6 March 1912, in Lady C. Lytton, *Letters of Constance Lytton*, pp. 229–30.
8 K. Marion, typescript autobiography, p. 213.
9 *The Times*, 2 and 4 March 1912.
10 *Votes for Women*, 23 February 1912.
11 Nevinson Journals, Bodleian Library, Dep. e 73/1, 4 March 1912.
12 *Evening Standard*, 5 March 1912.
13 See C. Pankhurst, 'My escape to Paris: a night in hiding', *Weekly Dispatch*, 8 May 1921; see also F. W. Pethick-Lawrence, *Fate Has Been Kind*, pp. 88–9.
14 Nevinson Journals, Bodleian Library, Dep. e 73/3, 23 November 1912.
15 *Evening Standard*, 7 March 1912.
16 *Votes for Women*, 8 March 1912.
17 *The Times, Manchester Guardian,* and *Morning Post*, 2 March 1912.
18 *Daily Chronicle*, 5 March 1912.
19 *Pall Mall Gazette*, 2 March 1912.
20 Fawcett Papers, vol. 3, Lady F. Balfour to M. G. Fawcett, 7 March 1912.
21 Gladstone Papers, Brit. Mus. Add. MSS. 45998, L. Harcourt to H. Gladstone, 4 March 1912.
22 Haldane Papers, MS. 6011, fol. 191, R. Haldane to E. Haldane, 5 March 1912.
23 *Pall Mall Gazette*, 6 March 1912.
24 *The Times*, 18 March 1912, letter to the editor from S. Buxton.
25 *Ibid.*, 22 March 1912, letter to the editor from E. Crawshay Williams, and *Pall Mall Gazette*, 6 March 1912, *The Times*, 18 March 1912, *Evening Standard*, 20 March 1912, and *H.C. Deb.* 5s. vol. 36, 28 March 1912, c. 671.
26 C. P. Scott, *Political Diaries*, 23 January 1912, p. 59.

27 W. S. Churchill to H. N. Brailsford, Home Office, 12 July 1910 (copy), in R. S. Churchill, *Winston S. Churchill*, vol. 2, Companion, part 3, 1911–1914, p. 1437.
28 *Ibid.*, p. 1447, W. S. Churchill, Memorandum, Not for Publication, 19 July 1910.
29 *Westminster Gazette*, 29 March 1912.
30 A. Kenney, *Memories*, pp. 174–5.
31 C. Pankhurst, *op. cit.*
32 *Votes for Women*, 13 September 1912.
33 See Pankhurst Papers, in the author's possession, various letters written by C. Pankhurst during 1912 and 1913.
34 E. S. Pankhurst, *The Suffragette Movement*, pp. 383–4.
35 A. Kenney, *op. cit.*, pp. 183–4.
36 *Evening Standard*, 15 April 1912.
37 *Votes for Women*, 12 April 1912.
38 *Ibid.*, 19 April 1912.
39 *The Times*, 23 May 1912.
40 *Evening Standard*, 8 June 1912.
41 F. W. Pethick-Lawrence, *op. cit.*, pp. 98–9.
42 From case for prosecution, Magisterial Enquiry, Oxford Assize Court, 26 July 1912, as quoted in *Votes for Women*, 2 August 1912.
43 *Ibid.*
44 *Evening Standard*, 22 October 1912.
45 *Votes for Women*, 30 August 1912.
46 Dame C. Pankhurst, *Unshackled*, p. 222.
47 *Votes for Women*, 19 July 1912.
48 F. W. Pethick-Lawrence, *op. cit.*, p. 99 and E. Pethick-Lawrence, *My Part in a Changing World*, p. 280.
49 *Evening Standard*, 22 August 1912.
50 *Daily Telegraph* and *Daily Mirror*, 23 September 1912.
51 E. S. Pankhurst, *op. cit.*, p. 392.

14 The Pethick-Lawrences Depart

1 F. W. Pethick-Lawrence, *Fate Has Been Kind*, p. 99.
2 Nevinson Journals, Bodleian Library, Dep. e 73/3, 23 November 1912.
3 *Ibid.*, Dep. e 74/3, 19 July 1914.
4 *Evening Standard*, 17 May 1912.
5 E. Pethick-Lawrence, *My Part in a Changing World*, p. 281.
6 Lansbury Papers, vol. 6, fols 151–3, F. W. Pethick-Lawrence to G. Lansbury, Clement's Inn, London, 26 October 1912.
7 *Votes for Women*, 18 October 1912.
8 *Ibid.*, 25 October 1912.
9 *Ibid.*
10 *Daily Herald*, 18 October 1912.

11 Nevinson Journals, Bodleian Library, Dep. e 73/3, 25 November 1912.
12 *Ibid.*, Dep. e 74/1, 23 December 1913.
13 *Ibid.*, Dep. e 74/3, 19 July 1914.
14 *Ibid.*, Dep. e 73/3, 23 November 1912.
15 A. Kenney, *Memories*, p. 79.

15   Bromley and Bow, and its Aftermath

1 Lansbury Papers, vol. 2, fol. 260, E. Pethick-Lawrence to G. Lansbury, London, 25 June 1906.
2 G. Lansbury, *My Life*, pp. 120–1.
3 E. S. Pankhurst Papers, Notebook 80B, unpaginated.
4 *Suffragette*, 15 November 1912.
5 Lansbury Papers, vol. 6, fol. 200, C. Pankhurst to G. Lansbury, Paris, 24 November 1912.
6 E. S. Pankhurst, *The Suffragette Movement*, p. 423.
7 *Ibid.*, p. 424.
8 *Daily Herald*, 18 November 1912.
9 E. S. Pankhurst Papers, Notebook 73b, p. 182; see also E. S. Pankhurst, *op. cit.*, p. 426.
10 *The Times*, 27 November 1912.
11 *Suffragette*, 29 November 1912.
12 Lansbury Papers, vol. 6, fol. 245, G. S. Jacobs to G. Lansbury, London, 27 November 1912.
13 E. S. Pankhurst Papers, Notebook 73b, p. 185.
14 *The Times*, 29 and 30 November 1912.
15 *Suffragette*, 13 December 1912.
16 *Ibid.*, 6 December 1912.
17 *Ibid.*, 13 December 1912.
18 *The Times*, 4 December 1912.
19 *Suffragette*, 29 November 1912.
20 PRO, HO 45.231366/3, Metropolitan Police Report on WSPU meeting held on Wimbledon Common, 8 December 1912.
21 PRO, HO 45.231366/10, Metropolitan Police transcript of speech by E. Pankhurst at the Pavilion Theatre, 13 January 1913.
22 Asquith Papers, Cabinet Letters, vol. 7, H. H. Asquith to George V, 22 January 1913.
23 *Ibid.*, H. H. Asquith to George V, 25 January 1913.
24 *Suffragette*, 31 January 1913.
25 *Ibid.*, 31 January and 7 February 1913.
26 *Globe*, 28 January 1913.
27 Nevinson Journals, Dep. e 73/3, 28 January 1913.

16   The Arson Campaign

1 *Morning Post*, 14 April 1913; also *Suffragette*, 20 December 1913.

2 PRO, HO 45.231366, speech by E. Pankhurst at the Pavilion Theatre, 10 February 1913.

3 *The Times*, 20 February 1913, *Pall Mall Gazette*, 21 February 1913, and Dame C. Pankhurst, *Unshackled*, p. 240.

4 Asquith Papers, Cabinet Letters, vol. 7, H. H. Asquith to George V, 12 February 1913.

5 *The Times*, 25 February 1913.

6 *Morning Post, Yorkshire Observer, Sheffield Daily Telegraph*, and *Morning Advertiser*, 20 February 1913.

7 *Yorkshire Post*, 20 February 1913.

8 *Observer*, 23 February 1913.

9 *Morning Post*, 13 July 1914, *Suffragette*, 26 December 1913.

10 Nevinson Journals, Bodleian Library, Dep. e 73/4, 16 March 1913.

11 Asquith Papers, Cabinet Letters, vol. 7, H. H. Asquith to George V, 7 March 1913.

12 *Ibid.*, 13 March 1913.

13 *Morning Post*, 21 March 1913.

14 PRO, HO 45.231366, Metropolitan Police transcript of speech by A. Kenney at the Essex Hall, 3 April 1913.

15 *Morning Post*, 13 July 1914, *Suffragette*, 26 December 1913.

16 E. R. Henry, Commissioner of Police of the Metropolis, to Acting Secretary, WSPU, 15 April 1913, as printed in *Suffragette*, 18 April 1913.

17 *Daily News*, 21 April 1913.

18 *H.C. Deb.* 5s. vol. 51, 2 April 1913, c. 437.

19 PRO, HO 45.231366/31, H. Samuel to R. McKenna, 3 March 1913.

20 *The Times*, 3 May 1913.

21 *Morning Post*, 9 May 1913.

22 *Ibid.*, 6 May 1913, *Evening Standard*, 15 May 1913.

23 PRO, HO 45.231366, transcript of speech by E. Pankhurst at London Pavilion, 3 March 1913.

24 *Suffragette*, 28 March 1913.

25 *Ibid.*, 18 April 1913.

26 *Ibid.*, 11 April 1913.

27 *Ibid.*, 2 May 1913.

28 *Morning Post*, 13 July 1914.

29 PRO, HO 45.236973/33, Secretary of State to Treasury, 8 May 1913.

30 E. Pankhurst to E. Smyth, 5 May 1913, as quoted in E. Smyth, *Female Pipings in Eden*, p. 214.

31 *H.C. Deb.* 5s. vol. 52, 6 May 1913, c. 2002.

32 PRO, Mepol 2/1551, Report, Constable F. Bunn, Epsom Station, 4 June 1913.

33 E. W. Davison, 'The price of liberty', article found in her private papers and published posthumously in *Daily Sketch*, 28 May 1914.

34 S. L. Thrupp, 'Millennial dreams in action', in *Comparative Studies in Society and History*, supplement 2, The Hague, 1962, p. 22.

35 *Sunday Times*, 15 June 1913.

36 *Suffragette*, 13 June 1913.

37 *Morning Post*, 13 July 1914.
38 *Suffragette*, 13 June 1913.
39 *Morning Post*, 13 July 1914.
40 *The Times*, 26 July 1913.
41 PRO, Mepol 2/1560, Report, Superintendent Sutherland, Vine Street Station, C Division, 29 July 1913.

17   The Great Scourge

1 *Suffragette*, 1 August 1913.
2 W. Acton, *The Functions and Disorders of the Reproductive Organs in Youth, in Adult Age, and in Advanced Life Considered in their Physiological, Social and Psychological Relations*, pp. 102–3.
3 F. W. Newman, 'Remedies for the great social evil' ['From the second part of the Tract of 1869, reprinted 1884 with a few omissions'], in *Miscellanies*, vol. 3, p. 273.
4 O. R. McGregor, *Divorce in England*, p. 68.
5 *Suffragette*, 8 August 1913.
6 *Ibid.*, 19 September 1913.
7 *Ibid.*, 15 August 1913.
8 *Ibid.*, 5 September 1913.
9 *Ibid.*, 19 September 1913.
10 *Ibid.*, 12 September 1913. See also C. Pankhurst, *The Great Scourge*, pp. 98–9.
11 Women's Suffrage Collection, Archives, Manchester Public Library, E. Pankhurst to S. Robinson, Bury St Edmunds, 15 August 1907.
12 *Suffragette*, 8 August 1913.
13 E. Pethick-Lawrence, *My Part in a Changing World*, p. 151.
14 C. Pankhurst, *op. cit.*, pp. 48 and 99.

18   The Arson Campaign, Continued

1 PRO, HO 45.236973/126, Police Report on WSPU meeting at Pavilion Theatre, 6 October 1913.
2 *Ibid.*
3 A. E. Metcalfe, *Woman's Effort*, p. 281.
4 PRO, Mepol 2/1566, Minutes, 1 October 1913.
5 *Ibid.*, Metropolitan Police Report, 13 October 1913.
6 *Ibid.*, 6 January 1914.
7 Arncliffe-Sennett Collection, vol. 25, P. Snowden to M. Arncliffe-Sennett, London, 15 October 1913.
8 *The Times*, 24 October 1913.
9 *Morning Post*, 13 July 1914.
10 *The Times*, 20 August 1913.
11 PRO, HO 45.236973/129, Police Report on meeting held by ELF of WSPU at Bow Baths, 13 October 1913.

12 PRO, HO 45.236973/139, Police Report on meeting of ELF of WSPU at Bow Baths, 5 November 1913.
13 *Daily Herald*, 6 November 1913.
14 E. S. Pankhurst Papers, folder 18, C. Pankhurst to E. S. Pankhurst, Paris, 7 November 1913.
15 *Suffragette*, 14 November 1913.
16 Pankhurst Papers, in the author's possession, E. S. Pankhurst to Dear Friend, Bow, 18 November 1913.
17 E. S. Pankhurst Papers, C. Pankhurst to E. S. Pankhurst, Paris, 27 November 1913.
18 Nevinson Journals, Bodleian Library, Dep. e 74/1, 30 November 1913.
19 *Ibid.*, 3 December 1913.
20 *Suffragette*, 12 December 1913.
21 Women's Service Collection, Fawcett Library, vol. 20, C. Pankhurst to Mrs Bradley, Paris, 17 November 1913.
22 *Morning Post*, 13 July 1914.
23 A. E. Metcalfe, *op. cit.*, p. 306.
24 *Suffragette*, 16 January 1914.
25 E. S. Pankhurst Papers, Notebook 82 Ib, unpaginated, minutes of meeting of the ELF, 27 January 1914. See also E. S. Pankhurst, *The Suffragette Movement*, pp. 516–17.
26 *Votes for Women*, 6 February 1914.
27 See NWSPU *Annual Reports*, 1906–1914, 'Subscribers'.
28 H. W. Nevinson, *More Changes, More Chances*, p. 316.
29 See Women's Suffrage Collection, London Museum 50.82/1132, E. K. Willoughby Marshall [a member of the bodyguard], typescript autobiography, 1947, p. 30.
30 E. Pankhurst to E. Smyth, 29 February 1914, in E. Smyth, *Female Pipings in Eden*, pp. 224–5.
31 E. Pankhurst to E. Smyth, 8 March 1914, in E. Smyth, *op. cit.*, p. 226.
32 *Glasgow Herald*, 10 March 1914.
33 A. E. Metcalfe, *op. cit.*, pp. 307–8.
34 *Suffragette*, 13 March 1914.
35 *Ibid.*, 1 May 1914.
36 A. E. Metcalfe, *op. cit.*, pp. 309–12.
37 *Suffragette*, 9 January 1914.
38 Collection of Nurse C. E. Pine, E. Pankhurst to Dear Friend, 29 January 1914.
39 PRO, HO 45.2491871, E. Pankhurst to 'The King's Most Excellent Majesty' (copy), Lincoln's Inn House, 25 February 1914.
40 *H.C. Deb.* 5s. vol. 63, 11 June 1914, cc. 521–2.
41 *The Times, Manchester Guardian*, 22 May 1914.
42 NAWSA Papers, Library of Congress, Anna Shaw on the Congressional Union, 27 July 1916, in A. Sinclair, *The Better Half*, p. 288.
43 *The Times*, 23 May, 27 June 1914.
44 *Manchester Guardian*, 25 May 1914.

L*

45 *The Times*, 13 June 1914.
46 *Ibid.*, 27 June 1914.
47 See Pankhurst Papers, in the author's possession, letters written by C. Pankhurst in 1914.
48 Interview with Miss Jessie Kenney, London, 29 July 1968.
49 See Kitty Marion Correspondence, London Museum, 50.82/1220–3, E. V. Fussell to Dear Old 'Clorf Ears!', Bristol, 19 April 1914, C. Breyer, otherwise 'Brer Rabbitt', to K. Marion, London 20 April [1914?], and M. M. Scholefield to My dear dear Auntie Maggie [K. Marion], Liverpool, 26 April 1914.
50 C. Pankhurst, 'Cat and mouse days: our friendly war with the police', *Weekly Dispatch*, 1 May 1921.
51 A. E. Metcalfe, *op. cit.*, p. 320.
52 *The Times*, 24 May 1914.
53 *Ibid.*, 8 June 1914.
54 *Ibid.*, 9 June 1914.
55 *H.C. Deb.* 5s. vol. 63, 11 June 1914, c. 528.
56 Asquith Papers, vol. 89, Misc. Letters, transcript of shorthand notes of deputation to Asquith of the East London Federation of the Suffragettes, 20 June 1914.
57 *H.C. Deb.* 5s. vol. 63, 11 June 1914, c. 532.
58 *Ibid.*, c. 1639.
59 A. E. Metcalfe, *op. cit.*, pp. 313–16.
60 *Suffragette*, 24 July 1914.
61 *Ibid.*, 10 July 1914.
62 *The Times*, 2 June 1914.
63 E. S. Pankhurst, *The Suffragette Movement*, p. 582.
64 G. Lansbury, *My Life*, p. 127; E. S. Pankhurst, *op. cit.*, pp. 583–7.
65 *Suffragette*, 3 July 1914.
66 *The Times*, 24 July 1914.
67 'Copy of the government's communication to wholesale newsagents', signed by Sir E. Troup, as printed in *Suffragette*, 31 July 1914.
68 *Suffragette*, 24 and 31 July 1914.
69 A. E. Metcalfe, *op. cit.*, pp. 316–17.
70 *Suffragette*, 7 August 1914.
71 Dame C. Pankhurst, *Unshackled*, p. 286.
72 See F. B. Smith, *The Making of the Second Reform Bill*, pp. 23, 26, M. Cowling, *1867: Disraeli, Gladstone and Revolution*, pp. 47–8, and A. Briggs, *The Age of Improvement*, chapter 5.
73 *Suffragette*, 7 August 1914.
74 E. J. Hobsbawm, *Primitive Rebels*, p. 58.

19   The End of the Militant Campaign

1 *Suffragette*, 19 June 1914.
2 *Ibid.*, 7 August 1914.

3 K. Marion, typescript autobiography, London Museum 50.82/1124, p. 268.

4 *H.C. Deb.* 5s. vol. 65, 7 August 1914, c. 2158.

5 *Ibid.*, 10 August 1914, c. 2265.

6 Women's Suffrage Collection, London Museum, folder: Demonstrations and Political Action, E. Pankhurst to Dear Friend, 13 August 1914.

7 Arncliffe-Sennett Collection, vol. 26, J. Allen to M. Arncliffe-Sennett, Rannock Station, Perthshire, 15 August 1914.

8 Women's Suffrage Collection, London Museum, folder: Violence and Imprisonment, Auntie Maggie [K. Marion] to Mrs Callender, 29 August 1914.

9 *Ibid.*

10 *Daily Telegraph*, 4 September 1914.

11 Flyer, WSPU meeting at London Opera House, 8 September 1914, in Nurse Pine Collection, London Museum 50.82/1022.

12 *Manchester Guardian*, 9 September 1914.

13 *Ibid.*

14 See flyers, Nurse Pine Collection, London Museum 50.82/1022.

15 C. Pankhurst, *America and the War* [pamphlet], a speech delivered at Carnegie Hall, New York, on 24 October 1914, pp. 5, 10.

16 E. Pankhurst, 'Why women should be mobilized', *Sketch*, 23 March 1915.

17 H. M. Swanwick, *I Have Been Young*, pp. 187–8.

18 K. Marion, typescript autobiography, London Museum 50.82/1124.

19 Lloyd George Papers, D/17/5/2, Stanfordham to D. Lloyd George, Buckingham Palace, 28 June 1915.

20 *Evening Dispatch*, 19 July 1915.

21 *Daily News and Leader*, 18 November 1915.

22 'Mrs. Pankhurst and the W.S.P.U.', 1 page printed manifesto, London, 1915.

23 *Weekly Dispatch*, 3 December 1915.

24 E. Smyth, *Female Pipings in Eden*, pp. 243–4.

25 *Britannia*, 2 November 1917.

26 *Independent Suffragette*, no. 2, September 1916.

20 Epilogue: The Vote, and After

1 *Parl. Pap.* 1918, vol. 14 (Cd 9239), *Report of the Women's Employment Committee, Ministry of Reconstruction*, HMSO, London, 1919, p. 8.

2 *Ibid.* (Cd 9164), *Report of the Board of Trade on the Increased Employment of Women During the War in the United Kingdom*, HMSO, London, 1919, p. 16.

3 *Ibid.*

4 *Women's War Work*, issued by the War Office, HMSO, London, September 1916, p. 7.

5 *Parl. Pap.* 1918, vol. 14 (Cd 9164), p. 9, and *Parl. Pap.* 1919, vol. 31 (Cmd 135), *Report of the War Cabinet Committee on Women in Industry*, HMSO, 1919, p. 81.

6 M. G. Fawcett to H. H. Asquith, 4 May 1916, as printed in *Common Cause*, 19 May 1916.

7 Women's Service Collection, Fawcett Library, Autograph Collection, vol. 1, Women's Suffrage 1915–17 (Part L), H. H. Asquith to M. G. Fawcett, 10 Downing St, 7 May 1916.

8 Consultative Committee of Constitutional Women's Suffrage Societies to H. H. Asquith, 4 August 1916, as printed in *Common Cause*, 11 August 1916.

9 *Observer*, 13 August 1916.

10 *H.C. Deb.* 5s. vol. 85, 14 August 1916, cc. 1451–2.

11 *Britannia*, 18 August 1916.

12 *H.C. Deb.* 5s. vol. 85, 16 August 1916, c. 1949.

13 Asquith Papers, Misc. Correspondence, vol. 17, W. Long to H. H. Asquith, 18 August 1916.

14 *Ibid.*, J. W. Lowther to H. H. Asquith, 1 October 1916.

15 *Parl. Pap.* 1917–18, vol. 25 (Cd 8463), *Conference on Electoral Reform, Letter from Mr. Speaker to the Prime Minister, 27 January 1917*, HMSO, London, 1917, p. 3.

16 *Ibid.*

17 J. W. Lowther, *A Speaker's Commentaries*, vol. 2, pp. 197–203.

18 *Parl. Pap.* 1917–18, vol. 25 (Cd 8463), pp. 2–8.

19 Holograph comment by M. G. Fawcett on reprint of Speaker's report, Women's Service Collection, Fawcett Library, Autograph Collection, vol. 1, Women's Suffrage, 1915–17 (Part L).

20 PRO, CAB 23/2, War Cab. 105, 26 March 1917.

21 *H.C. Deb.* 5s. vol. 92, 28 March 1917, cc. 469–70.

22 *Ibid.*, cc. 492–3.

23 *Ibid.*, c. 543.

24 *Ibid.*, c. 530.

25 *Ibid.*, c. 522.

26 *Ibid.*, c. 561.

27 *H.L. Deb.* 5s. vol. 27, 9 January 1918, cc. 448–9.

28 *H.C. Deb.* 5s. vol. 94, 19 June 1917, c. 1691.

29 *Ibid.*, vol. 117, 9 July 1919, c. 1847.

30 *Britannia*, 2 November 1917.

31 *Ibid.*, 21 June 1918.

32 *Ibid.*, 7 December 1917.

33 *The Women's Party* [leaflet], Arncliffe-Sennett Collection, vol. 28.

34 D. Lloyd George to A. Bonar Law, 21 November 1918, as quoted in F. Owen, *Tempestuous Journey*, p. 500.

35 D. Lloyd George and A. Bonar Law to Major S. N. Thompson, 10 Downing Street, 2 December 1918, as quoted in *Britannia*, 6 December 1918.

36 *Britannia*, 20 December 1918.

37 *Ibid.*

38 As quoted in D. Mitchell, *Women on the Warpath*, p. 371.
39 C. Pankhurst, *Pressing Problems*, p. 38.
40 C. Pankhurst, *The Lord Cometh!*, pp. vii and 6.
41 *Ibid.*, pp. vii and 5.
42 *Ibid.*, p. 3.
43 C. Pankhurst, *Pressing Problems*, pp. 35–6.

Selected Bibliography

Primary Sources

Printed State Papers

Census of England and Wales for the Year 1861, vols. 1, 2, London, HMSO, 1863.

Parl. Bills.

Parl. Deb., 3rd, 4th, 5th series, *House of Commons.*

Parl. Deb., 5th series, *House of Lords.*

Parl. Pap. 1916, vol. 16 (Cd 8189–90), *Royal Commission on Venereal Diseases, Final Report of the Commissioners*, HMSO, London, 1916.

Parl. Pap. 1917–18, vol. 25 (Cd 8463), *Conference on Electoral Reform, Letter from Mr. Speaker to the Prime Minister*, 27 January 1917, HMSO, London, 1917.

Parl. Pap. 1918, vol. 14 (Cd 9164), *Report of the Board of Trade on the Increased Employment of Women During the War in the United Kingdom*, HMSO, London, 1919.

Parl. Pap. 1918, vol. 14 (Cd 9239), *Report of the Women's Employment Committee, Ministry of Reconstruction*, HMSO, London, 1919.

Parl. Pap. 1919, vol. 31 (Cmd 135), *Report of the War Cabinet Committee on Women in Industry*, HMSO, London, 1919.

Parl. Pap. 1948–9, vol. 19 (Cmd 7695), *Royal Commission on Population Report*, HMSO, London, 1949.

Women's War Work, issued by the War Office, HMSO, London, September 1916.

Manuscript Sources

State Archives

Cabinet Papers, Public Record Office.

Home Office Papers, Public Record Office.

Metropolitan Police Reports, Public Record Office.

Other Archives

Asquith Papers (papers of Herbert Henry, First Earl of Oxford and Asquith), Bodleian Library, Oxford.

Balfour Papers (papers of Arthur James Balfour, First Earl of Balfour), Brit. Mus. Add. MSS.

Billington-Greig Papers (papers of Teresa Billington-Greig), Fawcett Library, London.

Blackman Papers (papers of Teresa Billington-Greig), owned by her niece, Mrs Mary Beatrice Blackman, of Chettle, Dorset.

Campbell-Bannerman Papers (papers of Sir Henry Campbell-Bannerman), Brit. Mus. Add. MSS.

Elibank Papers (papers of Alexander Murray, First Baron Elibank), National Library of Scotland, Edinburgh.

Fawcett Papers (papers of Dame Millicent Garrett Fawcett), Fawcett Library, London.

Gladstone Papers (papers of Herbert, Viscount Gladstone), Brit. Mus. Add. MSS.

Grey Papers (papers of Edward, Viscount Grey of Falloden), Public Record Office.

Haldane Papers (papers of Richard, Viscount Haldane of Cloan), National Library of Scotland, Edinburgh.

Lansbury Papers (papers of George Lansbury), British Library of Political and Economic Science, London School of Economics.

Lloyd George Papers (papers of David Earl Lloyd-George of Dwyfor), Beaverbrook Library, London.

Lytton, Lady Constance, typescript statement regarding prison experiences as 'Jane Warton', signed 31 January 1910, London Museum.

Marion Correspondence (correspondence of Kitty Marion), London Museum.

McKenna Papers (papers of Reginald McKenna), Churchill College, Cambridge.

Nevinson Journals (journals of Henry Woodd Nevinson), Bodleian Library, Oxford.

Pankhurst Papers (letters written by Emmeline Pankhurst, Christabel Pankhurst, E. Sylvia Pankhurst, and H. D. Harben), in the author's possession.

E. S. Pankhurst Papers (papers of E. Sylvia Pankhurst), Internationaal Instituut voor Sociale Geschiedenis, Amsterdam.

Women's Service Collection, Fawcett Library, London.

Women's Suffrage Collection, London Museum.

Women's Suffrage Collection, Archives, Manchester Public Library.

Minutes and Annual Reports

Fabian Society, *Special Report of the Proceedings of the Three Days Conference*, 9–11 June 1886, London School of Economics.

Independent Labour Party, *Report of the Fifteenth Annual Conference*, Derby, 1 and 2 April 1907.

Labour Party, *Proceedings, Annual Conference*, Belfast, January 1907.

Manchester National Society for Women's Suffrage, *Annual Report(s) of the Executive Committee*, 1867–1880, Manchester Public Library.

Minute Book of the Canning Town Branch, WSPU, 1906–7, London Museum.

North of England Society for Women's Suffrage, *Report(s) of the Executive Committee,* 1899–1905, Manchester Public Library.

Women's Social and Political Union [after October 1907, National Women's Social and Political Union], *First* to *Eighth Annual Report(s),* 1907–14, Fawcett Library.

Women's Social and Political Union [Women's Freedom League], *Report of the Second Annual Conference,* 12 October 1907, Fawcett Library.

Bound Collections of Letters, Newscuttings, and Miscellaneous Material

London Museum

Collection of Minnie Baldock.
Collection of Anne Cobden Sanderson.
Collection of S. Ada Flatman.
Collection of Caroline Hodgson.
Collection of Kitty Marion.
Collection of Nurse C. E. Pine.

British Museum

Collection of Maud Arncliffe-Sennett.

Newspapers and Periodicals

Dailies

Daily Chronicle	*Manchester Evening News*
Daily Express	*Manchester Guardian*
Daily Graphic	*Morning Advertiser*
Daily Herald	*Morning Post*
Daily Mail	*Observer*
Daily Mirror	*Pall Mall Gazette*
Daily News	*Sheffield Daily Telegraph*
Daily Sketch	*South Wales Daily News*
Daily Telegraph	*Sunday Times*
Evening Dispatch	*Sussex Herald*
Evening News	*The Times*
Evening Standard	*Westminster Gazette*
Glasgow Herald	*Yorkshire Observer*
Globe	*Yorkshire Post*
Manchester City News	

Weeklies and Monthlies

Britannia	*Review of Reviews*
Clarion	*Sketch*
Common Cause	*Suffragette*
I.L.P. News	*Suffragette News Sheet*
Independent Suffragette	*Votes for Women*
Labour Gazette	*Weekly Dispatch*
Labour Leader	*Women's Franchise*
Labour Record	*Women's Suffrage Journal*
Lancet	*Women's Suffrage Record*

Contemporary Articles, Pamphlets, and Leaflets

BECKER, LYDIA, *Directions for Preparing a Petition to the House of Commons*, 1869.

BIGGS, ANNIE, *My Prison Life and Why I am a Suffragette*, Croydon, 1907.

BODICHON, BARBARA LEIGH SMITH, *Reasons for the Enfranchisement of Women*, read at the meeting of the National Association for the Promotion of Social Science, Manchester, 6 October 1866.

BUDGETT, ANNIE, *Facts Behind the Press*, London, 1906.

DAVISON, EMILY WILDING, 'The price of liberty', article found in her private papers and published posthumously in *Daily Sketch*, 28 May 1914.

GLADSTONE, WILLIAM EWART, *Female Suffrage. A Letter from the Right Hon. W. E. Gladstone, M.P. to Samuel Smith, M.P.*, London, 1892.

GORE-BOOTH, EVA, 'The women's suffrage movement among trade unionists', in Brougham Villiers, *The Case for Women's Suffrage*, London, 1907.

GREG, W. R., 'Why are women redundant?', *National Review*, April 1862, as reprinted in *Literary and Social Judgments*, Boston, 1873, pp. 274–308.

HARDIE, J. KEIR, *The Citizenship of Women*, London, 18 May 1905.

Is Marriage a Failure? Women's Franchise League, 6th series, no. 1, n.d.

LEIGH, MARY, *Fed by Force, a Statement by Mrs. Mary Leigh, Who Is Still in Birmingham Gaol*, 1909.

NEWMAN, FRANCIS WILLIAM, 'Remedies for the great social evil' ['From the second part of the Tract of 1869, reprinted 1884 with a few omissions'], in *Miscellanies*, vol. 3, London, 1889, pp. 266–84.

PANKHURST, CHRISTABEL, *The Parliamentary Vote for Women*, Manchester, n.d. but clearly published 1906 or earlier.

PANKHURST, CHRISTABEL, *America and the War*, London, 1914.

PANKHURST, EMMELINE, *The Importance of the Vote*, London, 1907.

PANKHURST, EMMELINE, 'Why women should be mobilized', *Sketch*, 23 March 1915.

PANKHURST, RICHARD MARSDEN, *The House of Lords and the Constitution*, Women's Franchise League, 8th series, no. 1, n.d.

PETHICK-LAWRENCE, EMMELINE, *The New Crusade*, London, 1907.

PETHICK-LAWRENCE, EMMELINE, 'The purple, white & green', in NWSPU, *The Women's Exhibition 1909, Programme*.

SAVILL, A. F., MOULLIN, C. W. M., and HORSLEY, SIR V., 'The forcible feeding of suffrage prisoners', *Lancet*, 24 August 1912, pp. 549–51.

'What is woman's work?', *Saturday Review*, no. 642, vol. 25, 15 February 1868, pp. 197–8.

The Women's Party, n.d.

ZANGWILL, ISRAEL, *One and One Are Two*, London, 1907.

Contemporary Books

ACTON, WILLIAM, *The Functions and Disorders of the Reproductive Organs in Youth, in Adult Age, and in Advanced Life Considered in their Physiological, Social and Psychological Relations*, 3rd ed., London, 1862.

BILLINGTON-GREIG, TERESA, *The Militant Suffrage Movement*, London, 1911.

CHURCHILL, RANDOLPH, *Winston S. Churchill*, vol. 2, Companion, Part 3, 1911–1914, London, 1969.

LYTTON, LADY CONSTANCE, *Letters of Constance Lytton* (selected and arranged by Lady Betty Balfour), London, 1925.

MAYHEW, HENRY, *London Labour and the London Poor*, vol. 4, London, 1861.

PANKHURST, CHRISTABEL, *The Great Scourge and How to End It*, London, 1913.

PANKHURST, CHRISTABEL, *The Lord Cometh!*, London, 1923.

PANKHURST, CHRISTABEL, *Pressing Problems of the Closing Age*, London, 1924.

PANKHURST, CHRISTABEL, *The World's Unrest: Visions of the Dawn*, London, 1926.

PANKHURST, CHRISTABEL, *Seeing the Future*, New York and London, 1929.

PANKHURST, CHRISTABEL, *The Uncurtained Future*, London, 1940.

Reformers' Year Book: 1904, 1905, 1906 (Frederick William Pethick-Lawrence and Joseph Edwards, joint eds), London, 1904, 1905, 1906.

SCOTT, C. P., *The Political Diaries of C. P. Scott, 1911–1928* (Trevor Wilson, ed.), London, 1970.

SEWELL, ELIZABETH MISSING, *Principles of Education*, New York, 1870.

SMYTH, ETHEL, *Female Pipings in Eden*, London, 1933.

The Suffrage Annual and Women's Who's Who, 1913 (A.J.R., ed.), London, 1913.

Miscellaneous Contemporary Sources

Independent Labour Party, Directory and Branch Returns, Glasgow, 1896.

Women's Social and Political Union [Women's Freedom League], *Programme for Second Annual Conference, October 12, 1907.*

Autobiographies

Printed Autobiographies

ASQUITH, HERBERT HENRY, *Memories and Reflections, 1852–1927,* vols 1, 2, London, 1928.

FAWCETT, MILLICENT GARRETT, *The Women's Victory – and After: Personal Reminiscences, 1911–18,* London, 1920.

FAWCETT, MILLICENT GARRETT, *What I Remember,* London, 1924.

KENNEY, ANNIE, *Memories of a Militant,* London, 1924.

LANSBURY, GEORGE, *My Life,* London, 1928.

LOWTHER, JAMES WILLIAM (Viscount Ullswater), *A Speaker's Commentaries,* vol. 2, London, 1925.

MITCHELL, HANNAH, *The Hard Way Up,* London, 1968.

MONTEFIORE, DORA, *From a Victorian to a Modern,* London, 1927.

NEVINSON, HENRY WOODD, *More Changes, More Chances,* London, 1925.

PANKHURST, DAME CHRISTABEL, *Unshackled,* London, 1959.

PANKHURST, EMMELINE, *My Own Story,* London, 1914.

PANKHURST, E. SYLVIA, *The Suffragette,* London, 1911.

PANKHURST, E. SYLVIA, *The Suffragette Movement,* London, 1931.

PANKHURST, E. SYLVIA, *The Life of Emmeline Pankhurst,* London, 1935.

PETHICK-LAWRENCE, EMMELINE, *My Part in a Changing World,* London, 1938.

PETHICK-LAWRENCE, FREDERICK WILLIAM, *Fate Has Been Kind,* London, 1943.

SNOWDEN, PHILIP (Viscount Snowden of Ickornshaw), *An Autobiography,* vols 1, 2, London, 1934.

SWANWICK, HELENA MARIA, *I Have Been Young,* 1935.

Unpublished Autobiographical Manuscripts

GAWTHORPE, MARY, typescript autobiography, London Museum.

MARION, KITTY, typescript autobiography, London Museum.

MARSHALL, E. KATHERINE WILLOUGHBY, typescript autobiography, 1947, London Museum.

MITCHELL, HANNAH, typescript autobiography, London Museum.

Secondary Sources

Books

BANKS, J. A., *Prosperity and Parenthood,* London, 1954.

BANKS, J. A. AND OLIVE, *Feminism and Family Planning in Victorian England,* Liverpool, 1964.

BEALEY, FRANK, and PELLING, HENRY, *Labour and Politics, 1900–1906*, London, 1958.

BEST, GEOFFREY, *Mid-Victorian Britain 1851–1875*, London, 1971.

BLACKBURN, HELEN, *Record of Women's Suffrage*, London, 1902.

BRIGGS, ASA, *The Age of Improvement*, New York, 1959.

BURN, W. L., *The Age of Equipoise*, London, 1964.

BUTLER, DAVID, and FREEMAN, JENNIE, *British Political Facts, 1900–1960*, London, 1964.

CHURCHILL, RANDOLPH, *Winston S. Churchill*, vol. 2, London, 1967.

CLEGG, H. A., FOX, A., and THOMPSON, A. F., *A History of British Trade Unions Since 1889*, vol. 1, Oxford, 1964.

COHN, NORMAN, *The Pursuit of the Millennium*, London, 1957.

COWLING, MAURICE, *1867: Disraeli, Gladstone and Revolution*, Cambridge, 1967.

COXHEAD, ELIZABETH, *Daughters of Erin*, London, 1965.

DANGERFIELD, GEORGE, *The Strange Death of Liberal England* (2nd impression), New York, 1961 [first published London, 1936].

DRAKE, BARBARA, *Women in Trade Unions*, London, 1921.

FULFORD, ROGER, *Votes for Women*, London, 1957.

GORE-BOOTH, EVA, *Poems of Eva Gore-Booth*, London, 1929.

HOBSBAWM, E. J., *Primitive Rebels* (2nd ed.), New York, 1965.

HOUGHTON, WALTER E., *The Victorian Frame of Mind*, New Haven, 1957.

JENKINS, ROY, *Asquith*, 1964.

MCCORD, NORMAN, *The Anti-Corn Law League, 1838–1846* (2nd ed.), London, 1968.

MCGREGOR, O. R., *Divorce in England*, London, 1957.

MARRECO, ANNE, *The Rebel Countess, The Life and Times of Constance Markievicz*, London, 1967.

MARWICK, ARTHUR, *The Deluge*, London, 1967.

METCALFE, A. E., *Woman's Effort*, Oxford, 1917.

MITCHELL, DAVID, *Women on the Warpath*, London, 1966.

MITCHELL, DAVID, *The Fighting Pankhursts*, London, 1967.

NEWSOME, STELLA, *Women's Freedom League, 1907–1957*, London, 1958.

OWEN, F., *Tempestuous Journey*, London, 1954.

PELLING, HENRY, *Origins of the Labour Party*, London, 1954.

POIRIER, PHILIP, *The Advent of the Labour Party*, London, 1958.

RAEBURN, ANTONIA, *The Militant Suffragettes*, London, 1973.

READER, W. J., *Professional Men*, London, 1966.

ROVER, CONSTANCE, *Women's Suffrage and Party Politics in Britain, 1866–1914*, London, 1967.

ROVER, CONSTANCE, *Love, Morals and the Feminists*, London, 1970.

SINCLAIR, ANDREW, *The Better Half*, London, 1966.

SMITH, F. B., *The Making of the Second Reform Bill*, Cambridge, 1966.

STRACHEY, RAY, *The Cause*, London, 1928.

VICINUS, MARTHA (ed.), *Suffer and Be Still*, Bloomington, 1972.

Articles

COHN, NORMAN, 'Medieval millenarianism: its bearing on the comparative study of millenarian movements', *Comparative Studies in Society and History*, supplement 2, The Hague, 1962, pp. 31–43.

COMINOS, PETER T., 'Late-Victorian sexual respectability and the social system', *International Review of Social History*, vol. 8, 1962, pp. 1–66.

PANKHURST, CHRISTABEL, 'Why I never married', and succeeding weekly articles, *Weekly Dispatch*, 3 April 1921 to June 1921.

PETERSON, M. JEANNE, 'The Victorian governess: status incongruence in family and society', *Victorian Studies*, vol. 14, no. 1, September 1970, pp. 7–26.

SHEPPERSON, GEORGE, 'The comparative study of millenarian movements', *Comparative Studies in Society and History*, supplement 2, The Hague, 1962, pp. 11–27.

SIGSWORTH, E. M., and WYKE, T. J., 'A study of Victorian prostitution and venereal disease', in *Suffer and Be Still* (M. Vicinus, ed.), Bloomington, 1972, pp. 77–99.

THRUPP, SYLVIA, 'Millennial dreams in action', *Comparative Studies in Society and History*, supplement 2, The Hague, 1962, pp. 11–27.

Doctoral Thesis

MORGAN, DAVID, 'The Politics of Woman Suffrage in Britain and the United States of America, 1906–20', Ph.D. thesis, Cambridge, 1966.

Miscellaneous

Calling All Women [newsletter of the Suffragette Fellowship], London, February 1947–February 1968.

MCGREGOR, O. R., 'The social position of women in England, 1850–1914, a bibliography', *British Journal of Sociology*, vol. 6, no. 1, March 1955, pp. 48–60.

Other Sources

Interview with Miss Jessie Kenney, London, 29 July 1968.

Index

Craggs, Helen, 169
Crewe, Marquess of, 264
Croydon (Surrey), 190
Curie, Madame, 166
Curzon, Lord, 266

Daily Chronicle, 104–5, 160
Daily Graphic, 98, 111
Daily Herald, 182, 195, 218, 224
Daily Herald League, 218–19, 224
Daily Mail, 65, 68, 154
Daily Mirror, 61, 65, 74, 87, 111, 172
Daily News, 74, 102, 125, 154, 193
Daily Telegraph, 119, 249
Dangerfield, George, *The Strange Death of Liberal England*, 213, 237n, 257
Davies, Emily, 5–7
Davison, Emily Wilding, 125, 156, 167, 189, 198–201, Plate 9
Davison, J. E., 269
Derry (co. Londonderry), 231
Despard, Mrs Charlotte, 68–9n, 80–1, 84, 86, 90–2
Dickinson, W. H., 81–2
Dilke, Charles, 14
Disraeli, Benjamin, 11
divorce, 17, 77, 267
Dorr, Rheta Childe, 167n
Drew, Sidney, 194–5, 241
Drumcliffe (co. Sligo), 24
Drummond, Mrs Flora, 56–7, 63, 65, 79, 98, 103–4, 109–12, 152, 184–5, 191, 193, 214, 220–1, 230, 233, 250, 266, 268, Plates 4, 7
Dublin, 170
Dundee, 197, 231
Dunlop, Marion Wallace, 118, 120
Durham, 49

Earl, Mary Frances, 140

East End (London), 47, 58–60, 66–7, 70, 142, 180, 205n, 217
East London Federation of WSPU, 217–20, 223, 236–7n
East Lothian, 201, 222
Echo, 62–3
Edinburgh, 7, 95, 115, 197, 202
Edward VII, 123, 137
Edwards, Mary, 123
Elibank, Master of, 150–1, 162–3
Elmy, Elizabeth Wolstenholme, 69, 90–1
Emerson, Zelie, 218
Englishwomen's Review, 5
Evans, Dorothy, 229
Evans, Gladys, 170
Evans, Samuel, 65

Fabian Society, 17
Fabian Women's Group, 149n
Fawcett, Henry, 6
Fawcett, Mrs Millicent Garrett, 11, 25, 75–6, 79, 117, 127, 130–1, 154, 156, 160, 171, 256–7, 262
First Division, imprisonment in, 75–6, 98, 120–1, 125, 134, 166
Flatman, Ada, 115
Folkestone (Kent), 197
forced feeding, 123–30, 165–6, 195, 215, 235–6, 241–2, 244
Ford, Isabella, 28, 38, 58, 84n–5
Fox, Mrs Dacre, 242, 250–1
Franchise Act (1884), 25
Franchise Reform Bill (1913), 186–7
Francis, J. E., 198
Fraser, Helen, 105
Free Church League for Woman Suffrage, 149n
Free Trade League, 33
Freeman, Elizabeth, 140
Fulford, Roger, *Votes for Women*, xv

Galsworthy, John, 100
Garnett, Theresa, 126